BY SWORD
AND FIRE

BY SWORD AND FIRE

Cruelty and Atrocity in Medieval Warfare

Sean McGlynn

Weidenfeld & Nicolson
LONDON

First published in Great Britain in 2008
by Weidenfeld & Nicolson

1 3 5 7 9 10 8 6 4 2

A CIP catalogue record for this book
is available from the British Library.

ISBN-13 978 0 297 84678 9

Typeset by Input Data Services Ltd, Frome

Printed and bound in Great Britain at
Mackays of Chatham plc, Chatham, Kent

The Orion Publishing Group's policy is to use papers that
are natural, renewable and recyclable products and made
from wood grown in sustainable forests. The logging and
manufacturing processes are expected to conform to the
environmental regulations of the country of origin.

Weidenfeld & Nicolson

The Orion Publishing Group Ltd
Orion House
5 Upper Saint Martin's Lane
London WC2H 9EA
An Hachette Livre UK Company

www.orionbooks.co.uk

'But unfortunately the truth about atrocities is far worse than that they are lied about and made into propaganda. The truth is that they happen. The fact often adduced as a reason for scepticism – that the same horror stories come up in war after war – merely makes it rather more likely that these stories are true. Evidently they are widespread fantasies, and war provides an opportunity of putting them into practice ... These things really happened, that is the thing to keep one's eye on.'

GEORGE ORWELL, 'Looking Back on the Spanish War'

For my mother and
in memory of my father

CONTENTS

ILLUSTRATIONS

PREFACE

When the Armistice was declared at the end of the First World War, a conflict that had left over eight million dead, the poet Sir Henry Newbolt rather crassly exhorted his readers: 'Think of chivalry victorious.' The myth of chivalry has proven persistent. The allure of Chaucer's 'verray, parfit gentil knyght' remains irresistible for its image of a powerful warrior devoted to the ideals of bravery, honour, loyalty and self-sacrifice, all in the service not just of his lord or lady, but also for his role as protector of the weak, the elderly, the young and the defenceless. That Chaucer could describe his knight in such terms appears initially to military historians as a contradiction in terms: a gentle knight was not much use on the battlefield. Chaucer was writing in the second half of the fourteenth century, at a time when the ravages of the Hundred Years War and violent peasant uprisings had racked England and France with breathtaking brutality, as we shall see. Chaucer, with his high connections and travels across Europe, was well aware of these brutalities. His 'parfait, gentil knyght' was a call to an idealized version of knighthood, prompted by the horrors of endemic warfare and social unrest.

Chaucer was following in the tradition of a long line of medieval writers who sought to mitigate the excesses of war in the Middle Ages through an appeal to the nobler instincts of knights. This literary genre is the subject of Richard W. Kaeuper's book, *Chivalry and Violence in Medieval Europe* (1999), in which the author explores medieval writers' attempts at reform in calling for a return to the true values of chivalry. However, at the same time, other writers were calmly accepting – or, indeed, were encouraging – the waging of war against non-combatants as the most practical way to achieve victory, even going so far as to justify these measures as being in accordance with chivalric values.

The pragmatists retained their ascendancy over the idealists. This book examines what this meant for non-combatants in the wars of the Middle Ages and explains the rationale – the military imperative – that lay behind the atrocities committed.

I began studying medieval warfare in London just over twenty years ago, at a time when the revisionist school of medieval military historians there was making its important researches known. There are few who now believe that warfare in the Middle Ages was an amateurish and haphazard affair. However, the military atrocities of the age are still too frequently regarded as the natural outbursts of a violent age. The limitations of chivalry and the reality of medieval warfare have been the subject of exceptional scholarship by such medievalists as John Gillingham, Matthew Strickland and Christopher Allmand. This scholarship is deservedly acknowledged in academic circles, and at times I have drawn heavily on their work in their own particular fields. But the very nature of such research has perforce meant that it has been tightly focused in terms of period and region and that its audience has predominantly been a narrow, academic one. (Matthew Strickland's outstanding *War and Chivalry: The Conduct and Perception of War in England and Normandy, 1066–1217* (Cambridge University Press, 1996) is especially worthy of note here, not least because the research – originally in the shape of a PhD thesis – has taken the form of a book, albeit one designed for an academic readership.)

In this book I attempt to present the findings of recent research, including my own, in an accessible way to a broader readership that will demonstrate clearly that medieval atrocities were not simply the result of ill-disciplined soldiers sating their blood lust, or the abhorrent acts of aberrant knights acting out of character. I explain these atrocities in detail within their immediate and more general military context. In its geographical and chronological scope – ranging across the whole Middle Ages and the Latin world to encompass the crusading movement in the Middle East – I believe that this is the first book of its kind on this important subject.

The savagery of medieval warfare is widely acknowledged and understood; yet the idea of chivalry as an important and influential force in the conflicts of the Middle Ages somehow lives on in seemingly comfortable juxtaposition with this awareness. In *By Sword and Fire* I show that such notions of incongruent compatibility do not reflect the reality of the times. As far as the practicalities of war are concerned, chivalry has been showered with too much attention. It represented but one small facet of medieval warfare; for non-combatants, it was so small a part of warfare as to be inconsequential. Although, as Malcolm Vale has shown in his important study *War and Chivalry: Warfare and Aristocratic Culture in England, France and Burgundy at the End of the Middle Ages* (1981), chivalry remained (with notable exceptions, I would argue) practical and flexible for the nobility at war throughout the medieval period, for non-combatants it remained, as I hope to show, pretty much as irrelevant as it had always been. Chivalry was a cult and a code for a small elite; it was not designed for the masses in warfare, be they ordinary soldiers or non-combatants.

This book, then, concerns itself not with chivalry but with warfare, with the realities of conflict and what it meant for non-belligerents. The chapters on atrocities are introduced with a brief explanation of how the central operations of warfare – battles, sieges and campaigns – were conducted and the role they played within overall strategy. In this way, the background to the atrocity can be understood in the light of the overriding military imperative.

No less importantly, I wish to emphasize that the atrocities described by medieval chroniclers were not merely the excitable outpourings of monkish hyperbole submerged in biblical and religious symbolism; rather, for all the undoubted exaggerations of many of these accounts, they reflect the reality and brutality of medieval warfare as the great figures of chivalry pursued their military objectives by whatever bloody means they deemed necessary.

When I had just finished writing this book, I began reading George Orwell's essays. In his reflections on the Spanish Civil War of the 1930s, he comments on atrocity stories with his usual lucidity and perspicacity. These comments are reprinted at the beginning of this book; they summarize perfectly its conclusions.

Sean McGlynn
October 2007

ACKNOWLEDGEMENTS

A first book is traditionally the one most laden with acknow-ledgements. I shall not break with tradition. Academically, I obviously owe much to my teachers. In approximately reverse chronological order, I have been fortunate enough to study medieval history under Professors Peter Cross, John Gillingham, Janet Nelson, R. Allen Brown, David D'Avray and Christopher Harper-Bill. Fruitful and highly enjoy-able sorties into the sixteenth century and the world of teaching have been made under the guidance of Dr Susan Doran, Dr Michael Ryan and, right at the very beginning, Mr Tom Moran, who will be very surprised if this book ever falls into his hands: it was his small sixth-form library of Elton, Elliot, Hale and Parker that helped to start it all.

Over the years, while chiefly preoccupied with many other diver-sions, I have benefited greatly from the help and insights of many medievalists, whether through conversations and invitations to speak at seminars and conferences, or through correspondence and the pro-vision of publications in advance. These include Andrew Ayton, Matthew Bennett, David Crouch, John France, Alexander Grant, Len Scales, Matthew Strickland and Bjorn Weiler.

I should like to take this opportunity to thank my editors for their patience with me over some difficult years that have caused unavoid-able delays in the finishing of this book. I think it was Bismarck who said, 'Events are stronger than the plans of men.' I am also most grateful to George Moore for his study.

Many of the personal debts are greater still. My friends have long put up with avowals of near completion of projects offering either practical help or providing welcome opportunities to recharge my batteries: Stephen Forrow, not least for providing by far the most congenial accommodation in central London, complete with unlimited tea (thanks also to Kirsty); Robert Purves, a cheerful inspiration ever since the King's College MA days, who cannot be recommended highly enough as a great host and historical guide for Canada and America (I'll be back for the Buffalo wings you owe me); Dr Anthony Cross, one of Oxford's most down-to-earth fellows, always ready with tea and sympathy served with a great deal of common sense and enlightened gnosis; and Stephen Rigby(ski), international pedagogue extraordinaire, a fellow contrarian and atrabilious Jeremiah with a disturbingly similar *Weltanschauung*.

I am most grateful of all for the opportunity to express acknowledgement of my family. Sam, Maddy and Jenny May (*vide* 'many other diversions' and 'unavoidable delays' above) really are as good as people say they are; and Marie has always endeavoured both to encourage my work and to ensure that I keep things in perspective. My family will always be my proudest and most fulfilling association. Thank you.

None of this would have been possible without the constant support and incredible generosity of my parents over the last two decades. Sadly, my father did not live to see this book finished. I hope that my mother will accept the book and its dedication as a token of my neverending gratitude.

A NOTE ON SOURCES

Wherever possible, I have used the most accessible translations available of the original medieval sources. Aware of the prohibitive costs of many academic translations, I have attempted to include affordability as a criterion of accessibility. This has occasionally meant citing some rather dated translation sources which I have frequently updated and modernized in the hope of improving them for a modern readership. Where no translations in any form exist – most specifically for Ralph of Coggeshall, William the Breton and Anonymous of Béthune – I have provided one in the text.

Names – toponymic or otherwise – have largely been anglicized, 'de' being rendered 'of'. Many historical names are notoriously mutative (Sweyn, Swein, Svein, Sveinn, Sven); in such cases, I have settled as nearly as possible on the standard or most recognizable form in English.

The British Isles

SCOTLAND

Atlantic
Ocean

⚔ Battle
✦ Siege

Berwick ✦

North
Sea

Durham •

IRELAND

Irish
Sea

York ✦
Towton ⚔

ENGLAND

Dublin •

Chester •

Lincoln ⚔

Waterford
⚔

WALES

Ely •

Tewkesbury ⚔

• Bristol

London
•

Rochester ✦

Exeter •

| 0 | 50 | 100 | 150 miles |

| 0 | 80 | 160 | 240 kilometres |

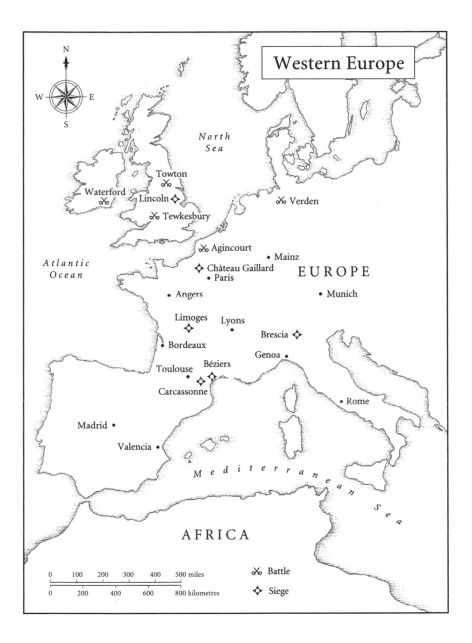

Western Europe

N
W   E
S

North Sea

Atlantic Ocean

Towton ⚔

Waterford ⚔

Lincoln ◈

Tewkesbury ⚔

⚔ Verden

⚔ Agincourt

• Mainz

◈ Château Gaillard

• Paris

EUROPE

• Angers

• Munich

Limoges ◈

Lyons •

Brescia ◈

Bordeaux •

Toulouse

Béziers ◈

Genoa •

Carcassonne ◈

• Rome

Madrid •

Valencia •

Mediterranean Sea

AFRICA

| 0 | 100 | 200 | 300 | 400 | 500 miles |
| 0 | 200 | 400 | 600 | 800 kilometres |

⚔ Battle

◈ Siege

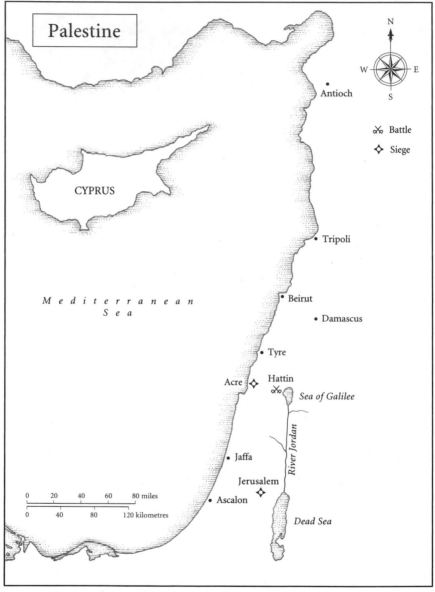

Palestine

1

VIOLENCE

INTRODUCTION

On 12 February 2002, Carla del Ponte, chief prosecutor at the war crimes tribunal at The Hague, accused Slobodan Milosevic, the ex-leader of Serbia, of 'medieval savagery' for his part in the sickening carnage that consumed former Yugoslavia in the 1990s. As I watched that war unfold on television during a decade that had also witnessed the genocide in Rwanda, I was struck by how little many aspects of warfare had changed over the course of world history. I have often questioned the accepted idea of a military revolution in Early Modern Europe, but was more willing to accept that perhaps the new tech-nologically driven military revolution at the end of the twentieth century really did mark a turning point in warfare. Yet in former Yugoslavia I was witnessing scenes of warfare that had been described in the pages of medieval chronicles: sieges, as at Sarajevo, where Serbian troops used donkeys to supply their troops in the hills around the invested city, from which heights the besiegers lobbed missiles onto a predominantly non-combatant population; the ravaging of the countryside, with troops burning, killing, stealing and raping their way across the land, the columns of smoke from razed villages punc-tuating the process of driving generations of families from their homes in a deliberate policy of ethnic cleansing; and the massacres, most notoriously at Srebrenica, where Muslim men and boys were murdered in their thousands. The parallels were striking; it seemed that in warfare there was nothing new under a blood-red sun.

Some scholars of the Middle Ages tend to mitigate common asser-tions and accusations of 'medieval savagery'. Their textual analysis of medieval chronicles raises objections of the contemporary sources' motives. Most records and annals were produced by monks and ecclesiastics; surely these would exaggerate the lamentable state of affairs in their time in pursuit of their vested interests? These were men of God who prayed for peace in well-ordered kingdoms; anarchy and warfare were God's punishment and judgement on a wicked people for deviating from the path of righteousness and holiness. More cynically, warfare was expensive to them: not only were they expected to supply men, money, food and transport for armies; they and their monasteries and churches were targeted by marauding troops in search of booty and supplies. What is more, as some medievalists have argued, what did these men of the cloth, secluded from the world in their rarefied cloisters, know about the business of warfare? (A good deal, actually, as we shall discover.) They spent their time chanting and producing beautiful illuminated manuscripts, full of woe and lamentation, the writing done by timid, even hysterical, clerics given to hyperbole.

This perception is a rare form of inverted chronocentrism. If, at the end of the twentieth century and beginning of the twenty-first century we observe and write with moral indignation about horrors being perpetrated which shock us to the core, why should it be so very different for the people of the Middle Ages? Everyday society was more violent then, and plague, disease and famine made death an ever-present reality; but this did not render the population of Europe immune to suffering, or any less disturbed by random, arbitrary violence. To suggest otherwise is to adhere to a more prevalent chronocentrism: that modernism is always best, more compassionate and civilized, and always an improvement on the past. Such neophilia has led to a ludicrous notion that has long held sway in scholarly circles, but is at last being banished by rigorous research and common sense, that before the Early Modern period parents did not hold such a strong, emotional bond with their children. The rationale for such nonsense has been that poverty, disease, hunger and infant mortality compelled parents to loosen their attachments of feeling, as there was such a poor return on their emotional investment. In other words, children were loved less because parents could not afford the anguish of frequent loss. This flies in the face of human nature. Similarly, we should not let the stories of brutality in this study be blunted by the wearing-down of the centuries. Death does not follow the laws of supply and demand; it is not to be devalued even in a flooded market. When we discuss the fear of medieval soldiers in facing mortal danger, we shall see it was no less real then than now.

Why, then, was medieval society so violent? Why did ordinary people demand spectacles of mutilation and execution? Were they made sadistic by the nature of their environment and harsh conditioning? In this chapter we shall explore how these impulses were in themselves largely driven by fear of random violence, and how societal views were shaped by the desire for stability. The following chapters will then discuss and analyse how and why atrocities took place in medieval warfare, in the environment of maximum violence. The purpose is to explain why these atrocities took place; this is not to exonerate or justify them but rather to reveal the military thinking behind them. The book will also hope to show that warfare, despite its purported 'revolutions' and undisputed technological leaps and bounds, retains its constant of misery. The chaos of war never restricts itself to soldiers in the field of battle. Once the Mars juggernaut has been unleashed, all who fall in its path can expect to be crushed. As one authority on modern warfare has noted, 'Organized violence creates its own momentum.'[1]

The geographical focus of this book is on England and France – but not exclusively so – and to well-attested events that allow for confident and detailed use of the contemporary sources of evidence. As the book's objective is explication rather than condemnation, I am largely spared the burden of deploying evidence to apportion explicitly moral guilt; if even the repulsive defendants at the Nuremberg trials could offer some form of defence, how much harder it would be to offer a full trial for war criminals in the medieval period with its limited documentation. (Disputes arising from military situations did gradually come to be settled in developing Courts of Chivalry as the Middle Ages progressed in time.) Even in the twenty-first century, the manifest culpability of Milosevic would not have guaranteed his conviction on all counts and to everyone's satisfaction. As it was, like so many war criminals, the 'Butcher of the Balkans' escaped judicial judgment and sentencing by dying a natural death in 2006.

To illustrate this point about culpability, we can delve back exactly one thousand years from the Milosevic trial to the infamous St Brice's Day Massacre in Anglo-Saxon England. Against the background of

Anglo-Danish warfare and tribute payments to the Vikings, in November 1002 King Ethelred II (the 'Unready') of England gave orders, according to the Anglo-Saxon Chronicle, 'for all the Danish people who were in England to be slain ... because the king had been told that they wished to deprive him of his life by treachery, and all his councillors after him, and then seize his kingdom'.[2] Henry of Huntingdon, writing a century later, confirms the massacre from eye-witness oral tradition: 'Concerning this crime, in my childhood I heard very old men say that the king had sent secret letters to every city, according to which the English either maimed all the unsuspecting Danes on the same day and hour with their swords, or, suddenly, at the same moment, captured them and destroyed them by fire.'[3]

The massacre takes on the characteristics of a major act of genocide, yet historians are uncertain as to just how extensive this pogrom really was. For a start, over one-third of England was under Danish control, including the cities of York and Lincoln, so Ethelred's mandate did not run there. In fact, hard evidence for the massacre comes only from Oxford, where Danes had taken refuge in vain in St Frideswide's Church. For the most part, it appears that the main casualties were new merchants and mercenaries. Only two victims' names are recorded, by tradition the married couple of Pallig and Gunnhild, prompting some historians to consider the massacre as little more than a political execution. Pallig, a Danish naval captain, had broken his pledge of loyalty to England and raided the southern coast; Gunnhild, sister to King Swein of Denmark, was living in England as a diplomatic hostage. But as these were high-ranking personages, it is to be expected that their names should be noted; medieval chroniclers were not concerned with the (unknown) names of the lower orders. One of Ethelred's later charters refers to the slaying of the Danes. Swein, possibly in partial revenge for his sister's death, made deep incursions into England in the following year. Clearly, fatal violence was inflicted upon some Danes in southern England in 1002, but whether it constituted a political crime of mass murder, a pre-emptive strike against a potential fifth column, a legal execution of a traitor and a small number of hostages or a local manifestation of millenarianism and ethnic hatred exacerbated by economic factors is not certain. It is likely that all these elements were present to some extent; but the most significant underlying factor is the King's role in unleashing the violence against a targeted group. The atrocities examined in this book are much clearer in their magnitude and certainty, but equally diverse in motivation.

CRIME AND PUNISHMENT

Medieval society was violent; and it was a society organized for war. Some historians have wondered not so much at its violence but at its periods of peace. Relatively quiescent phases did occasionally occur. In relative terms, the thirteenth century in England, from *c.*1220 onwards, equates in many ways to the nineteenth century. Both periods experienced a mid-century dip into war – the Baronial War and the Crimean War – but otherwise full-scale military conflicts did not encroach too deeply upon people's preoccupations. However, in both cases, the following centuries seemed to make up for lost time, as the Hundred Years War and the World Wars more than negated the earlier peace. Thirteenth-century England might have been peaceful; thirteenth-century Britain most certainly was not. The border wars on the Celtic fringe were escalating with ever more brutalities. In 1230 alone, the chronicles tell us of: an ambush in which twenty thousand Irish soldiers were slaughtered (the figure is obviously inflated); Welsh prisoners being decapitated and their heads sent to the English king; and, in revenge for this deed, Prince Llewelyn embarking upon a series of savage raids across the border into England, during which he was accused of sparing no one, even burning alive women and girls who had taken sanctuary in churches. So even in this 'quiet' century, war and violent death were not banished. Even in periods of relative peace, war was forever in the forefront of a monarch's thoughts.

Not all society was militarized, but military matters touched upon all aspects of society. In England, for example, all men (and boys over twelve) were subject to call-up to the national levy in times of danger for the country. Anyone physically capable of bearing arms was expected to answer the call when given; those who failed to respond could expect a life of servitude and culvertage (degradation of a vassal to the position of a serf). Local and municipal militias were also organized, such as those to guard London or watch the coast for invasion. These militias were reorganized by Henry III's Assize of Arms in 1181, making no distinction between feudal and non-feudal elements. In the thirteenth century, archery practice at the butts became compulsory in England, the statutes of Winchester (1285) and Cambridge (1388) being but two attempts by the Crown to compel men and youths to train with bows and arrows. These reforms were emulated on the continent, especially during the exigencies of the Hundred Years War, when rulers ushered in laws to direct subjects away from games towards more martial pursuits: Charles V of France prohibited pastimes that did not involve military training; James I and II of Scotland banned football and golf.

In the shadow of the castles, those formidable fortresses that dominated the landscape as symbols of power and authority, peasants worked in the fields with agricultural implements that could easily serve as weapons; these were ever at hand should an argument turn violent, and so the murder rate was a high one. Recourse to violence was easier in an age without a local police force pounding the beat and when courts could be prohibitively expensive.

Perhaps the greatest influence on modern perceptions of violence in the Middle Ages has been Jan Huizinga's famous *The Waning of the Middle Ages* (1919), the first chapter of which is entitled 'The Violent Tenor of Life'. Huizinga paints a colourful but bloody picture of life in the late Middle Ages: his is a Europe of lepers and deformed beggars, processions of self-flagellants and, most of all, public executions announced by ceremony and fanfare. These executions were 'spectacular displays with a moral. For horrible crimes the law invented atrocious punishments.' An appropriate punishment to fit the crime was uppermost in the eyes of the law: thus arsonists might expect to be burned to death. But harshness could be tempered by human emotion. Final speeches of condemned men could prompt tears from the crowd assembled for the carrying out of the court's sentence. One of the victims of the 1411 Burgundian terror in Paris begged the hangman to embrace him, a request witnessed by 'a great multitude of people, who nearly all wept hot tears'. Huizinga explains how crime was 'a menace to order and society, as well as an insult to divine majesty. Thus it was natural that the late Middle Ages should become the special period of judicial cruelty', a reference to the harsh and deliberately terrifying and inventive punishments meted out to malefactors.[4] The people's investment in social order encouraged their exultation and enthusiasm at ending any perceived threat to it; medieval accounts tell of brigands being bought for money so their quartering and execution could be witnessed in front of an ecstatic home crowd, a form of transfer market for executions. At a hanging in Paris in 1427, the victim is harangued by a high official who not only prevents a last confession to a priest, but who also, working himself up into a frenzied state of self-righteousness, physically attacks not only the condemned man but the hangman as well (for granting spiritual reconciliation). The executioner, unnerved by events, botches the hanging; the rope snaps and the condemned man falls to the ground, fracturing some ribs and a leg. He is then forced to drag himself back up to the scaffold for completion of sentence.

Huizinga relates how late medieval society deteriorated from previous ideals held in a golden age of chivalry, where concerns for justice and mercy loomed higher in medieval man's conscience. While correct in ascribing a 'violent tenor' to medieval life, Huizinga is wrong to consider it a phenomenon of the late medieval period. There was never a golden age of chivalry, as accounts in this book will demonstrate. Nor was earlier medieval society much less brutal in character. Spanning the entire Middle Ages, in different times and in different places, we can see both waxing and waning in the prevalence of violence, but nothing that amounts to a golden age or anything like it. In a notorious case from the late sixth century, Gregory of Tours imparts the story of Sichar and Austregisel. During a night of drinking a retainer of a priest was killed. As the priest was Sichar's friend, Sichar and his followers took up arms in vengeance but were worsted by Austregisel's contingent. Sichar, a casualty of the encounter, made his escape, leaving his wounded retainers behind in the priest's house, where they were slaughtered by Austregisel's men. These then stole goods from the house. Sichar later recovered the goods by force, killing not only a certain Auno, in whose house they were stored, but also his son, brother and some slaves. Another of Auno's sons, Chramnesind, swore vengeance and refused Bishop Gregory's placatory intercession of compensation. As the ensuing feud escalated, both families suffered woundings, mutilations, deaths of retainers and slaves, and the burning of homes. A legal solution was finally settled between the two families and peace was restored. The families were reconciled and resumed the habit of socializing over convivial dinner and drinks.

Sichar, possibly drunk, made the gauche comment that Chramnesind should be grateful to him for killing his relatives, as the consequent compensations and inheritances had left him a rich man. For his egregious insensitivity, Sichar received from Chramnesind an axe in his head. Chramnesind hung his body on the fence post of his house.

Such private wars as these abated during the high medieval period, only to re-emerge with renewed vigour in post-Black Death Europe, reflecting a central period when comparatively strong government stamped upon any diminution of its controlling status. But this did not mean any reduction in local or judicial violence. What was important to all elements of society at all times was the difference between legitimate and illegitimate violence, and the need for the former to suppress the latter. Those in power were expected to exercise violence in pursuit of social order, in a pre-Weberian form of condoned violence in pursuit of social stability. There was little point in villagers appealing to the better nature of a group of marauding brigands to spare their homes and chattels; far better for the authorities to hang them, thereby sending out a strong message to deter further bandits while obviously also preventing this particular group from causing any further problems.

Medieval society is frequently, if restrictedly, viewed in terms of its three principal orders: the *bellatores*, *oratores* and *laboratores* – those who fought, those who prayed and those who worked. The last of these is typically regarded in terms of peasantry, but actually encompasses the middle and mercantile classes. In exploring medieval violence, we shall have cause to address each: the Church through its opinions, practices and attempts to limit the violence; the warriors through images of kingship, political control, and the practice and culture of war; and, first of all, the *laboratores* through their personal exposure and attitudes to criminal violence.

Visual violence, in its cautionary and minatory forms, was ubiquitous in the medieval period. Barbara Tuchman's classic study *A Distant Mirror: The Calamitous Fourteenth Century* (1978) makes this gruesomely clear:

> The tortures and punishments of civil justice customarily cut off hands and ears, racked, burned, flayed, and pulled apart people's bodies. In everyday life, passers-by saw some criminal flogged

with a knotted rope or chained upright in an iron collar. They passed corpses hanging on the gibbet and decapitated heads and quartered bodies impaled on stakes on the city walls. In every church they saw pictures of saints undergoing varieties of atrocious martyrdom – by arrows, spears, fire, cut-off breasts – usually dripping blood.[5]

Entertainment was also very often violent. Sometimes, like today, it was the offshoot of a sporting event. In the early thirteenth century Roger of Wendover reports a wrestling match that erupted into a full-scale riot, with extensive damage to property. The ringleader was executed and his leading cohorts had their hands and feet amputated. By modern standards, this was a zero-tolerance society. Violence was commonly the explicit purpose of the entertainment. Even football originated as campball, the camp designating a field of battle, an apt term to apply to some of these early, highly aggressive games. More blatant still were games with animals. One involved the chasing of a pig by men with clubs, the aim being to beat the poor animal to death; another, its match in subtlety and intellectual elegance, involved nailing a live cat to a post so that competitors could headbutt it to death. (Brutal as these pastimes were, they are not so very different from festival entertainments that persisted in Spain until at least the end of the twentieth century.) The links between play and punishment could be close, as we shall see later.

Literature also chose violence as one of its central themes. Chivalric works are replete with knights being cleft from shoulder to saddle. Morality tales were hardly any less scary. One recounts how a woman eloped with a monk. She is found *in flagrante delicto* by her outraged brothers. They castrate the monk, hurling the dismembered parts into her face and force her to eat them. Then she and her lover are drowned. Extreme as this sounds, the reality of punishment was not so very different; it is hard to determine here whether art is imitating nature or vice versa: the case of Abelard and Héloïse comes painfully to mind. Judicially, there are similarities as well with the unfortunate end of Hugh Despenser the Younger in 1326: he was forced to experience castration and to watch as his genitals were cast into flames before his own final execution. Such forms of execution were devised to reflect the crime of sodomy. (At this time Portugal held more liberal views

9

towards homosexuals: here punishment was not a life taken on the gallows but a life spent serving in the galleys.)

With few prisons and no police force, severe punishment was deemed invaluable as a deterrent to crime; the more extreme the crime, the more extreme the punishment it warranted. Expectations exceeded Old Testament notions of an eye for an eye. Capital punishment for non-violent crimes was normal: in France, counterfeiters could expect to be boiled alive in a cauldron. Political crimes, especially those of treason, were dealt with particularly harshly: by the thirteenth century in England, treason was punishable by disembowelling, hanging, drawing, quartering and burning at the stake.

Where temporal powers failed or were unable to prosecute, God stepped in. Medieval chronicles are never short of stories of divine retribution for human failings; mankind brought war, famine, pestilence and all manner of calamities upon himself through his lassitude, moral turpitude and persistent sinning. More often than not, divine punishment was directed at those who had offended against the Church or religious sensibility. Abbot Suger relates from 1119 the fate of Enguerrand de Chaumont. Having destroyed some lands belonging to the Church of Notre Dame in the archdiocese of Rouen in Normandy, Enguerrand was struck down by a serious illness. For a long time he was racked by 'continual bodily pain, which he deserved but could not bear'; he died 'having learned too late what was due to the Queen of Heaven'.[6] Sometimes divine intervention was instantaneous. Anglo-Norman records tell us of the pickpocket caught in the act of thieving by the crime-busting St Ecgwin, who trapped the criminal's hand in the purse from which he was stealing, and then caused the hand to shrivel up. Even minor digressions were not overlooked. The otherwise dependable Roger of Wendover offers the cautionary tale of the washerwoman who took in laundry on a Sunday; for this outrage she was tormented by little black pigs who sucked her dry. Society expected transgressors everywhere to meet with just retribution, whether divine or secular.

Manor rolls from medieval England show that deaths from manslaughter were far more frequent than accidental deaths. Protagonists of violent crime came in all shapes and sizes, from normally docile, henpecked husbands to abused women, and from drunken old brawlers to the most prominent grouping, young men. Most killers, whether guilty of manslaughter or murder, were young male adults; they often had accomplices; their victims were predominantly male; and both perpetrator and victim were usually poor. If this is not so very different from our own day, the development of the law to deal with these offenders is. Although it does not lie within the scope of this study to explore legal and judicial issues, it is necessary to draw attention to legal responses to criminal violence, as this reveals much about approaches and responses to the problem of violence in medieval society.

Crime figures for our own high-tech, bureaucratic times are sufficiently dubious and malleable to render medieval crime rates even more problematic. Thirteenth-century evidence suggests that for every twenty villages there was one annual killing. As already mentioned, tools of all varieties, especially knives, were ever at hand, and the lack of medicinal knowledge and good practice could make even a minor wound potentially dangerous. Common, too, were other violent crimes such as rape and arson. Arson was particularly feared and condemned in a world of timber and straw. Thirty-five people found guilty of the great fire that destroyed Norwich in the 1270s were hanged and burned, the fate also of the Carlisle arsonist two decades later in 1292. John Hudson's recent monograph on the formation of the common law in Anglo-Norman and Angevin England notes how most minor infringements and disputes would never surface in the sources. However, he shows how some of these minor difficulties and petty circumstances did develop into major cases. The mother of Hugh of Moreville (one of Thomas Becket's assassins) had her advances to a young man thwarted. In revenge, she contrived a situation in which it appeared (falsely) that the young man was about to attack her husband with a sword, and she publicly accused him of such. For this he was condemned to death; he was boiled alive. (Boiling, a favoured French method of execution, was more common in the Channel Islands than in mainland England.) Malice and ill intent towards neighbours were to be instrumental in later inquisitorial procedures.

It was the collective responsibility of communities to maintain law and order in their vicinity and to bring criminals to justice. Punishment could also be communal. William the Conqueror enforced the *murdrum* (murder) fine: if an unrecognized body was discovered, it was presumed to be French; unless nearby villages could prove otherwise, they were subjected to a monetary penalty, which could be very onerous. Through a system of frankpledge and tithings (in which groups of ten freemen were responsible for the actions of the others), and through peer pressure and punitive authority, order was largely maintained. Judgment could only be passed down and sentence carried out if the culprit had been apprehended. Flight after the deed was common and, given the draconian punishment waiting, often sensible. Those who avoided justice were outlawed and, if subsequently caught, could be executed immediately their outlawry was established.

Of those relatively few cases of wrongdoing that came to court, trial by ordeal or battle was commonly undertaken. Ordeal took the forms of water or burning iron; the latter was the standard test for women, while men confident in their prowess and strength tended to opt for battle. Neither ordeal was undertaken lightly. 'Fear of God, the elaborate ritual build-up, the certainty of physical pain in trial by hot iron, the potential of execution following failure, could all encourage submission in the hope of a settlement which would at least leave one alive and unburnt.'[7]

Both ordeal and battle called upon God's judgement; both employed violence in the process of determining justice. Ordeal by water offered reasonable chances of success: over sixty per cent of those taking it passed. It involved the immersion of a suspect in a large pit of water. The water had been blessed and thus purified. If the suspect sank beneath the surface it signified that he or she was accepted by the pure water and was therefore innocent; if the suspect floated, the water had rejected him and he was therefore guilty. This process of dipping is more familiar to modern eyes from pictures of witch hunts in the Early Modern era. The chances of success in ordeal by water could be dramatically improved if those undergoing it counter-intuitively exhaled before submersion. The hot iron left more to chance. The accused was made to carry a burning rod over a defined number of spaces; the hand was then bound for three days. When the binding was removed, the hand was inspected. If the hand was healing cleanly the suspect was innocent; if the hand was infected, he was guilty. In the 1170s a defendant by the name of Ailward requested either judicial duel or ordeal by fire, but was offered only ordeal by water. He failed the ordeal and, before a large crowd, he was mutilated, losing his eyes and testicles. By this time the use of ordeal had been extended, the water form taking priority as it offered an instant judgement. The legal reforms of Henry II, as laid down in the Assizes of Clarendon and Northampton, stipulated the loss of a foot and the right hand for those failing the ordeal.

Trial by battle was a Norman introduction to England. It was more popular than ordeal by water, the water form being associated with a lower status. Battle is rather a grandiose term for what was in effect a wrestling and bludgeoning act. The usual weapon was a wooden staff. The early thirteenth-century legal treatise known as *Bracton* (officially entitled *On the Laws and Customs of England*, it was largely written before its attribution to the supposed author, Henry Bracton), commented that for trial by battle a good set of incisors was important to a successful outcome. The weapons were not obviously lethal, as death in combat would prescind the failed duellist from the necessary judicial punishment. In the late twelfth century, the sacrist of Canterbury cathedral oversaw a duel between two peasants, disputing an accusation of theft; he hanged the vanquished party. The use of champions was strictly limited and was more common in clerical disputes between men of the cloth, who were fortunately (for them) forbidden to shed blood.

As the legal system developed, so greater emphasis was placed on the death penalty. This usually entailed hanging. A spectacular example of this is given in the Anglo-Saxon Chronicle from 1124, when forty-four thieves were hanged in one mass execution. Of the gruesome methods of despatch available and utilized, the nobility abhorred hanging as the worst death of all, as it denoted common criminality and low status. Women could expect to be burned to death, as Alice of Wheatley was in the early thirteenth century for the murder of her husband. Infanticides were torn apart by four wild horses. Clemency meant commuting the death penalty to mutilation: eyes, noses, ears, hands, feet and testicles were the most frequent payments for life; in many cases, mutilation was the standard, mandatory sentence. Henry I, outraged at deficiencies in his coinage, had the moneyers' testicles and right hands cut off. Such leniency could also serve a purpose: the survivors were a living testament to the harsh justice meted out to wrongdoers. Deterrence – either through death or mutilation – was an essential element of medieval spectacles of punishment. Public executions and displays of outlaws' heads in prominent places were

13

both common and exemplary, and survived long after the Middle Ages and its barbarities had faded away.

The right to exercise capital punishment was a fundamental prerogative of authority. Despite St Thomas Aquinas's judgement that capital punishment was the preserve of princes (who attempted jealously to guard this right), this licence was claimed and exercised by a number of authorities, chiefly lords and towns. The primary motivation in such an appropriation of rights was the authority, and hence power, that it conveyed; the gallows communicated not only threat, but also ultimate power over life and death. Overenthusiastic use of the death penalty led to reform and greater centralization in England. Cases such as the Abbot of Evesham's court executing a thief over 4d prompted a government response to such severe sanctions against petty theft; by a statute of 1278/9, 12d became the measure of a man's life. Diversity of authority facilitated diversity of execution. A recent study of attitudes to capital punishment in England between 1200 and 1350 reveals a wide range of methods, often based on local traditions concentrated along the south coast; here felons were flung from the cliffs of Dover, buried alive, or left on an isolated rock to drown by the tide.

Much as society ardently supported the death of malefactors, there were signs of resentment at rich man's justice and the impersonal handing down from high of the ultimate penalty. When, in 1285, rape was made a capital felony, 'jurors immediately ceased to convict laymen of it, though they remained willing to convict men in holy orders, who could save their lives by claiming benefit of clergy'.[8] In 1292 a fourteen-year-old thief from Westmoreland in north-west England was saved from hanging by two judges who took two years off his age. Dramatic rescues and clerical interventions sometimes cheated the hangman. Ironically, in 1293 two hangmen who helped a condemned thief escape the gallows were themselves hanged. Research by Henry Summerson shows that as the death penalty became more widely imposed, so revulsion for it grew as it failed to represent a sense of balanced justice. He cites an appalling case from 1258, in which a woman from Woodstock was sentenced to the gallows for theft. Not only did she claim to be able to prove her innocence, she was also heavily pregnant. (Pregnant women were normally executed only after having given birth.) The court emptied, people refusing to participate in the carrying out of the sentence. It seems that people wished a violent end for violent people; petty thieves merited severe punishment, but not to this extreme.

The Church usually aided and abetted the full vigour of the justice system, but occasionally it mitigated excessive sentencing. Many a felon was condemned to death in a Church court. In the late twelfth century Ranulf le Taburer was sentenced to the gallows by a court of the Abbey of Glastonbury in Somerset for theft; after burial he was exhumed and hung from a tree. As in all areas of medieval government, Church and State worked hand in hand. Being men of peace, the clergy relied on swift retribution against wrongdoers as a means of protecting the Church. Clerical courts, as we have noted, commonly ruled on secular crimes; criminous clerks, however, claimed exemption from secular courts. Some recent research into homicide in the ecclesiastical court of fourteenth-century Durham in north-eastern England sheds new light on this area. In 1370, Archdeacon William de Beverley stood accused of malicious homicide (the victim being his niece's husband). His trial was recorded in a twelve-thousand-word episcopal register. The archdeacon's presentation and manipulation of five well-prepared and co ordinated eyewitnesses enabled him to successfully defend himself against the charges, but at great cost to his own reputation, which was further tarnished in an unusual, follow-up secular trial. He was acquitted and, officially, exonerated; but William felt it prudent nonetheless to move to Westminster for his personal safety. The close co-operation between episcopal and royal authorities in this case demonstrates the vested interests of both in the maintenance of social order, and that in medieval communities 'the condign punishment of individuals, lay or clerical, who transgressed social *mores* sometimes mattered more than the strict preservation of jurisdictional boundaries'.[9]

Later medieval England is often depicted as being as anarchical as the country, like Europe in general, degenerated in the wake of the systemic shock from war and plague: the Hundred Years War and the Black Death. Estimates for medieval England suggest violent crimes at the annual rate of twenty per hundred thousand of population, ten times the rate of the nineteenth century. However, this may be over-stated, especially for the late medieval period. In nearly a century of correspondence, the Paston Letters (1424–1518) reveal that the family experienced only twenty-six cases of violence to themselves or their neighbours (including injuries incurred from sporting events or incidents). One explanation for this benign environment (which should emphatically not include the border regions) is, paradoxically, war. War destabilizes society like few other phenomena, but prior to the 1450s England was fighting its war in France, not in England. The result was relative peace at home and the opposite for war-torn Europe, where a state of war encouraged further acts of non-military violence. Thus, during particularly intense phases of the Hundred Years War, many potential and actual lawbreakers were exported to the continent, where their violent tendencies were rewarded rather than condemned. But it should be remembered that many killings involved not weapons of war but everyday implements, normally associated with work. In her study of violence in East Anglia during the period 1422–42, Philippa Maddern has calculated that over one-quarter of murder cases involved such tools, while many others involved no weapons at all. Two examples illustrate the point: in 1428, while John Wysbeche was working alongside John Colley clearing out a drain, Wsybeche struck down and killed Colley with his turf shovel; a trial from 1434 examined the death of Richard Tarcel, killed by Elesius Tomesson wielding a hedge stake.

Public executions continued apace, a warning to those who offended God and his divine order. Although premeditated and unintentional homicides were differentiated, violent intent was foremost in a jury's mind. Thus two dissimilar cases from medieval England met with the same judgement. In one, Richard Fayrcock and Martin Budde were found guilty of calculated murder. They buried their victim in a deep grave, carefully arranging and camouflaging the soil to prevent detection. Both were condemned to hang but Budde, pleading clergy, escaped Fayrcock's fate. When Thomas Elam attacked Margaret Perman in his attempt to rape her, he broke three of her ribs and bit off her nose. Her wound became infected and she died; Elam was hanged for murder, although this was not premeditated. However, perhaps the extent of violent crime is not so important as the extent of violent, public punishment against all forms of crime: approximately eighty per cent of all executions in England were for non-violent offences, predominantly property crime.

By and large, similar attitudes to violence in both rulers and ruled existed throughout Europe. Here, as in England, monarchs held their position by divine right, and so punishment for acts against the body politic drew on themselves divine retribution. Ideas on punishment went back to Roman times (the Holy Roman Empire of the Middle Ages essayed to imitate its more illustrious classical predecessor) and to the early Church, with its long line of martyrs. In Europe we can perhaps discern some earlier appearances of punishments that were to develop later in England, such as the commutation of the death penalty to mutilation: for example, in the early seventh century the Visigoths sometimes used blinding as an alternative to capital punishment. As discussed, mutilation had a visual, minatory effect, but it also conveyed other intentions. Sometimes these were unsubtle but effective: a thief without hands was unlikely to resume his career as a pickpocket. Other times the intent was more subtle: at least one early medieval source justifies blinding so that the guilty party could not see the damage he had wrought, and so take no satisfaction in it.

Certain crimes had designated punishments, as with mutilation for counterfeiters in England, boiling in France. In Europe and in the Byzantine Empire, blinding was inflicted upon political criminals and became increasingly widespread from Charlemagne's time. As a form of mutilation, it allowed the offended ruler to display clemency for crimes that warranted death: the sources praise Charlemagne and Pippin who, having quelled revolts in 786 and 792, had the conspirators blinded instead of killed. Similarly, over three centuries later, the French chronicler Suger notes the mercy of Henry I of England towards a chamberlain who attempted to kill him: the chamberlain suffered blinding and castration, instead of hanging as the crime merited. On occasion, the process of inflicting such terrible wounds did result in actual death. One contemporary account of King John's murder of his rival and nephew Arthur of Brittany mitigates his culpability by explaining that John had only castrated Arthur, the victim dying from shock. It is interesting to note how varying forms of punishment developed their own theological justification: blinding, for instance, was couched in terms of the repudiation of divine light that God had showered on his temporal prince.

A recent groundbreaking study by Trevor Dean, *Crime in Medieval Europe* (2001), reveals similarities in crime patterns to England, but also differences in judicial approach. Again, the influence of imperial Rome is to the fore, with England diverging from Europe to construct common law and frankpledge later declining with the greater social mobility of the fourteenth century. However, the later medieval period saw areas of convergence: trial by ordeal receded as lawyers trained in universities grew in influence; and central, monarchical authority took an ever greater role in persecuting criminals. But Europe generally pursued a more inquisitorial line, perhaps not surprisingly influenced by ecclesiastical inquisition processes. This permitted the creeping inclusion of torture into criminal cases.

By the thirteenth century, torture was becoming an established measure in France, Italy and Germany; by the fourteenth century it was common procedure. At first, judicial torture was carefully regulated and could be applied only once, but inevitably it was increasingly employed with fewer and fewer safeguards. Initially, confessions elicited by torture had to be ratified beyond the confines of the torture chamber, but such refinements were frequently dispensed with. In late medieval Venice and Paris torture was the norm in theft trials; distorting limbs, fracturing bones and even death from its excessive application are all recorded. Understandably, 'some suspects clearly confessed to anything in order to end the pain'.[10] Sometimes, as in Florence in 1369, written complaints were made about the all too early recourse to torture in criminal trials. It is possible that such reactions occasionally had some effect; in Paris in 1488 the record reveals that increasing pressure from relatives and friends meant that only twenty out of six hundred prisoners underwent torture. However, torture, unlike punishment, was rarely public; it was a disreputable means to an end that did not warrant publicity. After all, the vile methods of torture might, in the end, have been applied to victims ultimately cleared of the crime under investigation. In 1376 in Vauvert, a suspected counterfeiter was put to the rack three times before being set free. Another case from the same century concerns Finuccio de Marti, who was tortured four times for tax evasion before being released by the judge.

As with modes of capital punishment, the variety of tortures was seemingly limited only by imagination; indeed, some torture techniques were adapted for public execution. No doubt there was also a diabolical exchange of ideas between the military and civil spheres.

Unlike punishment, torture did not command universal popular approbation, but, as a window into medieval attitudes, it reveals to what
frightening extremes the authorities would go in sanctioning official
forms of violence in their quest for law and order. Techniques ranged
from the most intricate and inventive devices to simple non-
interference (neglect, exposure, starvation) and were often combined
with the death penalty.

Impalement was common. It was for this that Vlad III Dracul of
Walachia earned his sobriquet of 'the Impaler' in the mid-fifteenth
century. Vlad, the inspiration behind Bram Stoker's *Dracula*, learned
this method from his time spent in the Turkish courts as a youth.
One story relates how some visiting Muslim ambassadors to Vlad's
court did not doff their caps to the prince when they were presented
to him; Vlad had their caps nailed to their heads. Throughout his
territory corpses of his victims were to be seen suspended on
huge stakes on which they had been impaled. Other forms of
impalement included the 'Dice', an inquisitorial device in which the
victim was extended on the floor and bound or held down. A metal,
spiked die was tightly tied to a heel and forced into the flesh from
pressure applied by a screw. Pressing, *peine forte et dure*, offered a
blunted variation: the victim, again stretched out, was subjected to
immense weights being placed on his body, crushing the breath out
of it.

Fire was used in the execution of women and heretics, but it was
also applied in torture. Executions could either be hastened by oil (and
later gunpowder) or protracted by faggots (especially green ones). A
detailed account from the sixteenth century offers a gruesome narrative of death by burning, the victim being John Hooper, Bishop of
Gloucester:

> But even when his face was completely black with flames, and his
> tongue swelled so that he could not speak, yet his lips went till they
> were shrunk to the gums; and he knocked his breast with his hands
> until one of his arms fell off, and then continued knocking with the
> other while the fat, water and blood dripped at his finger ends ...
> Soon after, the whole lower part of his body being consumed, he fell
> over the iron that bound him ... His nether parts were consumed,
> and his bowels fell out some time before he expired.[11]

The whole, grisly process took, in this case, forty-five minutes. This was the fate of thousands of medieval victims, from lowly criminals and heretics, to famous historical figures such as Gilles de Rais, Joan of Arc and John Hus; it was also the fate of many victims of warfare, especially those who died in atrocities consumed by flames in the churches in which they had sought sanctuary. The fortunate ones, such as the garrison of Petit-Andely in 1203, died from smoke inhalation. The application of fire in torture was obvious. Branding by iron, and boiling and frying, are frequently attested to in the sources. One form was to place the victim in stocks, grease their bare feet, and literally fry the victim's soles. The body's most sensitive parts were exposed to flames; grilling occurred on gridirons over fires; boiling could be in a cauldron, in a suit of armour, or localized, as when boiling water was poured into a high leather boot.

Suspension and stretching were central to medieval torture practices. The pulley torture, or squassation, entailed suspending the victim using a pulley system; heavy weights were attached to the feet. If no responses were elicited by whipping, the victim was drawn to the ceiling and then dropped precipitously almost to the floor before being jerked to a sudden, bone-juddering halt, the countering forces of pull ensuring a violent jolting of the body. The rack was one of the most commonly employed forms of all torture. Two rollers that moved in opposite directions when operated by levers attached the victim, stretched upon a frame. The distending of the body could lead to dislocation and even dismemberment. Other methods involved tourniquets of thin cords with wooden or iron bars that were twisted around fingers or limbs so that they cut into the flesh, even reaching bone. While on the rack, the victim might undergo water torture in which water was forced slowly down the throat causing massive bloating and even drowning. An accompaniment to the rack was the scavenger's daughter: a hinged ball of iron hoops into which the accused was compressed to an almost impossible degree, sometimes causing blood to spurt from all the orifices.

Torture on the wheel normally preceded execution. Tied on his back to a cartwheel, the victim's body was smashed and broken up by the wielding of a heavy club or another heavy wheel. The severity and intensity of the beating was controlled to regulate the duration of the suffering, starting with the limbs and progressing in the hope of extracting a confession or details of accomplices. Breaking on the wheel remained popular long after the Middle Ages; the State was still sending men and women to this fate in Prussia in 1850, so we should not think exclusively in terms of 'medieval barbarity'. John Taylor, an Englishman travelling through Germany in 1616, witnessed the execution of a father found guilty of axing his daughter to death. He recorded the agonizing stages of execution. The 'arch-hangman' picked up a coach fore-wheel . . .

> . . . took it up by the spokes, and lifting it up with a mighty stroke he beat one of the poor wretch's legs in pieces, (the bones I mean) at which he roared grievously; then after a little pause he breaks the other leg in the same manner, and consequently breaks his arms, and then he stroke four or five main blows on his breast, and burst all his bulk and chest in shivers, lastly he smote his neck, and missing, burst his chin and jaws to mammocks.[12]

In its diversification, torture ranged from the obvious to the ingenious. Even whipping and beating offered a multiplicity of tools and methods for flagellants. Like whipping, the pillory was torture as punishment. The prisoner, forced into an immovable position for days on end, was subjected to a public response. For a sympathetic crowd, the pillory was punishment enough; however, if popular opinion deemed the punishment insufficiently harsh, death could (and sometimes did) result from the barrage of missiles hurled at the prisoner, whose head was extremely exposed. Almost anything could be utilized as a missile, even dead cats. Simply being left in a cold, vermin-infested cell, lying in human and rodent excrement, deprived of food and compelled to drink urine constituted an effective form of torture.

At the other extreme lay the torture of the rope and the torture of the rats. Both these are attested to in sixteenth-century sources and were probably derived from ancient practices. The rope method involved the victim being dragged naked back and forth along the top of a taught rope which thereby sawed into his flesh. The rat method, seemingly known to all ghoulish schoolboys, was quite literally a variation of being eaten alive. An iron bowl was placed upside down over the victim's stomach and genitals. Under this bowl were placed dormice or rats; on top of it a fire was lit. The rats, desperate to escape the heat, would attempt to gnaw their way through the victim's flesh and hence into his entrails. Other uses were found for animals. The thirteenth-century chronicler Matthew of Paris depicts a prisoner tied to a tree confronted by a horse being made to trample him with his hooves. A particular vile use of a dog in conjunction with an execution will be examined in the section on political punishments.

Some recorded tortures were either probably figments of a twisted imagination or were unique in usage. One thirteenth-century account informs us of a lady being tied up naked in a sack with a large number of cats. Unsurprisingly, this failed to extract a confession; surprisingly, we encounter variations of this macabre procedure in later medieval Germany. Most bizarre of all is a reference from the fifteenth-century writer Hippolyte de Marsillis to what I presume we must call the goat torture: the prisoner's bare feet were soaked in brine and then licked by goats; apparently this resulted in 'an indescribable torment'.[13] However, the disturbing creativity of human sadism, then and now, means that even the most bizarre and seemingly preposterous torments cannot be entirely discounted.

The violence of the medieval world perversely inspired the medieval imagination, but in a deeply religious world, invention was not always called for. The Bible, with its Old Testament atrocities and New Testament martyrs, offered more than spiritual guidance and inspiration. Antiquity also furnished plenty of ideas and a treasure trove of pain, as in the horrific accounts of the torture of the Maccabees and other victims; the Latin edition of Josephus' first-century *The Jewish War* was widely read in the Middle Ages. Authority, in both its judicial and political manifestations, was ready to deploy whatever force it deemed necessary in pursuit of justice, social order and continuing control; and all so much the better if the Bible offered precedents. Medievalists have rightly drawn attention to chroniclers drawing on biblical inspiration for their accounts of atrocities; but, as we shall discuss later, this does not necessarily mean that such accounts should be dismissed out of hand.

In such a biblical society, it is not surprising to learn that it was not only property and violent crimes that met with harsh responses. Two offences that incurred violent retribution were blasphemy and sodomy. In 1472 the Estates of Provence blamed blasphemy for God's infliction of epidemics and other evils upon the region. Blasphemy could be punished by the tongue being bored through with a red-hot poker, although this was reserved for the worst, most recalcitrant offenders. A first transgression was punishable by a day in the stocks followed by a month in prison subsisting on bread and water; a second offence merited the pillory on market day and the splitting of an upper lip; a third the splitting of the lower lip; and a fourth the severance of the entire lower lip. Finally, the tongue would be cut out. An excruciating variation in Germany was to have the tongue split. However, blasphemy was notoriously difficult to stamp out and, as reformation tendencies seeped into the population, sacrilegious acts increased: in 1501 in Florence a gambler was hung for the defacement of an image of the Virgin Mary with horse dung. Homosexuality, as a perverse inversion of God's divine order and plan, met with harsher responses, as we have already seen. Encouraged by the Church, legislation against sodomy grew increasingly harsh until by the fourteenth century the death penalty became standard punishment, usually in the form of burning or, less commonly, being buried alive. Such punitive judgment was infrequently passed, one exception being Bruges which, between 1450 and 1500, averaged one execution for homosexuality per year.

If blasphemy, like sodomy, was not rigorously persecuted, one reason could be that although, as a rule, society disapproved of the former and was repulsed by the latter, neither posed as direct or as menacing a threat as property or violent crime. These latter crimes rarely evoked calls of leniency from the public at large; indeed, the Crown was often criticized for leniency and for issuing royal pardons, as when it offered life in the royal army in place of execution. For many people clemency only encouraged further wrongdoing by its mitigation of deterrence. Bowing to public opinion in England in 1389, Parliament successfully petitioned for restrictions of pardons for violent crimes.

The influential notion forwarded by Michel Foucault that punishment in the Middle Ages was predominantly physical because society was pre-capitalist is misleading for, from the twelfth century onwards, Europe began a remarkable economic transformation and became increasingly monetized, allowing for the greater use of the payment of fines and compensation (if and when judicially stipulated). The number of prisons also grew in the later medieval period, stimulated by the Church, which should not shed blood and which therefore had to find alternative forms of punishment. I suspect that this development has another, overlooked stimulus: as armies grew in size and wars became ever more endemic, so more provision was necessary for the detention of growing numbers of prisoners of war who awaited the payment of their ransom in gaols. Imprisonment was, in any case, reserved for lesser crimes, or as a holding place until execution, this ultimate sanction remaining a very public event.

As already seen in England, the form a criminal execution took could vary from place to place. The standard methods of hanging, decapitation and burning dominated throughout Europe, but these were augmented by various traditions and innovations. Public hangings could be large, as with the above-mentioned case of forty-four thieves recorded in the Anglo-Saxon Chronicle, hung in Leicestershire in 1124. Some executions reveal interesting details: when Gilbert of Plumpton went to the gallows in 1184, he wore an iron chain around his neck and his eyes were covered with green clay. If a crowd was, at the last moment, denied the spectacle of an execution, occasionally there was some gruesome compensation. In England in 1221, Thomas of Eldersfield was reprieved from hanging at the last moment; in a show of mercy, he was blinded and castrated instead: 'the eyes were thrown to the ground, the testicles used as footballs, the local lads kicking them playfully at the girls'.[14] Crowd participation was part of the event. Hanging was rare for women, bourgeois and nobility; the latter classes were traditionally decapitated as a concession to a swifter death. A woman hanged in Paris in 1445 drew great crowds, such was the novelty; the hanging of a burgher of Malines in 1423 was the first such for over a century. By the late fifteenth century hanging became the most usual form of judicial execution for men, with burning also common. Trevor Dean's research into crime in late medieval Italy has come up with these examples of executions in 1490s Ferrara in northern Italy:

Here we find a peasant burned to death for impregnating his sister and for bestiality with asses, a seventeen-year-old from the suburbs burned for sodomy, another peasant hanged for theft and incest with his sisters, an eighteen-year-old hanged for thieving during public celebrations of a ducal marriage, two more peasants hanged for homicide, and soldiers hanged for robbery and counterfeiting. In addition, an eighty-year-old draper convicted of sodomy and sentenced to death by burning was spared his life, and a teenage wife convicted of strangling to death her husband's nephew escaped from prison while awaiting the death penalty.[15]

We can discern here a pattern of punishment: hanging for ordinary crimes; burning for sexual crimes that required purification of the body. In the case of Ferrara, the harsh sentencing of sex crimes may have been influenced by the contemporaneous events in nearby Florence, then under the control of the puritanical Savonarola.

In his massive, brilliant study *Rituals of Retribution: Capital Punishment in Germany, 1600–1987* (1996), Richard Evans enumerates the various forms of public execution in the Early Modern period. The German basis for capital punishment was derived from and stipulated in the *Constitutio Criminalis Carolina*, the legal codification by Emperor Charles V from 1532. We have encountered breaking on the wheel for (predominantly) male murders. The number of blows was specified in the sentence and could be top down, i.e. from the head, for a more merciful execution, or bottom up, prolonging the death agonies of the worst offenders. In a display reminiscent of Vlad Dracul the Impaler's methods, the head was then severed and placed on top of a pole, while the decapitated trunk was bound to a cartwheel which was then placed horizontally on top of another pole; here it was left to rot very publicly. Forgers, prisoners, blasphemers, witches, heretics and sodomites (the last of these were considered to be synonymous) could expect burning at the stake, so that only ashes were left; these were then totally disposed of. The code favoured drowning for women, usually in the form of being lowered from a bridge and held under until dead. The somewhat incredible torture of the woman in a sack of cats is echoed in the code here: notorious women criminals were to be lowered into water in a sack containing a cat, a hen and a snake (the last tending to be a pictorial representation). Unusual as this may sound, there is at least one report from the Hundred Years War of a soldier being executed by being placed in a sack with a dog and then drowned. Like fire, water was believed to have purifying properties, drowning therefore being considered particularly appropriate for moral crimes. Burial alive also sometimes came into this category, the code specifying such a sentence for women guilty of infanticide. As with perhaps the majority of medieval death sentences, this process was more elaborate than its name suggests. The guilty woman was lain in a shallow grave and covered in thorns; the grave was then filled in, starting with the feet. At some point, again mimicking Vlad Dracul, a stake was driven through the woman's heart, 'perhaps to prevent the body from returning from the dead in a reflection of folk beliefs about vampirism',[16] fears more prevalent in central and eastern Europe than in the west.

The deliberate, hoped-for deterrence of execution called for as much suffering as possible to prolong the dreadful spectacle. The condemned person was frequently dragged to the place of execution, all the while undergoing whipping and beating by the guards and crowds; in Germany and elsewhere, the journey entailed having flesh ripped out by red-hot tongs. The execution could also be designed to protract the dying process. Estrapade, the hurling from a great height, was adapted to this intent. The criminal was left alive after the drop, with his body broken and in agony, to die of starvation; reports tell of how, unable to move, the dying criminal would sometimes resort to autophagic extremes, the eating of his own flesh. Boiling alive could also be dragged out as a death: the offender was slowly lowered into a vessel of bubbling oil by a rope under his arms, his flesh being boiled first from his feet and then slowly upwards; if he was fortunate, the pain would cause the condemned man to pass out in the early stages. With executions like this, it is obvious how torture and capital punishment had an interchange of forms.

Decapitation was an easy death by comparison, and hence the method favoured by the higher ranks. John Taylor, who gave us the eyewitness account of breaking on the wheel, was also present at a beheading: 'The fashion is, that the prisoner kneels down, and being blinded with a napkin, one takes hold of the hair of the crown of the head, holding the party upright, whilst the hangman with a backward blow with a sword will take the head from a man's shoulders so nimbly, and with such dexterity, that the owner of the head shall never want the miss of it.'[17] This picture of professional proficiency should not obscure the fact that there were plenty of bungled beheadings. It would seem that the sword was more accomplished than the axe in this act and as such was the offender's preferred mode of despatch. Dismemberment was also fairly common for the nobility, but this was reserved for political crimes, chiefly treason and rebellion.

The above details are all variations of a theme, the common thread being a visual demonstration of ritual killing demanded by a majority of the population. Even so, the similarities are more striking than the dissimilarities: Charles V's code has much in common with the fourteenth-century *coutumiers* of France, which in their own turn build on thirteenth-century traditions, such as found in the *Coutumes de Beauvaisis*. Everything went to serve a policy of deterrence, even after death. Long after sentence had been carried out, the bodies of criminals were left on public display to inhibit other potential wrongdoers; whether corpses left on the gallows, or heads on pikes, or quartered parts prominently exhibited in different parts of a kingdom or city, the price of crime was shown as a high one and one continually advertised to the public at large.

No general observations are universal, and so it is possible to encounter exceptions that prove the rule. Depending on the nature of the crime and on whether the convicted man was having a 'good' death, sympathy could be evoked from the assembled spectators. As mentioned earlier, last-minute rescue attempts were not unheard of, one efficacious resort being the reprieve that came with an offer of matrimony. Executions that were motivated to further a political faction were sometimes publicly opposed, as no offence had been perpetrated against the people. In 1315 in the western Italian city of Siena, the authorities attempted to amputate a foot from each of six men from an opposing party who had entered the city in violation of a biased law, but the city (at least partisan elements of it) rose in riot against this measure. Leniency, however, was only rarely tolerated, and was especially resented by ordinary people when it was granted to the nobility: in Siena in 1374 a threat to riot ensured that clemency granted to a noble family of brigands was rescinded. As the case of the unfortunate Thomas of Eldersfield demonstrates, the crowds gathered for an execution were not squeamish. The corpses of executed criminals often became playthings, notably for youths, who dragged them around, kicked and beat them, and severed body parts. Many of these youths would go on to become soldiers.

Despite the pervasive brutality of this period, there is evidence to suggest that the number of death sentences was declining by the fifteenth century. One possible explanation for this might have been the reluctance to assist what nature and war had done to population levels; plague, famine and endless military conflicts had depleted workers in the field and manpower for the army, the latter recruiting increasing proportions of criminals. Alternatively, there may simply have been a drop in the crime rate. A further reason was the development of an ever more legalistic and literate society that spawned theories on which crimes deserved what punishment, allowing more detailed delving into a case and greater complexity in judicial procedure. Claude Gauvard's study of the death penalty and the late medieval *parlement*, France's highest court, shows that between 1387 and 1400, of nearly two hundred criminal cases heard at the court, only four men were condemned to death. The family of one of these men, to avoid the shame of a public hanging, saw to it that the guilty party was instead secretly drowned one night. That this was a noble court helps to account for the few death sentences passed. In the majority of cases, privately negotiated agreements meant that there was a decreasing recourse to the hangman. In this way, the court offered a conciliatory process to honour avengers without initiating a blood feud between the victim's family and that of the accused.

The court adapted the premise of an eye for an eye into its workings, but 'the death penalty was used more frequently as part of an argument than it was in reality'.[18] Lesser jurisdictions – dealing with 'lesser' people – did not lean so heavily this way. The influence of Roman law remained strong, Seneca's assertion that the more severe a punishment the greater its effect on people informed the thinking in most courts. Medieval jurists made juridical and philosophical arguments for the deterrent effect and didactic moral message of capital punishment and its efficacy in preserving social order. The population at large wished to participate in the dissemination of this message and effect, and did so through attendance and participation at public executions.

In discussing violence in the medieval world, a brief foray into the domestic environment is merited. Here the violence is generally perceived as more directed against the individual than against society, but not always. The nature of medieval record-keeping and the illiteracy of most people require us to examine this field through court cases. While this permits us to discover official views on domestic violence (and the official view can be expected to at least partly mirror the popular view), it affords our only opportunity to consider violence within the household. Perceptions are far more ambiguous here, given that most domestic violence was meted out to women, and a woman's legal standing left her at a great disadvantage (although not to the degree that is commonly supposed). As Philippa Maddern has written of females and violence in the Middle Ages: 'Their place in the moral hierarchy of violence was low; men who beat their wives, according to fifteenth-century views, merely affirmed natural and normal order, whereas wives who attacked their husbands were seen as unnatural traitors against their lords.'[19]

This notion is reinforced by the Statute of Treason of 1352 in England which declared that a woman killing her husband was guilty of a treasonous act. So even in this sphere of violence there was concern for the stability of the social order. For this crime, as with many others, a woman would be burned alive; this sentence was last carried out in England as late as 1789. (The unfortunate woman was Catherine Murphy, burned at Newgate on 18 March for coining, which was considered high treason. By this time, women could normally expect to be strangled before the burning.)

Women as perpetrators of violent crime and murder appear in court records many times fewer than men, proportionately forming an average of ten per cent of cases in Europe. The one violent crime for which there is an inversion is infanticide. Of all the many social, economic, cultural and moral pressures that drove a mother to kill her child, perhaps the most telling was the preference for boys in medieval society. In fourteenth-century Catalonia, eighty per cent of infanticide victims were girls: 'Girls were a cost and a liability, so were extinguished; boys were an asset and a benefit, so were preserved.'[20] Thus, even from birth, females were more vulnerable to violence than males. We have already noted Charles V's legal code's penalty for infanticide, but punishment varied, especially according to whether the case was heard before a secular or ecclesiastical court, the latter emphasizing repentance over punishment. Thus in Italy, where infanticide came under secular jurisdiction, we hear of a case from Bologna in 1344 in which a guilty mother was beheaded, while a mother in late medieval England was sentenced by a Church court to penitential processions. England also seems to have entertained mitigating circumstances more readily: in 1342 one Alice was incarcerated to await the King's grace, judged to having been in a state of insanity when she killed her young son. For all of their disadvantages in law, women were less likely to receive corporal or capital punishment for certain offences, and far more likely to receive pardons.

Married women were vulnerable to violence, but not to the extent that modern perceptions hold. Intra-familial murders were very low indeed, especially when compared to modern society; as Barbara Hanawalt explains, 'With the family as the basic unit of peasant economy, one would no more consider killing one's wife than one's ox.'[21] (The 'rule of thumb' precept – husbands could beat their wives if the stick was no thicker than a thumb – does not come from the Middle Ages as some commonly suppose.) James Brundage has shown how canon (Church) law attempted sensitive adaptations of biblical patriarchal authority, addressing areas such as St Paul's command that wives should subject themselves to their husbands in all things and that while husbands should love their wives, wives should fear their husbands. In a form of corporal trickle-down effect from the king, superiors had the right to chastise inferiors whether they were women, servants or children. At the degree ceremony for Master of Grammar in medieval universities, the newly qualified master was given a rod with which to beat a boy as part of the ceremony; the Rule of Benedictine monasteries permitted abbots to whip monks.

However, wife-beating was frowned upon and discouraged, although clerical wives could be more harshly treated, the mid-twelfth-century *Summa Parisiensis* authorizing severe, but not lethal, beating for wives of the clergy. Wives could obtain legal separation from their spouses on grounds of cruelty: in late fourteenth-century Paris, Guioche Grivoul received a court warning to cease assaulting his wife with clubs and knives, on pain of excommunication, a fine, a separation and the wife laying claim to her share of their property. Appeals on such grounds were almost unheard of (as low as 0.02 per cent of divorce cases in England). Economic difficulties were often cited as the basis for matrimonial violence. In the western French city of Angers in 1367 a man who had lost half his property in pursuit of a litigation case was, as a result, driven temporarily irrational; he beat his wife and attempted to defenestrate his children. For this he was manacled at home for six months. That there was a degree of equality in judicial punishment is borne out by Hanawalt's various studies. These demonstrate that in late medieval England husband killers and wife killers were equally likely to be found guilty (twenty-nine per cent each in all cases); fifty-two per cent of men convicted of killing a relative were hung, while fifty per cent of women were.

One area in which there was great injustice for women was rape. The writings of misogynistic monks portraying women as stereotypical temptresses and latter-day Eves twisted some opinions into expressing the view that some women deserved to be raped, and the accused frequently resorted to the effective defence of besmirching the moral character of his victim. Rape, as an offence against the king's peace, was a serious crime, but one with an extraordinarily high acquittal rate. Questions of proof of consent, the lack of witnesses, and the reluctance of an all-male jury to pass a death sentence (which was applied to rape in England only in 1285) all conspired to mitigate punitive legislation. A number of studies highlight this glaring injustice. In the English Midlands between 1400 and 1430, of 280 rape cases, not one led to a conviction. For the country as a whole in the first three-quarters of the thirteenth century, of 142 prosecutions only one resulted in so much as a fine (two others, as clerics, were dealt with – how we do not know – by the more lenient Church courts). It was a similar story for Europe as a whole: in Brescia between 1414 and 1417 of over 400 criminal sentences only four were for rape; in fourteenth- and fifteenth-century Cerisy, of 344 violent crimes appearing in the courts, only eight were rape cases; and fourteenth-century Nuremberg records only eight rapes in over 700 crimes. No wonder, then, that in medieval Europe, 'Of the crimes perpetrated against women, rape stands out for the apparent ineffectiveness of the law.'[22] Given these attitudes, it is only to be expected that the number of rapes increased many times over in war zones when the disincentives to rape were so feeble in peacetime.

The victim of rape had little recourse to justice and so might look to her own protection. The violence of a woman against a man was abhorrent to received ideas of the social order, but exceptions could be made for self-defence: a trial in England from 1438 acquitted Joan Chapelyn, who had killed the rapist assaulting her (the fact that the rapist was a Frenchman undoubtedly helped her case). But even suicide was condemned as a means of escaping rape. Sometimes justice was dealt out by the victim's outraged family, but authorities were persistently stamping down on private feuds. What little help there was available came from spiritual intervention, if we are to believe the sources. In 1345 a widowed noblewoman fell pregnant after a rape assault; she turned to the Franciscan friar Gerard Cagnoli for assistance and miraculously all signs of her pregnancy disappeared.

With this last example we encounter another aspect of medieval attitudes towards violence and justice. The population looked to the authorities to administer violent retribution as a deterrence to wider, criminal violence; we have also encountered guilty parties meeting with divine punishment; but sometimes the feeling of people was that judicial chastisement was not only too severe but represented a miscarriage of justice. As a remedy to this, they occasionally took the law into their own hands, aiding prisoners to escape or calling on the hangman to spare the offender; where it was particularly vocal, the authorities at times did heed this barometer of public opinion and granted the condemned person his life, lest public disorder break out. But the supplication of divine help and subsequent miraculous intervention formed an equally powerful influence on society's need for an equitable system of justice. The sources are replete with examples of this, undoubtedly promoted by the clerical writers, who encouraged belief in the efficacy of prayers and the more material offerings to the saints and the Church. The emphasis on forgiveness meant that even the guilty could hope for grace.

Examples exist from all of medieval Europe; they range from events that can be explained in practical ways to the completely inexplicable (not to mention improbable). In England in the late 1170s, a defendant soundly beat his accuser in a trial by battle, his success being attributed to his having invoked the aid of St Thomas Becket the Martyr; but the defendant had also undergone a three-day crash course in combat immediately prior to the trial. From Norwich in East Anglia in 1285 we have the case of Walter Eghe, who was hung for theft. When he was cut down from the gallows and taken to be buried, it was soon apparent that he was not dead. He took sanctuary in a church and received a royal pardon, his wondrous recovery being taken as a divine sign of his innocence. (Walter was more fortunate than a thief hung in Oxfordshire in 1335: not fully despatched by the hangman, he was buried alive.) In 1291 William Crak was hanged for multiple homicide (thirteen murders) in Swansea in south Wales. He invoked the aid of Thomas Cantiloupe before a heavy rope with a slip knot was placed around his neck and the ladder was quickly removed 'so that he would die at once'[23] (by the breaking of his neck). When strung up, William fouled himself, as victims usually did, and went limp. He was carried to church on the ladder used to hang him. His face was black and swollen; his eyes protruded; his neck, throat, nose and mouth were bloody; and his tongue was livid and thick, having been lacerated by his teeth. Yet St Thomas Cantiloupe brought him back to life. This St Thomas was bishop of Hereford until his death in 1252. He was the nearest thing to a medieval liberal, and takes the credit for saving a number of guilty offenders on the gallows. Another of his successful interventions took place in Lincoln in 1291, responding once again to a gallows appeal.

Prison walls were no guarantee against saintly assistance to incarcerated parties. In early twelfth-century England, the Bishop of Ely wrote of one Bricstan, wrongly imprisoned (or so he believed) for financial crimes. Five months after his arrest, in a well-organized and carefully co-ordinated gaolbreak, Saints Benedict, Ethelreda and Sexburga sprang Bricstan from his prison cell. In Angevin times, a shoemaker by the name of Robert the Putrid escaped purgation of ordeal by water when, having prayed to St Edmund, he offered the saint (i.e. the Church) his best ox as a *quid pro quo;* consequently, his name miraculously failed to materialize on the prepared trial list. In 1170, to settle a case of debt and violence, one Ailward was made to undergo ordeal by water. He failed and was mutilated: his eyes were put out and he was castrated. 'Fortunately for Ailward, his devotion to St Thomas at length restored him to wholeness, although his new testicles were small and one of his eyes no longer multi-coloured but black.'[24] God's mercy could go against public order. One Oxford pickpocket was sentenced to death to general applause. However, the intervention of some monks, praying to the relics of St Ecgwin, successfully entreated the saint's help to save the thief from hanging.

In times of calamity and desperation, people looked to the heavens for help. Unsurprisingly, then, the turbulent fourteenth century saw an explosion of thaumuturgical interventions, providing sufficient material for a book-length study of this phenomenon, Michael Goodich's fascinating *Violence and Miracle in the Fourteenth Century* (1995). The author notes how 'in times of great fear and distress, the innocent suppliant appeals for divine aid against the exigencies of a violent and unjust world'.[25] Charged with murder in 1323, the innocent Bernardo Nuctii made a vow to renounce all sin to Nicholas of Tolentino; he made good his escape past seven guards. At Die in 1390, the execution ladder broke causing the horses to flee in panic; the condemned man was offered a second trial and was freed. In 1384 a crowd of three hundred spectators watched a forger make a sacred vow before being hung from the bridge at Lansberg; he fell into the water and despite being bound hand and foot managed to reach safety. A similar story is told from Châteauneuf in 1395, where a bound child killer was sentenced to drowning in a river; however, she resurfaced on a sandbank with her hands miraculously freed. More often than not, though, it was the innocent who were saved by divine involvement.

Occasionally, heavenly aid did not go quite far enough. In 1369 in the north-western French city of Le Mans, Guillaume le Breton survived several attempts to hang him. At each attempt the halter broke and Guillaume made a lengthy drop to the ground. This was taken as a sign of celestial aid, so Guillaume was spared the gallows and transported back to prison on a carriage. During the return journey the carriage was involved in a serious accident in which Guillaume was critically hurt; as a result of this, he died soon after in his cell. The physician attending him put cause of death down to injuries sustained in the falls from the gibbet and in the carriage crash.

So far, we have observed medieval perspectives on violence in society without reference to wars. This facilitates a point of reference for atrocities in warfare, what today we would call war crimes. It has been seen how even in times of normality, medieval society was constantly exposed to exemplary violence in many brutal forms which society itself demanded. Torture was seldom public, except in executions where it was designed to prolong the killing process and maximize the death agonies (anticipating by centuries the draconian pamphlet from London in 1701, *Hanging Not Punishment Enough*), but it existed primarily as a widely utilized judicial measure. These levels of violence jumped exponentially in times of war, not just on the obvious field of battle but wherever troops marched. Violent crime also increased in the wake of war, a feature noted in most societies in most times, whether it be English soldiers returning from defeat in France at the end of the Hundred Years War in the early 1450s, or when they returned again at the close of the wars of William III and

Queen Anne 250 years later. War does more than provide a cloak for the criminal activity of soldiers; it offers a time of opportunity for all, and not just for those with base motives. During the Scottish invasions of northern England in the early fourteenth century, large numbers of animals and amounts of grain were stolen in thefts designed and timed to look as if Scottish raiders were responsible. In a subsistence economy at the best of times the loss of an ox or horse could have a dire effect on a household. Unsurprisingly, then, these raids 'did not merely furnish people with the opportunity to take advantage of disturbed local conditions in order to engage in criminal activities; they must have also provided strong incentives to those who had been deprived of their goods to replace animals and foodstuffs that had been carried off, and crops that had been burned'.[26]

Conditions of war imposed great strains on vulnerable elements in society, leaving them exposed to an environment in which the rule of law counted for little. In times of peace, visual exemplary violence was condoned, brutal and widespread; but it was as nothing compared to times of war, when the lessons of violence were applied on an altogether grander scale.

2

WAR

THE KING AS JUDGE AND EXECUTIONER

At the head of the medieval system of justice and government stood the king. With him lay the ultimate sanctions of power: the authority to make war or peace, and the authority to order death or grant life to his subjects, from the lowest to the highest of them. He was encouraged – expected – to wield his sword to protect his people from criminals and from enemies. He was the foremost knight and the final arbiter of justice; in both forms, he was the most powerful life giver or life taker in the land. He was warrior, judge and executioner.

The peace of the realm was the king's peace. The severity of a monarch was praised if it rendered his kingdom safe. Much like today or any time when there are perceptions of ruptures in the social fabric of society, medieval folk looked back to earlier times as periods of law-abiding order, a golden age secured by a ruler who respected tradition and who did not stay his hand in meting out fatal justice to lawbreakers. To defend his nation from enemies, a monarch's legislative and judicial ability had to be matched by his martial prowess, for not only was he head of the country's judiciary, he was also the commander-in-chief of that country's army. These two elements – the legal and military – combined with a third: sacerdotalism, or the priestly nature of kingship. Medieval (and later) theory deemed a ruler to have inherited his temporal authority from God, and so he reigned by divine right. His duty to uphold the laws of the land, maintain the peace and protect his people from mortal enemies was therefore a sacred one. Breaking the king's peace offended people, king and God; it was up to the monarch to prevent such inversions of the natural order of society.

Thus the king's responsibility was not just to his people but directly to God. This divine hierarchy granted the monarch heightened powers both politically and mystically, the latter including miraculous healing capabilities. The first lines of a royal letter or command reminded all that the monarch was king 'by grace of God'; this was no empty formula, but a phrase pregnant with unbounded authority, claiming God as the ultimate source of royal power. Whatever the king did, in theory he could do so in God's name.

This sacerdotal element of kingship was established at the coronation. Drawing on Old Testament precedents, the ceremony imbued the king with dual authority in both the lay and clerical spheres. The papacy attempted to play down the resemblance of a coronation to the sacrament of Holy Orders, but without success. In England and France, the crowning ceremony involved anointment with chrism, the holy oil employed in episcopal consecrations. French coronations also saw the administering of an oil, conveniently 'sent' from Heaven, and used at Clovis's baptism in 496. Not to be outdone, in the fourteenth century the English wondrously 'discovered' a phial of oil that St Thomas Becket had received from the Virgin Mary; the oil became a feature of English coronations thereafter. This fusion of powers dominated medieval ideas of kingship and has been much studied since (most notably in Ernst Kantorowicz's *The King's Two Bodies: A Study in Medieval Political Theology*). It was a short step for medieval theologians and political observers, raised on belief in the Holy Trinity, to articulate the king as two forms in one: the body corporeal (mortal), and the body politic (immortal and divine). The emperor Frederick II was not alone in contending that failure to perform royal wishes amounted to blasphemy, something that should be borne in mind when we encounter soldiers carrying out their king's orders to massacre prisoners or indulging in other atrocities.

As Vicar of Christ (a title also taken by Pope Innocent III in the early thirteenth century at a time of competition between temporal and spiritual influences), and as a viceregent of theocratic government, the monarch's primary objective was maintaining the king's peace, not least so that the faithful could concentrate on serving their God. If a crime was not directed simply against the people or the king but against God as well, then this implied that upon the king was imposed the onerous duty of ensuring that peace was enforced for God. It therefore followed that the application of violent royal justice was divinely sanctioned. A king with blood on his hands could raise them to his people as proof of his efforts on their, and God's, behalf; he could expect acclamation in return.

Henry I of England received such praise. Henry does not have a martial reputation. Not for him a colourful royal sobriquet such as 'Lionheart', 'Hammer' or 'Conqueror'; instead he must settle for 'Beauclerc', a testament to the efficiency of his administration and bureaucracy. However, as Warren Hollister has shown, amongst contemporaries and following generations he earned renown as a fierce lawkeeper, keeping his subjects safe by harsh measures against malefactors. To modern eyes these measures are extreme; various historical opinions have condemned Henry as a 'savage, ruthless man' with a 'reputation for brutality', his 'reign of calculated terror' being 'terrible and barbaric'; but in twelfth-century England his divinely inspired policy of zero tolerance was greeted much more favourably. Henry was merely fulfilling his coronation promise to keep peace throughout his domain. Two centuries later, Edward II's failure to do likewise was highlighted clearly and shamefully in the deposition articles set out against him.

Henry I's policy of 'tough on crime, and a whole lot tougher on criminals', met with a hugely popular and supportive press, at complete variance with modern condemnation of his brutal methods. Leading churchmen of Henry's day were fulsome in their praise of Henry's policies: Eadmer declared that 'great good immediately resulted'; Robert of Torigny lauded the King for keeping the peace 'by the point of the sword'; a monk from Peterborough in central England uses the Anglo-Saxon Chronicle to voice his approval of Henry's mutilations of moneyers, as 'it was done very justly'.[1] Henry's constituency was truly a flog 'em and hang 'em one.

Henry's great protagonist, the larger-than-life (in all respects) Louis the Fat of France, was not to be outdone in upholding law and order in his own realm. When, in 1109, Guy of la Roche-Guyon and his children were murdered by his brother-in-law William, Louis was swift in striking with the sword of justice. His friend and biographer Abbot Suger tells us how the King ordered that William and his followers be punished 'by a carefully chosen and shameful death'. When William and his men were seized, their fate was terrible.

Attacking them with swords, they piously slaughtered the impious, mutilated the limbs of some, disembowelled others with great pleasure, and piled even greater cruelty upon them, considering it still too kind. No one should doubt that the hand of God sped so swift a revenge when both the living and the dead were thrown through the windows. Bristling with countless arrows like hedgehogs, their bodies stopped short in the air, vibrating on the sharp points of lances as if the ground itself rejected them. The French hit upon the following unusual revenge for William's unusual deed. When alive he lacked a brain, and now that he was dead he lacked a heart, for they ripped it from his entrails and impaled it upon a stake, swollen as it was with fraud and evil. They left it set up in a conspicuous place for many days to make public their revenge for this wickedness.

The corpses of William and several of his companions were then tied with ropes to harrows and pieces of fences, which had been fitted for this purpose, and were cast upon the river Seine. And if nothing managed to keep them from floating all the way to Rouen, they would exhibit there how treachery had been avenged.[2]

Here we see coming together many of the elements already discussed: the emphasis on highly visual and gruesome punishment as a warning; the encouragement of extreme brutality by the king; and an abbot of the Church's approbatory applause for the 'hand of God' in 'piously' slaughtering the guilty. There is also here the presence of xenophobia, as the men killed were Normans and not Frenchmen. This was not some spur-of-the-moment act of bestial madness, but something ordained from on high. How easy, then, in the chaos and heat of war, for appalling acts of savagery to be perpetrated.

The reactionary similarities between Henry and Louis disguise a growing divergence between English and continental ideas on kingship. In France, Germany and elsewhere, theocratic monarchy exercised much greater influence than in England, paving the way for later absolutism. This in part explains why anti-heretical measures against the Cathars in southern France received such strong royal support, as these formed another facet of divine law and order. It also helps to account for the relative (to England) lack of active political opposition against French kings in particular; although the French baronage failed to unite sufficiently to offer a common front and programme against royal encroachments, when serious rebellions did occur their intention was largely to change government policy rather than to threaten the king himself. The French looked on horrified at later medieval England's penchant for killing its kings, they themselves not acquiring the taste for judicial regicide until later in their history.

In England, rising against the monarch, although acutely serious, was rendered less shocking by the slightly less theocratic and more feudal nature of kingship there. Feudalism, for all its emasculation by modern deconstructionism, remains a useful term to designate the essential contract at the heart of hierarchical society. 'Good faith' (*bona fides*) was required on both sides of the personal, political covenant between lord and master. Thus if a king, especially in a state like England, failed to uphold his end of the bargain – law and order, good governance, defence of the realm, etc. – he risked being brought to account in the most practical of ways for not maintaining his side of the bargain. When an English king confused his theocratic and feudal roles it fostered crisis within his realm. Even when feudalism was on the wane, in later medieval England, theocratic monarchy was still exercised under limits, as the reign of Richard II shows.

Theory is one thing, reality another. What really mattered to a ruler was preservation of power; for this he had to employ violence widely but intelligently. Weakness sent out all the wrong signals. This late medieval passage from England warns rulers to remember

> How kings [who] kept neither law nor peace
> Went soon away in many different ways
> Without thanks of God at their decease.[3]

Plentiful violence well directed by the king was approved; arbitrary, inconsistent violence was not. Philippa Maddern has categorized three areas of justifiable violence as used by the king in his role as a judge. First, his position of established authority, especially in respect of that authority bestowed upon him by God, sanctioned his acts of punitive force. Secondly, this violence had to be directed in pursuit of a good cause – peace and order, for example. Thirdly, this violence could also be directed only against certain people, namely the criminal and wicked.

The king was permitted – indeed, encouraged – to express emotional outrage in his judgement: 'The king's anger was as unquestioned as the wrath of God; it could be coupled with it.'⁴ But he had to channel his fury appropriately. As the deity's representative, the king's anger (*ira regis*) was meant to reflect God's anger (*ira Dei*) in its projection, accuracy and proportion. This also applied to God's mercy, the dispensing of justice allowing for displays of clemency. Just as the king's ruthlessness could be praised, so too could be his mercy. When Philip II of France defeated his enemies at Bouvines near Lille in 1214, Roman law and French custom sanctioned his use of the death penalty for those guilty of rebellion and *lèse-majesté*; but Philip refrained from implementing the death penalty. His royal biographer, the sycophantic panegyrist William the Breton, records Philip's humane mercy to his prisoners and applauds his astonishing forgiveness and pity. Of course, such acts of leniency could be promoted as much as public executions; they were frequently driven by political or propaganda considerations. For a king, it was good to be feared; but being loved and respected was also a source of political capital. As Pope Clement IV advised Henry III in a letter from 1265, after the King's success against the baronial revolt, 'Human forgiveness will entice more of your men back to love than harsh punishment would, since the lust for revenge sates the hatred of a few but irritates that of the many.'⁵

Female intercession was another route to mitigating justifiable kingly anger. The most famous example of such an intervention is that of the Burghers of Calais, related by Froissart in his colourful, bloody chronicle of the early stages of the Hundred Years War. In 1346, Edward besieged and took Calais in northern France. Edward, a hardened and successful warrior, wanted a general massacre of the citizens as a warning to any towns that might consider resistance in the future. His war council advised against such a move, echoing the similar advice given to King John over a century earlier at the siege of Rochester in 1215, alerting him to the danger that the English might receive similar treatment at the hands of the French should the campaign later suffer any reversal in fortune. Edward was only partially placated. In return for sparing the majority, he demanded a sacrifice by a minority; six men from Calais were to be offered up for execution. The bells of Calais rang out, calling its citizens to a general assembly. Six burghers from the town's hierarchical elite, including its richest man, Eustace de

Sainte-Pierre, stepped forward as the town's sacrificial victims to appease the wrath of the English king. Stripped to their shirts and breeches, and roped together by their necks, they advanced from the town towards Edward. They knelt before him, imploring him to spare their lives. Edward, however, was resolute and ordered that their heads be struck off. Edward's queen, Philippa of Hainault, moved to pity by the wretched spectacle, threw herself on her knees before her husband, despite her advanced pregnancy, and tearfully beseeched his mercy for the men, in the name of the love he bore for her. Of course, Edward relented, and the men were freed. The episode did Edward's fierce reputation no harm: his propagandists saw to that. Edifying as this tale of emollience is, it was not typical: one medieval commander who, out of pity, permitted an enemy garrison to escape, was beheaded. Such measures did not encourage battlefield restraint towards one's enemies.

In his account of the Burghers of Calais, Froissart throughout emphasizes Edward's great anger, stoked not least by the losses that his own men had incurred at the siege; thus his wrath was both justifiable and understandable. The God of the Old Testament furnished an abundance of examples displaying how angry retribution was directed for the good of men; as kings and lords represented legitimate authority in the world, rulers could dispense violent retribution against those who sinfully flouted their will. Society presumed on witnessing manifestations of violent anger from its rulers, understanding, as Richard Barton has shown in his study of aristocratic anger, that 'they might grow righteously angry when evil threatened their positions or the areas under their protection', and those that resisted their authority 'would come to be seen as sinful, as deserving recipients of zealous rage'.[6] Such an understanding has clear military implications; from here it is but a short step to brutal battlefield actions mandated by medieval generals. The expression of anger and violence was accepted in the course of executing hierarchical authority; this being so, it was reserved for the *bellatores* and denied the *laboratores*, the lower orders thereby relying on the upper ones to wield the sword, rather than the pitchfork, of justice.

Keeping the masses under the thumb was one strand of control, maintaining the peace amongst the nobility was another, altogether weaker, one. Recourse to violence amongst the higher ranks was an early option in any dispute, and moved beyond crime and punishment in its scope. The threat to greater disorder was always present as arguments readily escalated from individual acts to feuding and private war. In his famous work *Feudal Society* (1940), Marc Bloch argued that medieval people were subjected to 'ungovernable forces'; living so 'close to nature', they had little control over it. 'Behind all social life, there was a background of the primitive, of submission to uncontrollable forces, of unrelieved physical contrasts'; epidemics, famines and 'constant acts of violence' led to a state of 'perpetual insecurity'.[7]

Against such an unstable background, it is not unexpected that when a man of power had the ability to affect the course of events by force he did so. The popular literature of the time was no discouragement, being excessively bloodthirsty, the endless feuding and warmaking in the widely read *Raoul de Cambrai*, for example, ending only with the deaths of all the protagonists. The only potential curb to violent anarchy was royal authority, which attempted to control aristocratic aggression, acting not out of altruistic motives but out of self-preservation. As Richard Kaeuper has perceptively noted, 'When lords at all levels, and townsmen as well, sallied forth in arms to settle their own grievances, a long tradition of private rights buttressed by the ethos of chivalry ran headlong against a developing theory of public authority vested in kingship for the common weal.'[8]

With society so often in a febrile and precarious state, it did not take much to spark off major incidents. Much of the kindling for blood feuds came from the family tree. Most families defined themselves through both immediate kin and in-laws, making for a large grouping, widened further still by frequent remarriages. When just one member of this extended family fell into a dispute, the collective familial group could easily be sucked into an escalating imbroglio. Fiery male youths, accountable for most violent crimes and acting on violent impulses, would often initiate a bitter dispute; but just as often they were acting on the cynical orders of family greybeards, the latter deliberately creating an incident *ex nihilo* from which they foresaw political or financial gain.

In recent years, feuds have spilt as much ink as blood. The efforts of many scholars to neatly categorize and define feud as separate from various forms of private war and public disorder should not distract us from the fact that all such terms can blur into one; what concerned the medieval ruler was the ever present danger and likelihood that a feud would escalate beyond family neighbourhoods to engulf entire regions. One thesis for the origins of the Wars of the Roses in England lays the blame on baronial factionalism and feuding. Although the modern consensus inculpates Henry VI's incompetence as the cause of the wars, the telling point is that this incompetence was most clearly manifest in Henry's inability to suppress the various regional feuds in the first instance, and so prevent them from escalating into something altogether larger. In Germany, the long-running feud between the archbishops of Cologne with their secular neighbours culminated spectacularly and bloodily with the Battle of Worringen in 1288. The inevitability of spiralling, reciprocal violence was increased by medieval theories, first propounded by St Augustine, that a war waged to avenge an injury was just, thus actually encouraging a war to develop from a feud. None of this was conducive to the king's peace; feuding, for all its acceptance in culture as a justifiable process in many disputes, did not make the king look good.

A brief look at some blood feuds throughout medieval Europe will show how the image of feud as being the result of impulsive, hot-blooded men in pursuit of swift vengeance and honour covers just one corner of the canvas. Instead, it shows how frequently and readily was the recourse to violence by men in pursuit of coldly calculated aims, with self-aggrandizement usually the goal. Benjamin Arnold's study of the dynamics of princely power, *Princes and Territories in Medieval Germany* (1991), clearly reveals how feuds were manipulated towards land-grabbing or well-tuned checks to opponents and competitors. 'Feuds amongst the lords were so prevalent that it is tempting to subordinate all the institutional, dynastic, and judicial explanations for the evolution of princely command to the insistent political rhythms of intestine conflict ... Nearly every prince inherited a set of quarrels, which had to be prosecuted by armed force as a virtual normal function of regional politics.'[9]

In the 1140s, Bishop Otto of Freising complained that things were now so serious that men plundered and burned all year round. Long-lasting disputes among the powerful included: the dukes of Bavaria with the archbishops of Salzburg; the counts of Tirol with the bishops of Bixen and Trent; the counts of Holland and Guelders with the bishops of Osnabrück; the margraves of Brandenberg with the archbishops of Magdeburg; and the dukes of Brunswick with the bishops of Bremen, Hildesheim and Halberstadt. (Given this level of secular–ecclesiastical conflict, it is hardly surprising that the Reformation began in Germany.) A lesser but still serious feud in the 1150s between the Counts Widekind and Folkin of Schwalenberg with Abbot Wibald of Corvey was raised in the royal court. The counts had attacked the abbot's town of Höxter, destroying its defences, sacking it, and then demanding a large ransom. Royal authority ordered the Abbot and town to take their vengeance. The feud lingered on until a leading vassal of the Abbot was murdered, for which Count Widekind was exiled by Duke Henry the Lion, having first paid compensation and having lost his ducal castle. The prevalence of feuding in Germany can be linked to the lack of strong, central authority; levels of feuding were not so high in England, where monarchy had a stronger grip.

Lay and religious feuds were also common in France (although to a lesser extent than in Germany) where the protagonists habitually vied with each other over financial rights, such as tolls and tallages. In these disputes, monasteries could find their lands and people plundered, livestock stolen, crops and houses burned; sometimes monks were killed. As elsewhere and in Germany, lords and lesser knights latched on to any pretext for pillaging their neighbours' lands. With the Crown, the Church was the biggest institutional landowner in medieval Europe, and hence its lands were contiguous to those of any number of lords who enviously eyed ecclesiastical property and wealth. Germany, with its hundreds of principalities and mini-statelets, was far harder to govern than the more centralized kingdoms such as England and France, where there were more successful attempts at limiting and formalizing feuds, as through ordeal and trial by battle. Malcolm Vale recounts a case from Valenciennes in northern France in 1455 when an incident of insult to a personal reputation led to a trial by combat before Philip the Good of Burgundy. Although it was fought according to strict regulations, the outcome was nevertheless gruesome: the loser 'was beaten senseless with a staff by his assailant, his eyes were gouged out, and he was drawn on a hurdle – still alive – to be hanged from the gibbet by the public executioner of the town'.[10]

Such trials had evolved from royal limitations on feuding in France, stemming primarily from Louis IX's ordinance of 1258 which restricted the rights of nobility to engage in private wars, tournaments and even single combats. In 1304, Philip the Fair issued a further ordinance, at Toulouse, a region of southern France notorious for its incessant private wars; he felt compelled to moderate it only two years later in acknowledgement of the nobility's determination to settle differences through violence. Eventually, through royal regulations of sanctioned combats, the French monarchy was at least seen as exercising some form of control while limiting the possibilities of disputes growing out of control. The nobility did not lightly relinquish what they considered to be their birthright to wage private war; the king would not relinquish his God-given duty to preserve peace in his lands. In 1323, Charles IV the Fair had the opprobrious Jourdain, Lord of Casaubon, executed for pursuing private war. Jourdain admitted to the killing of men, women and children, the destruction of crops and properties, and robbing churches and abbeys; but he attempted to defend himself by declaring it was all done on his own territory to help his war effort. Feud and private war were often invoked to cover a multitude of sins and excesses.

The weaker the central authority, then, the greater the propensity to indulge in private wars and feuds. Before William the Conqueror established his dynasty on the English throne in 1066, he had first to survive a perilous period through his minority as the duke of Normandy. During his minority ducal power was understandably weak, and the duchy was riven with feuds against a background of numerous power struggles. In this near state of anarchy, many atrocities were committed. One occurred at a wedding feast held by William de Bellême; invited by his lord, William Giroie attended, only to leave without his eyes, ears or genitals.

As a relatively closely controlled kingdom, England generally saw less in the way of vicious, large-scale feuds, these being more prominent in the early and late medieval periods when royal authority was compromised. Richard Fletcher's recent study of blood feud in late Anglo-Saxon England reveals how feuding could intensify and extend to encompass political ambitions, chief amongst which was, paradoxically, the preservation and perpetuation of dynasties. The feud that Fletcher analyses began in 1016 and lasted three generations. In the year it started, Earl Uhtred and forty of his retainers, under a passage of safe conduct, were murdered, the Earl dying in a royal hall when Thurbrand the Hold leapt upon him from his hiding place behind a wall hanging. Ealdred, Uthred's son, avenged his father but was himself killed in 1038 at the hands of Thurbrand's son Carl; the pair's attempt at reconciliation was dashed when a night of drink was followed by a morning of murder. (Note the resemblance to the feud between Sichar and Austregisel.) The feud ended only in 1073 when most of Thurbrand's grandsons and great-grandsons were massacred by Earl Waltheof, great-grandson of Uthred. Waltheof may have used the pretext of the blood feud to make a pre-emptive strike against his dynastic enemy, whom he feared was on the point of rising in rebellion. Waltheof himself rebelled against William the Conqueror in 1075, for which he was publicly decapitated. The Crown had the last word.

Feuds could be ended by the complete annihilation of the foe; more often they were settled by compensation and royal intervention. In the early medieval period, financial recompense was the less honourable path, symbolizing an inability or disinclination to pay the full debt of honour, which could be cancelled only by the shedding of blood. As the Middle Ages progressed, royal restrictions on blood feuds tended to reverse this situation. Even when royal authority was diminished in fifteenth-century England – a time which saw the violent feuds of Poynings against Percies, Wydvilles against Nevilles, and Staffords against Harcourts – bastard feudalism permitted avenues that allowed for financial settlements to end disputes, as happened in the private arrangements between Henry Pierpont, Thomas Hastings and Henry Ferrers in 1458. As private warmaking continued, so did private peacemaking.

Any sizeable violent activity in a kingdom was a dangerous distraction for a ruler; large-scale unrest could attract unwanted attentions as a focus of discontent and divert valuable time and sources away from the ruler's own military plans. For any prince, the most iniquitous form of war came in the shape of domestic uprisings. Treason and rebellion against the king was not lightly undertaken, not just because of the military resources the king had at hand, but also because it was an act against the Lord's anointed. In England, where, as we have seen, the idea of theocratic kingship was not held as highly as in Europe, rebellions were so frequent very few English monarchs escaped them. Before the further development of treason laws in Edward I's time, every reign from 1066 to 1272 suffered rebellions to dethrone the king. A ruler had to play his hand carefully against potential threats, for although he was ruler by the grace of God, he could lose his temporal authority if he acted against the law as a tyrant. Some political treatises held that tyrants should be overthrown by their subjects, others that this should be left to God. In the earlier medieval period, this second view was often held by the Church, which anathematized rebellions against God's appointed representative; later, however, the Church was just as likely to label an oppressive king (i.e. one that taxed them heavily or failed to protect Church property) as a tyrant. Condemnation or approbation could depend largely on the prevailing political situation and anticipation of which side was likely to win.

The danger of violent unrest did not lie exclusively with the aristocracy, as events in fourteenth-century England and France were to show dramatically. The 1381 Peasants' Revolt in England, retold in Alistair Dunn's revealing book *The Great Rising of 1381* (2002), actually comprised as many discontents from the lower middle classes as the lower ones; it also involved some rich Londoners. Their demands for social reforms – including the abolition of serfdom – were coupled with political ones. When they marched on London they decapitated the Chancellor, Archbishop Sudbury and the Lord Treasurer, Robert Hales. In Suffolk the same fate befell Sir John Cavendish, Chancellor of Cambridge University and Chief Justice of the King's Bench, and John Cambridge, Prior of Bury St Edmunds; their heads were spiked on lances and made to perform a macabre puppet show, in which they chatted and kissed each other. When Richard II's government retook control of the situation, its response was uncompromising: on London Bridge, as elsewhere, the heads of royal ministers and lawyers were replaced by those of Wat Tyler and other rebel commanders; where rebels had been buried at St Albans, Richard personally supervised the exhumation of the bodies and had them re-strung up on the gibbet in classic warning mode.

The Jacquerie of 1358 in France makes the Peasants' Revolt mild by comparison. The uprising was named somewhat ironically after 'Jacques Bonhomme', the familiar and genial French nickname for a peasant. Peasant unrest was endemic in France in the confusion of war and military defeats for the French; it was heightened by heavy taxation, one of the main causes of the revolt in England. The French problem was exacerbated further by the weakness of the Crown at this stage, unlike England under Edward III basking united in the afterglow of great victories in France. The acute sufferings of the French peasantry from plague, deprivation and war erupted in the Jacquerie, the most murderous of all fourteenth-century risings. It was truly a revolutionary class struggle at its most bitter.

Ordinary people blamed those who ruled them for total failure. It was barely two years since their king, John II, had been captured by the English at Poitiers; recovery from the Black Death was slow; and companies of mercenaries and brigands rode at will across the land. Law and order had broken down most calamitously of all in the regions worst afflicted by the Hundred Years War, but it was about to collapse completely. Froissart wrote of the Jacques, 'These evil men, who had come together without leaders or arms, pillaged and burned everything and violated and killed all the ladies and girls without mercy, like mad dogs.'[11] He tells of how one knight was bound to a post while his pregnant wife and daughter were gang-raped and killed before his eyes; he himself was then murdered in the most sadistic fashion. Another knight was roasted alive on a spit while the members of his family were forced to watch before their own deaths. They elected their own king, Jacques Bonhomme, to lead them in their inchoate struggle.

Though it was just a fortnight in duration, the backlash under Charles of Navarre was felt for years. This shocking inversion of the social order prompted a response of solidarity amongst the aristocratic classes beyond the boundaries of France in a savage repression of a savage revolt. Charles himself was credited with the execution of three thousand rebels in one day; elsewhere, claims Froissart with even greater exaggeration, seven thousand were despatched in a few hours. The (no doubt) inflated figures give an indication of the level of punitive slaughter; so many were executed they had to be strung up in bunches. A concatenation of crushing factors conspired to launch the Jacquerie, but it is surely relevant that it burst out at a time when France was, in effect, without its king.

The aristocracy posed a greater threat to the Crown. Robert Bartlett has identified three main types of aristocratic rebellion. One form was individual, instinctive and visceral, a hot-blooded response to royal encroachment or denial of patronage or expected reward. More threatening was a general aristocratic movement agitating in support of a rival ruler, usually a member of the ruling dynasty. Most hazardous of all, perhaps, was a rebel movement with an aristocratic programme of reform, of the type that led to Magna Carta in 1215. Open rebellions gradually decreased as medieval rulers increasingly stamped out private wars by impressing their authority; the weaker the ruler, the greater the threat of revolt. In the earlier period, fighting against the king was not always considered treasonable so long as formal defiance (*diffidatio*) had been declared. But from legal and political developments emerged the notion that warring against the king connoted warring against the public realm and its good, thereby denying rebels the cover of fighting a private war.

In England, all taking up of arms against the king became treasonous during Edward I's reign. Initially, executions for treason were carried out against only Welsh and Scots who were considered rebels in England, but by Edward II's reign political executions were becoming common for the first time since the eleventh century. Indeed, unlike Europe, for nearly two centuries not a single member of the nobility was punished by death or mutilation for political crimes, so benign was royal policy. Undoubtedly, the extensive ties of kinship amongst the hierarchy helped stay the king's avenging hand. Lesser ranks were not so privileged: rebellious garrisons were hanged by Stephen at Shrewsbury in 1138 and by Henry III in 1224 at Bedford.

Edward II's disastrous reign dramatically altered this culture of clemency towards the nobility, when an orgy of high-ranking political executions transformed politics in England. In 1322, there were no less than twenty political hangings and decapitations. Of Edwardian executions, the most famous were: Piers Gaveston, run through and decapitated in 1312, his body not receiving final burial until 1315; the Younger Despenser who, in 1326, was hung from a fifty-foot-high gibbet, disembowelled alive, and then beheaded; and King Edward II himself, in 1327, tradition claiming that he was murdered by thrusting a red-hot poker up his anus, a comment on his alleged homosexuality.

Such executions would not have surprised the Scottish and Welsh. English imperialist attitudes towards the Celtic fringe fostered the enforcement of harsh measures against rebels from an early stage, reinforced by Edward I's new treason laws. It is from this time that we become familiar with some of the most gruesome and famous executions in England. In 1282, Prince David of Wales was drawn, hung and quartered, and his internal organs burned in a fire. William Wallace's execution was another ritualized death. Drawn by a horse's tail to his place of execution, he was inflicted with different punishments for different crimes (treason tended to attract to the guilty party a plethora of other wrongs). For felony, robbery and murder, Wallace was hanged until nearly dead, and then disembowelled; for sacrilege, his viscera were burned; for treason, his body was dismembered and displayed throughout the north: his head was impaled on a spike on London Bridge, his right arm was exhibited in Newcastle, his left at Berwick, his right foot at Perth, his left at Stirling. Edward I – the Leopard, the Hammer of Scots – considered even mockery as a form of *lèse-majesté*. One medieval chronicle implies that his sack of Berwick on the Scottish border in 1296 was in response to the insults that he suffered from the town's ramparts: jibes, gestures and buttock-baring. In its laws on treason, France trailed England by a few decades. Following his victory against the Flemish at Courtrai in 1328, Philip III treated the enemy as traitors in true bloody Edwardian style.

Where crime constituted countless individual acts and tragedies, rebellion was an act of war that could easily concentrate divergent political discontent into a central and focused attack on the Crown. The monarch therefore did not hesitate to punish it publicly like other crimes, but in the most extreme form imaginable, as the grotesque spectacles of the deaths of Prince David and William Wallace demonstrate. In France, treason was also punishable by quartering, but here the favoured method was by four horses pulling the offender apart; in England and Germany, the blade was preferred (in Germany, the executioner struck the offender over his mouth with his disembowelled innards or heart). In early fourteenth-century France, Philip the Fair had his daughter-in-law's lovers executed for treason: they were flayed alive, then quartered, beheaded and strung up. In 1330, King Charles of Hungary and his wife Elizabeth survived an assassination attempt by a baron called Felician. Elizabeth lost four fingers of her right hand, for which she became known as 'Cripplehand'. Felician was killed on the spot, but his men and accomplices were dragged around the streets and squares until they died with the flesh stripped away from the bones; their remains were chopped up and scattered about the streets for dogs to eat (and thus denied

Christian burial). As with Wallace, Felician's head and limbs were displayed throughout the kingdom.

One of the most inventive and repulsive executions on record emerges from early twelfth-century Flanders. It occurs in the aftermath of the murder of Count Charles the Good. The fate of the rebels involved in the murder included hanging, decapitation and being bound to a wheel fixed to a tree. This last device was employed for one Burchard. He was 'delivered over to the greedy appetite of ravens and winged creatures, a miserable death of a choice kind. His eyes were pecked out and his whole face torn to shreds by the birds from above, and his body was pierced a thousand times by arrows, lances, and javelins from below. He died a very vile death, and his remains were thrown into a sewer.'[12]

On 5 May 1127, twenty-eight rebels were hurled in their armour to their deaths from the tower at Bruges Castle. The chronicler Galbert of Bruges tells us that even with their hands tied behind their backs and despite the great height, some remained conscious for a while after striking the ground. Louis the Fat, who oversaw this precipitation, arranged the most shocking execution of all, reserved for a ringleader named Berthold. The death was devised to be as demeaning as possible. Berthold was strung up from a gallows but kept alive; a dog was suspended close by him. The dog was beaten repeatedly and turned its anger and fear on Berthold; when struck, it savaged Berthold, 'eating up his whole face ... It even befouled him with excrement.'[13] Abbot Suger notes approvingly that it was a wretched death for a wretched man.

THE KING AS WARRIOR

Of all the king's roles, the one of warrior was paramount. Very few medieval monarchs could combine a successful reign with poor military leadership or a poor military reputation. The strength of divine or legal right to power depended largely on the more practical ability to back that right with hard force, as recent studies have demonstrated. Kelly de Vries shows how military authority could displace political authority and how success in war could lead to success in politics.

Citing the example of Harold Godwinson's accession to the throne of England in 1066, he perceives the potential weakness in this might-is-right approach: there was 'one problem with military legitimacy as the foundation for medieval rule: it could always succumb to one who proved to be more militarily legitimate'.[14] A king with military charisma was in a much stronger and more secure position than one without. As Matthew Strickland has observed, 'There can be no doubt that one of the king's primary functions – arguably *the* primary function – remained as warleader, and that his *virtus* continued to be a vital ingredient in his military and political success, as it was still felt to be when Machiavelli wrote his *Prince*.'[15] A study by Richard Abels has shown how the fortunes of the late Anglo-Saxon state waxed and waned with the military abilities of its kings; monarchs who performed badly on the battlefield or, like Ethelred, shunned it altogether, courted political failure.

Like all nobles, the king was raised and trained to fight. His ultimate role was defence of the realm, and so the kings who were the most competent at war were the ones who were most admired. This admiration has carried through to the present day: for England, William the Conqueror, Richard the Lionheart, Edward I, Edward III and Henry V conjure up glorious images of iconic national warleaders; the pictures we have of John, Henry III, Edward II, Richard II and Henry VI are altogether different and more derogatory. Success in war brought with it political capital; confidence in – and fear of – such kings led to increases in loyalty, royal revenue and order in the kingdom. Being the head of government meant more than being chief executive; all the kings of medieval England were directly involved in military activity in the field; and all but one or two fought in the thick of battle. Harold, Richard I and Richard III were killed in combat; Henry I, Stephen and Henry VI only narrowly avoided the same fate. Sir John Fortescue, the fifteenth-century commentator on English governance, wrote, 'Lo! To fight and to judge are the office of a king.'[16]

A convincing display of royal martial ability conveyed reassurance to subjects as this indicated that the king was able to smite down not just political enemies but also the enemies of law, order and justice. The admiration for Edward IV in the thick of battle in this account of his return to England in 1471 is evident: 'The king, trusting verily in God's help, our blessed lady's, and Saint George, took to him great hardness and courage ... wherewith ... he manly, vigorously, and valiantly assailed them; [and] with great violence, beat and bore down before him all that stood in his way.'[17] The pressure to perform in war was therefore immense; it pushed kings to being ruthless so that they could be effective, and this need to be successful resulted in some extreme actions in warfare.

One way of examining a king's military role and contemporary attitudes to this role is to compare and contrast two great royal enemies and their reputations: Richard the Lionheart (1189–99) and Philip Augustus of France (1180–1223). Of the two, Richard has by far the more illustrious reputation as a military leader, reflecting his fame as a legend during his own lifetime. The early thirteenth-century *The History of William Marshal* claims that although French knights were the most highly regarded in Europe, thirty English knights under Richard's command would happily take on forty French ones. Medieval chronicles were almost unanimous in their praise of Richard: he was not only 'the most victorious' of kings, but also 'pious, most merciful and wise', 'He did right to all and would not allow justice to be perverted', 'He had the valour of Hector, the magnanimity of Achilles; in courage he was the equal of Alexander and Roland.' Even his Muslim enemies said of him that his 'courage, shrewdness, energy and patience made him the most remarkable ruler of his times'.[18] So elevated was his reputation that he appeared in visions to saints ascending into Heaven. Here was the epitome of chivalric kingship, a monarch who quite literally led from the front, who bested his enemies everywhere, who was brave and concerned for his men, who was in turn chivalrous and ruthless, and who led the Third Crusade to within sight of the walls of Jerusalem. For a long while Richard has been traduced by historians, especially those keen to eschew military history and instead measure a king's greatness by his bureaucratic output and book-keeping; but thanks mainly to the scholarship of John Gillingham, the view of most historians is now closer to that of contemporaries. (That great warrior king Edward III is currently undergoing a similar rehabilitation.)

Philip II of France, in contrast, suffers by comparison. Despite his martial appellations that denote his military success, 'Augustus' and 'Conqueror', his contemporaries were far more ambiguous in their views of him. Bertran de Born, the famous soldier and troubadour (and borderline psychotic belligerent), chides Philip as being 'too soft ... hunting sparrows and tiny birdies' instead of engaging in the manly pursuit of war; he 'looks like a lamb to me', laments Bertran.[19] English historians have been particularly scathing: Philip exhibited 'unattractive traits, [he was] lustful, authoritarian, cynical, suspicious, and treacherous'; his 'nervous disorder' predisposed him to 'underhand intrigue', he was guilty of 'cruelty' and 'treachery'; he was 'timid', 'not a great soldier', 'not an outstanding warrior'. Philip quite manifestly lacked the military charisma exuded in abundance by Richard. Yet Philip was not only the greatest of the Capetian kings; he was one of the most important monarchs in French history. He earned his sobriquets by military means, vastly extending royal power throughout France, kicking the English out of Normandy, and defeating his imperial enemies at Bouvines in 1214, a victory that resounds through French history and memory. As if in compensation, some French historians have unconvincingly attempted to paint Philip in the same incandescent light as Richard, but even those that recognize his 'talents as a soldier' also acknowledge his unappealing personal traits as an 'unscrupulous' and 'cautious, cynical and distrustful man'.

How can two hugely successful military kings leave such differing reputations to posterity? The explanation has already been alluded to in the quotes; the answer lies in image as seen through the lens of chivalry. The two kings were diametrically opposed in character and outlook: Richard was extrovert, gregarious, athletic, energetic, generous and colourful in the best traditions of a chivalrous warleader sharing bonhomie with his men; Philip was none of these things. The French king not only lacked these attributes of Richard, his physical presence did not promise heroic material; a pale, sickly child who grew into a fat, prematurely balding young man, Philip was not the stuff of chivalric legend. But the psychological perceptions were more debilitating for Philip's standing; his grandfather Louis the Fat was also bald and so obese he could only mount his warhorse with help, and even then with difficulty, but he gloried in his deserved esteem as a bellicose king. The image of Richard as the open, honest and true soldier and Philip as the sly, masterful, manipulative Machiavellian, may be simplistic but it has much to recommend it. In the Middle Ages the former qualities were prized over the latter, less chivalrous ones, and so Philip's propagandists made futile attempts to portray Philip in the same manner as Richard's did the English king. The French royal biographers Rigord and William the Breton adorned Philip with the grandiose, imperialistic overtones of 'Augustus' and likened him to Alexander the Great, charging improbably into battle far ahead of his more timorous men. However, even their hyperbolic descriptions of Philip's martial prowess could stretch the dictates of chivalric literature only so far and they could never make up the differences in personalities and deeds of the kings by quill and vellum. Ironically, it was these expected dictates of chivalry that forced Rigord and William to engage in a forlorn endeavour of contesting style over style rather than style over substance.

Philip's esteem suffered heavily on the Third Crusade. Contrary to a popular view, this was not Richard the Lionheart's crusade; he and Philip undertook joint leadership of this massive enterprise, which throws into relief the contrasting styles of military leadership of these two leaders of the Latin west and contemporary views of them in a combat setting. They led their forces together at the siege of Acre on the Mediterranean coast, the opening military engagement of the crusade; here an atrocity by Richard, to be discussed later in this book, occurred. By the summer of 1191, crusading forces had been besieging the vital seaport of Acre for nearly two years. Philip arrived first in April to a warm but low-key reception. The besieged Muslim garrison in Acre, dreading the arrival of the two most powerful Christian kings, were greatly relieved to see Philip sail into view with only a paltry six ships of men and provisions. However, it should be noted that the bulk of the French forces were already at the siege. Richard turned up six weeks later with twenty-five ships and many more following, arriving to a rapturous welcome. Philip had been complaining about Richard's tardiness, tut-tutting Richard's lack of commitment to this holy cause and delaying the essential task of taking Acre. Yes, Richard was a bit late, but he came up with some good excuses: in the short time between Philip's arrival at Acre and his own, Richard had conquered a kingdom, sunk a huge supply vessel ferrying relief to the beleaguered Muslim garrison, and even got married! How typical of the man, enhancing his contemporary reputation for flair and brilliance. He brought with him men and materiel, morale-boosting news of recent victories, and a honeymoon bride. No wonder people were astonished by him and admired him in equal measure. How could the dull Philip compare with this? As ever, he was in Richard's shadow.

And so contemporaries recognized. At Messina in Sicily, en route to the Holy Land, a sudden crisis prompted characteristically decisive action from Richard; donning his armour, he led his men to subjugate the city immediately, 'more swiftly than any priest could sing Matins' wrote one chronicler in praise.[20] And Philip's instinctive reaction to this unexpected outburst of violence? The same source relates that 'The French, unsure of what their lord the king would do, were running about looking for him, when he rushed out of the conference place to take refuge in the palace'; no wonder 'the king of France was jealous of the king of England's success'.[21] Even the Arabs perceived the difference between the two, one Arab chronicler of the siege writing: 'The king of England was a very powerful man amongst the Franks, a man of great courage and spirit. He had fought great battles, and showed a burning passion for war. His kingdom and standing were inferior to those of the French king, but his wealth, reputation and valour were greater.'[22] These were the perceptions of the time and they have passed down to the modern age. Now, as then, Philip is compared unfavourably to Richard, something which is bound to leave the French king's military reputation lost somewhat murkily in the shade.

Opinions continued in this vein at Acre. Philip paid his knights three gold coins a month, so Richard paid his four. The result was, of course, that Philip lost men (and face) to Richard, diminishing his standing further. A fervently pro-Ricardian writer effused: 'King Richard was universally extolled. It was declared that he surpassed everyone. "This is the man whose arrival we longed for," they [the crusaders] said ... "The most outstanding king in the world, more skilled in warfare than any other Christian, has come." ... Everyone's hope hung on King Richard.'[23]

This must have been very galling for Philip who, as a master of poliorcetics (siegecraft), had assiduously participated in the siege operations. The sources confirm that Philip, immediately on reaching Acre, mounted a horse and rode amongst the host and around the city to see from which side he could best test the enemy's defences. From thereon Philip oversaw the investment that included the building of belfries and artillery pieces, one of which was named 'the Evil Neighbour', moat-filling and the digging of a mine in preparation for storming. One French-led storm attempt pressed the Muslim garrison very hard, but it was the bombardment that was particularly effective. Muslim, French and English sources all attest to the efficacy of Philip's barrage; the garrison was forced to fiercely defend breaches and lamented the ceaseless battering that caused walls to crumble and structures to collapse, all of which increased the defenders' exhaustion. French sapping also played its part, allowing an assault (when Richard was incapacitated by illness) that came close to success.

Eventually the garrison, fearing being put to the sword in a successful storm that would surely follow the devastating bombardment, capitulated. The Continuator to William of Tyre's chronicle summed up the operation succinctly: 'The king of France's siege engines had broken down the walls of the city so much that it was possible to get through and engage in hand-to-hand fighting, while the renown of the king of England and his deeds so terrified [the Muslims] that they despaired of their lives.'[24] The success at Acre was therefore a joint effort, with Philip making a significant and telling contribution to the victory. The two kings were playing to their strengths. When Saladin's relief force arrived to attack the besiegers from its base on the heights above Acre, Richard rode out to tackle the Muslim army while Philip continued to batter the walls. Philip was never going to outshine the brilliant Richard, but Philip's role as a successful crusading king at Acre should have left his reputation greatly enhanced amongst contemporaries. That it did not owes much, as indicated above, to the perceptions of chivalric behaviour and esteem.

Soon after taking the city (and his share of spoils), Philip abandoned the crusade and left for home. This sudden departure dismayed the crusaders. Contemporaries wrote of 'contempt and hate' and 'immense opprobrium', 'how shameful and outrageous' it was, and even of 'frightened rabbits'. The departure was disastrous for Philip's standing; for many, it negated his contribution to the fall of Acre. No longer had he been an asset but, according to Richard of Devizes, the English king was 'burdened with the king of the French and held back by him, like a cat with a hammer nailed to its tail'.[25] Even though he left the bulk of his forces at Acre, the eventual failure of the crusade to take Jerusalem was laid at Philip's door.

None of the reasons supplied for Philip's action redound to his advantage. The best that his propagandists could come up with was his suspicion of Richard's talks with Saladin, his illness and his fear of poisoning (Philip was paranoid about assassination). His malady, arnoldia, is well documented; but to leave the greatest undertaking of the age because one's hair and nails were falling out was hardly going to promote Philip's image as an heroic general. When Richard also fell ill, he had himself carried on a litter to shoot a crossbow bolt symbolically at the walls of the city, thereby reassuring his troops. Touches like this made Richard the hero without equal.

Other explanations for Philip's departure included his jealousy of Richard and his distaste for Richard's arrogance. The real reason, recognized by some chroniclers, was hardly less flattering; it was purely political and motivated further by the opportunities open to him back home with Richard absent in the Holy Land. Unchivalrous as this was, it was a wise recognition on Philip's part that Richard was the better commander; and Philip did indeed make military headway until Richard's return. But even a pro-Ricardian source has this to say in mitigation: 'Yet the king of France's reputation should not be completely blackened. He had expended a great deal of effort and expense in that country, in storming the city. He had given aid and support to a great many people, while the very authority of his presence had brought about more quickly and easily the completion of that great undertaking.'[26]

Part of Philip's strength as a general was to acknowledge his own weaknesses and his enemy's strength, and to act on it. Had Philip succumbed to the pressures of knightly behaviour and engaged in single combat with Richard, the chroniclers would have loved it and the fanfare for chivalry would have blown loudly and joyously. Militarily, it would have been a total disaster for France, with their royal champion an overweight poodle flung into the arena against England's pitbull terrier. Richard knew this and over the years of Anglo-French conflict he would taunt Philip mercilessly with challenges to duel.

Richard's embodiment of the medieval view of the king as a warrior translated into real military capital for the English monarch: his reputation weakened the resolve of his enemies; his leadership qualities inspired his soldiers and encouraged others to serve him. Conversely, this should mean that Philip was hampered by his less bellicose character, but was this so in reality? Clearly Richard's military record speaks for itself. But whatever advantages he gained by leading from the front were negated by his death, in action, at the siege of Chalus Chabrol near Limoges in 1199. The consequences for his kingdom and empire were disastrous. He was succeeded by his incompetent younger brother John. Revisionist attempts to re-evaluate John as a good king, on account of his efficient bureaucracy, and to rescue him from his malign reputation, have been rebutted by recent scholarship. John, whose sobriquet of 'Softsword' (*Mollegladium*) reveals his aversion to war, was a poor general and hence a poor king. He shared many unattractive personality traits with Philip and, like him, disdained direct involvement on the field of battle. The difference that counted was Philip's awareness and understanding of all things military, and his appreciation of simple but important values such as consistency, determined intent and man-management. John lacked all of these and the result was that Philip's generalship defeated John time and again. Within five years of John's accession to the throne in 1199, Philip had accomplished the long-held dream of the kings of France and annexed Normandy. He went on to even greater glory at the epoch-making Battle of Bouvines in 1214.

Had Richard been alive it is debatable whether Normandy would have fallen at all. Philip's disinclination to personal risk had served him well; Richard's risk-taking had reaped huge dividends until it acted spectacularly and mortally against him. John not only lost all Richard had won, he even nearly lost the crown of England itself to the French in 1216; France was served both by Philip's military achievements and by the stability of his reign. Philip came close to death at Bouvines, a battle he had tried to avoid; after this experience, he left military campaigning to his more belligerently inclined son, Louis the Lion. Despite his accomplishments in war, Philip was not happy to let actions speak louder than words. Kings were very conscious of the image they portrayed and Philip was no exception; but attempts to depict him in Ricardian mode were unconvincing. On one occasion William the Breton implausibly describes Philip as biting at the bit to get stuck into action, being restrained only by the wise counsel of his advisers, who warn their king against the folly of reckless bravery: 'Go . . . while we hold back the enemy. Our deaths would be a light loss, but in you rests the hope and glory of the entire kingdom; for as long as you remain safe and well, France has nothing to fear.'[27] Philip was only too ready to take this sound advice. Timid and even pusillanimous though this might have been, it was good sense for the king to avoid danger whenever possible; Philip's staying power proved to be an invaluable, if not inspiring, military asset.

As warrior kings, Richard and Philip demonstrated contrasting styles. Richard's insights were arguably more brilliant and he was unequalled as a leader of men; but Philip's conquests affirm his own methods. What they shared was a deep understanding of the nature of warfare and the way it should be fought, and also the key attribute in a leader of the ruthless determination necessary to obtain objectives. This was seen in stark terms by Richard's treatment of the garrison at Acre and Philip's treatment of non-combatants at Château Gaillard during his conquest of Normandy. They matched each other tit for tat in vicious reprisals. When Philip massacred a large force of Richard's Welsh mercenaries, Richard hurled three prisoners to their deaths from the rocky heights of Château Gaillard and blinded fifteen others, leaving one with an eye to lead them to the French king. Philip, not to be outdone, responded in exactly the same fashion, 'so that no one', asserted William the Breton, 'would believe him less than Richard in strength and courage'.[28] Each attempted to intimidate the other; neither was too quick to show mercy, as this would be interpreted as a sign of having been intimidated. As in the sphere of crime and punishment, mercy was valued if sparingly used; in warfare it also had its uses, but if too readily resorted to it was a fatal sign of weakness and lack of resolve. The warrior king, as *rex irae*, was more to be feared than a merciful one. The implications for warfare were frightening.

THE CHURCH AND JUST WAR

In the summer of 793 the Vikings arrived at Lindisfarne monastery off the north-east coast of England.

> Like stinging hornets they overran the country in all directions, like fierce wolves, plundering, tearing and killing not only sheep and oxen, but priests and deacons, and choirs of monks and nuns. They came to the church of Lindisfarne, and there they laid all waste with dreadful havoc, trod with unhallowed feet the holy places, dug up

the altars, and carried off all the treasures of the holy church. Some of the brethren they killed; some they carried off with them in chains; many they cast out, naked and insulted; some they drowned in the sea.[29]

Medieval chronicles are crowded with such attacks on churches and monasteries. As centres of wealth and priceless artefacts they were obvious targets for pillaging; as economic centres, they could provide ransacking troops with grain, wine, horses and other forms of supply so necessary for an army on the move.

That the Vikings were pagans and roundly condemned as such for their barbaric activities did not mean that the Church was safe from its Christian brothers. The very things that attracted the Vikings attracted Christian troops in the Latin west. Although the latter did not inflict such heavy mortality rates upon ecclesiastics and the religious, these rates remained appreciable. We have already glimpsed – and we shall see again – how sanctuary for criminals was a flexible concept; in times of war it could be a meaningless one. The vulnerability of religious establishments can be shown by the events in the 1216–17 French invasion of England. Even in this relatively restrained war, fought between chivalrous, Christian knights, the principal abbey of St Albans was plundered by both sides in the space of a few weeks: stores, horses and money were seized, in one case under the threat of razing the monastery and entire town to the ground.

Despite such acts being sacrilegious and even condemned as war crimes, the prospect of Church wealth was too tempting to resist; here was a ready source of pay and provision for the troops. Church writers portrayed the perpetrators as blasphemous, ungodly barbarians, but the intent was very rarely anti-religious. Statues, images and altars were not wantonly destroyed, but broken to extract the valuable stones and metals with which they were embedded, while vestments, wall hangings and altar cloths were easily transportable forms of wealth. Even kings, the vicars of God, got in on the act, as the supposedly saintly Henry III did in 1231. During the Welsh uprising of that year, Prince Llewelyn's forces are recorded as having spared neither churches nor ecclesiastics, and burned several churches, even when women and children had taken refuge in them. King Henry III of England responded by plundering a pro-Welsh Cistercian abbey and burning many of its structures; he spared the abbey itself only when its abbot paid him 300 marks to save the building in which the community had invested so much time and labour.

This last example demonstrates how churches and monasteries might be attacked for reasons other than financial ones. In 1194 Philip Augustus destroyed churches in Evreux in northern France as an act of revenge against the town's citizens after Count John (later King John) had massacred the French garrison there. Destruction was often directed against religious establishments under the patronage of an enemy, damaging the patron's reputation and the economic benefits with which the establishments provided him; also, as with Henry III in Wales, it was directed against partisan houses, a problem that faced John during his reign, when monasteries poured out anti-royalist rhetoric. In his perceptive study of attacks on churches, Matthew Strickland has written: 'Religious foundations, which often served as the necropolis of a noble family, might be deliberately targeted precisely because they were tangible symbols of an opponent's status and prestige ... [A]ssaults on churches marked not simply the negation of an immense investment of capital and labour but a psychological blow which highlighted a lord's inability to defend his own.'[30] Thus Henry's violence against the Cistercian abbey in Wales was much more than a mere display of vengeful spite.

The Church had to rely on more than prayerful invocations for protection. It had to turn to the temporal world of politics and warfare, seeking benefactors who provided not only wealth but also the means to defend that wealth, thus involving themselves in the power politics of the age and widening the scope of warfare. From the pope in Rome to abbots of provincial houses, the Church needed swords and shields to guard against violation; as a great landowner, it raised money and troops not only for its feudal lord but also for its own use, often deploying these for its own personal ends as demonstrated by the ecclesiastical–secular feuds in Germany. Even its churches could be built with defence in mind, splendid examples still standing today in the Languedoc. When secular help was lacking, the Church sometimes took direct action, as Richard Hodges reveals in his account of the sack of the Italian monastery at San Vincenzo al Volturno in 881. The monastery was attacked by Arab mercenaries who had been in the employ of the Duke of Naples, one Bishop Athanasius. The monks, forewarned of the troops' advance, assembled with arms at the bridge entering the monastery, determined to fend off the assault. A ferocious battle ensued in which the monks acquitted themselves well, killing many of the mercenaries. Despite their effective defence they were betrayed by their slaves (so the source informs us); the Arabs fired and plundered the monastery, and put to the sword those monks who were unable to escape.

As the Middle Ages progressed, such expressions of the Church militant became increasingly rare as the Church grew ever more dependent on secular protection, so much so that, by the fourteenth century, it had become a bone of contention for some commentators. In the *Disputation Between a Clerk and a Knight*, a sparring dialogue for supremacy between the secular and religious worlds, the knight reproves the clerk for the protection he and his brethren enjoy: 'Whilst the kings fight risking their lives and property, in order to defend you, you lie in the shade and dine luxuriously – then, you may indeed call yourselves lords, whilst kings and princes are your slaves.'[31]

Clearly the Church had, for the most part, a vested interest in peace. Individual bishops, like those who feuded in Germany and Bishop Athanasius in the above paragraph, and on many occasions the collective Church itself, pursued explicitly military aims, but its wealth and personnel were exposed and vulnerable in times of war. Motivated by not only this but also genuine abhorrence at Christians spilling the blood of other Christians in endless private and dynastic wars, the Church instigated the Peace of God and the Truce of God in a forlorn attempt at limiting the effects of war. The Church's concerns are distinctly expressed by the Peace of God (*Pax Ecclesie*) of the late tenth century. It attempted to defend the Church's interests by prohibiting acts of violence or war against clergy, pilgrims and Church property; it extended its cover to women, peasants, merchants and livestock (which in their turn contributed to the Church's income). During a council held at Bourges in 1035, the Archbishop decreed that all Christian men of fifteen years and above should swear an oath to uphold the Peace. From this emerged the Truce of God (*Treuga Dei*) in the early eleventh century. The Truce attempted to restrict the extent of warfare, banning it from Saturday nights until Mondays (later extended to Thursdays) and also at Lent, Advent and a host of vigils and feast days. By the end of the century it was established throughout the entire Holy Roman Empire and was confirmed at the Council of Clermont in 1095. Ironically, this papal council, called by Pope Urban II to declare the launching of the First Crusade, pressed for peace in Christian Europe so that a united front could make war against the Muslims in the Holy Land. More than just an embryonic, proto-peace movement or a disingenuous pursuit of vested self-interest, these initiatives helped to establish a convention of what was permissible in war and adumbrated the chivalric code. They expressed admirable ideals: 'The Peace sought to protect certain classes and their goods at all times, the Truce was an attempt to stop all violence at certain times.'[32] Although these were of some help in curtailing private wars, such ideals were given short thrift on royal battlefields where kings were the highest authority.

One real consequence of the measures to limit conflicts was the strengthening and reassertion of ducal and royal power in France and other kingdoms where law and order had to some extent broken down; in England, especially post-Conquest England, the strength of central administration and royal control meant that the movements had less impact here. In France and elsewhere, the Church was attempting to make up for deficiencies in a ruler's maintenance of the king's peace; rulers of fissiparous and fractious territories were happy to co-opt the Church in reasserting central authority. Matthew Bennett suggests that ecclesiastical peace councils were less a sign of government weakness and more a supplementation of the endeavours of authorities to enable means of conflict resolution. In this way the Church subtly appropriated to itself in Rome an increased moral authority over temporal affairs and powers as an arbiter of peace.

The Church's peace movement ran out of steam in the twelfth century as it was replaced by the consolidation of royal power and the king's peace. In mid-twelfth-century England, however, when King Stephen's grip on power was weakened by civil war (the 'Anarchy'), the Church was once again very active in promoting peace measures. Ironically, at the same time the Church was becoming more militant towards the enemies of God and later, by association, enemies of the Church. The success of the First Crusade, culminating in the bloodbath at Jerusalem in 1099, spurred the papacy to harbour ambitions in the Middle East. The crusading movement, perhaps the defining phenomenon of the Middle Ages, pervaded every aspect of medieval life.

Ultimately, it relied on the men of Latin Christendom to fight wars against the infidel.

The peace movements had sought to constrain violence, but did not actually condemn the act of fighting itself; the crusaders had few restraints placed upon them. In 1054 the Council of Narbonne prohibited warfare between Christians: 'Let no Christian kill another Christian, for there is no doubt that he who kills a Christian spills the blood of Christ.'[33] Now the Church was exhorting the faithful to take up arms and spill the blood of Muslims in the Holy Land and Spain, granting indulgences – including automatic entrance into Heaven for martyrs – to all who did so. Indeed, killing unbelievers was a meritorious act in itself. The Jews were soon caught up in the bloodletting as pogroms against these 'killers of Christ' erupted from the violent religious fervour generated. Soon came the turn of pagans in northern Europe and heretics, especially the Cathars of southern France, where the Albigensian Crusade was even more of a cynical land-grabbing exercise than the expeditions to the Middle East. The crusade against the Cathars was followed up by the Inquisition, employing and innovating the dreadful methods of torture already discussed, and developing methods of informing, denouncing and terrorising that were to play such a part in the state-led persecutions of Stalin's Russia and Hitler's Germany.

Politics and religion became ever more fused and by the later Middle Ages the papacy was launching blatant crusades against its political opponents, thereby devaluing the movement further. Thus the Church, instigators of the peace movement and its ranks full of holy men who genuinely prayed for an end to wars and violence, played its full role in spreading death and destruction within Europe and beyond its boundaries. The observation that 'Men never do evil so completely and cheerfully as when they do it from religious conviction'[34] was borne out repeatedly in the Middle Ages. In 778 at Verden, the great Holy Roman Emperor Charlemagne had 4,500 pagan Saxon prisoners decapitated in cold blood. His biographer Einhard has little to say on the matter, opining only that you could do as you pleased with rebels; the fact that they were non-Christian made their deaths even more inconsequential. Further examples of religious atrocities in warfare will be examined in our look at Jerusalem, Béziers, Acre and Hattin, which will also show that there were far more to these atrocities than mere religious fanaticism, and that it can be too easy simply to blame the Church militant for them.

The Church did more than pray for victories and shout from the sidelines; it did more than write in support of one side and condemnation of the other and use its pulpits for propaganda purposes; it did more than provide soldiers, money, transports and provisions for armies: it took an active and very real interest in the conduct and art of warfare, and its personnel often took an active part in the actual fighting itself. What is manifestly evident is that it is wholly inaccurate to say that the only literate class of the day exclusively comprised monks and clergy who 'had little comprehension of military matters, and even less interest in . . . strategy and tactics'.[35] Just as William of Poitiers, Villehardouin and Joinville were fighting men who took up the quill to write about war, so also did monks such as William the Breton, Roger of Wendover, Orderic Vitalis, Abbot Suger of St Denis and many others. Monastic and ecclesiastic writers came from the same class as their fathers, brothers, cousins and patrons who made up the *bellatores*, the order of fighters, so it was only natural that they should be familiar with the martial world.

The Church's own language was frequently couched in combative terms as the serried ranks of religious fought a spiritual battle against the forces of Satan. *Turma*, for example, a Latin word denoting a body of troops, is found throughout medieval chronicles; it is also employed for groups of monks, such as those of the monastery of St Maurice at Agaune, who were engaged in the round-the-clock worship that has been considered a powerful ritual weapon. Just as the Church fought on one front, so rulers fought on another. The castle-building Abbot Marcward of Fulda opined, 'Not that it is proper that monks should inhabit anything but monasteries or fight battles other than spiritual ones; but the evil in the world cannot be defeated except by resistance.'[36]

The Church's interest was more than intellectual and spiritual; as landowners responsible for furnishing their lords with soldiers and as leading players in the world of politics, the Church hierarchy necessarily had a practical understanding of military affairs. At the turn of the thirteenth century, Bishop Hugues of Auxerre would gather knights about him to discuss military lessons from Vegetuis's *De Re Militari*, a classical text highly valued as a checklist or handbook on war by some medieval commanders. Many of the Church's hierarchy came from a background of soldiering while others retired from active service into monasteries. The Church hired mercenaries and had its own military divisions; in its military orders – the Knights Templar, Hospitaller and Teutonic Knights – it even had its *milites Christi* (knights of Christ), highly effective warrior monks. Never had the Church been so militant.

Clergy came under the nominal protection afforded to non-combatants, but many clergy exempted themselves from this category. Active ecclesiastical participants in warfare ranged from the highest to the lowest, from Bishop Odo of Bayeux vigorously swinging his club over his head at the Battle of Hastings as depicted in his famous tapestry (he wielded a club and not a cutting weapon for as a churchman he was forbidden from spilling Christian blood), to the bald priest who, according to Suger in *The Deeds of Louis the Fat*, was given a courageous spirit by God enabling him to lead and inspire a successful assault on the castle of Le Puiset. Leading churchmen often found themselves in positions of command in armies: in 1298, Anthony Bek, Bishop of Durham, was a commander in the English forces at Falkirk; in 1214, Guérin, Bishop Elect of Senlis, as commander of the French rearguard, was instrumental in the victory at Bouvines. In 1346 Archbishop Thoresby of York helped to lead the English in their defeat of the Scottish army at Neville's Cross; this had no deleterious affect on his reputation as a devout peacemaker who was blameless in his private life, a 'bishop who took his episcopal duties seriously'.[37]

Thomas Hatfield, Bishop of Durham (1345–81), was less circumspect about his military role; his seal portrays him not as a churchman but as a warrior knight mounted on his charger. High-ranking clergy could fall victim to the perils of war. In 1056 in England, Leofgar, who had sported his warrior's moustache as a priest, after his consecration as bishop of Hereford, 'forsook his chrism and his cross, his spiritual weapons, and seized his spear and sword, and thus armed went campaigning against Griffith, the Welsh king; and there he and the priests with him were slain'.[38] At the Battle of Ashingdon in 1016 Bishop Eadnoth of Dorchester and Abbot Wulfsige of Ramsey were amongst Cnut's victims.

The violence of the medieval world did not exempt men of the cloth from being either victims or perpetrators. Within the Church there were many men whose ferocity went beyond inquisitorial methods and actions taken against heretics. In the twelfth century Earl David of Huntingdon's infant son was killed by a cleric; the cleric was tied to the tails of four horses and torn apart. More commonly, the protection of holy orders permitted violent and criminal religious to hide under the habit and vestments of benefit of clergy and so escape judgment in secular courts. A study of clerical violence during the baronial war in mid-thirteenth-century England reveals the enormous extent of this phenomenon and reinforces the claim that gangs of criminals were often led by churchmen of all ranks. One of the most feared outlaws in Edward I's reign was Richard de Folville, a rector and leader of the notorious Folville gang. He began his life of crime in Lincolnshire by robbing one of the King's judges and murdering a magnate. His brothers in the gang had high connections that enabled them to buy royal pardons or escape punishment by joining the army; Richard's crimes against the King were so great his clerical status was of no benefit to him: armed men dragged him from a church and he was immediately decapitated. A recent book on outlaws and highwaymen from the Middle Ages onwards observes: 'The records reveal so many thugs in holy orders that . . . the astute professional malefactor may well have regarded clerical status as a useful qualification.'[39] For all its efforts to achieve peace, the medieval Church, with its crusaders, statesmen, inquisitors, criminals and warriors, was no stranger to violence and warfare.

The Church – and later political theorists – had long concerned its intellect with the problem of what constituted a just war, although it was not until the twelfth century that it truly developed and not until the thirteenth century that an agreed definition was arrived at with the help of St Thomas Aquinas and Pope Innocent IV. The theories of just war laid down that a war was just only if: it was declared by a legitimate authority; it was fought for a just end, such as redressing a wrong or reclaiming one's possessions or persons; it was motivated by a genuine desire for peace and justice and no alternative means were available; it was undertaken in self-defence.

The font of all thinking on just war was St Augustine. For Augustine, war was the price of peace and therefore inevitable for a just ruler whose hand would be forced into action by the wickedness of his enemies. The Church fathers did not consider wars to be incompatible with Christianity; Isidore of Seville did not even consider just wars to be regrettable. 'Provided that the purpose of war was just', explains J. M. Wallace-Hadrill, 'it could be waged; and peace, itself the justification for war, was the supreme realization of divine law.'[40] Thus a king, charged by God with keeping the peace in his kingdom, would no more shirk from harsh measures in warfare than he would from administering punishment to criminals. *Jus in bello*, laws concerning the conduct of war, were therefore not as important as *jus ad bellum*, the just right to declare war. Augustine wrote that 'war is waged that peace may be had'; thus 'the justification of war ... lay not in the manner in which it was conducted, but in its end'.[41] This opinion – that the ends (of peace) justified the means – obviously hampered attempts to restrain excessive acts within a just war. What constituted a crime in any other circumstances could be defended if perpetrated in the cause of a war that was just, as legal theorists essayed to make clear. Raymond of Pennaforte defines arson as a criminal deed, but if an incendiary acts 'at the command of one who has the power to declare war, then he is not to be judged an incendiary'; conversely, Nicholas of Tudeschi opines that 'knights who take part in a war without just cause should rather be called robbers than knights'.[42]

The trouble with the theory was the practice; anyone who waged war did so under a self-justifying banner and to the exhortations of apologists and propagandists. All wars were just, and on all sides; therefore all sides were free to prosecute the war in the way they saw fit. In his monograph on the just war in the Middle Ages, Frederick Russell doubts that theories of just war had much effect; 'might made right' and for soldiers, 'when their cause was just, there were only vague moral limits on their conduct'. He concludes:

> [J]ust war theories have had the dual purpose of restraining and justifying violence, essentially a self-contradictory exercise. Either the just war was a moral and religious doctrine, in which it was deprived of coercive but not normative force, or it was a legal concept that served as a cloak for statism. It remains an open question whether just war theories have limited more wars than they have encouraged.[43]

The Church's theories to limit the effects of war were likewise contradicted by its practice. Even though its aims were modest (quite unlike the desperate optimism in 1928 of the Kellogg–Briand Pact in prohibiting war a solution to disputes), that it failed should only be expected. We have seen the importance of war to medieval society; theories to limit it would not stand up to the Mars juggernaut.

CHIVALRY AND THE LAWS OF WAR

Despite the Church's implementation of the Peace of God, it was less interested in the conduct of warfare; once just war had been declared it was necessary to employ whatever means to hasten its end. The impetus for restraint in war came in equal measure from the Church and the belligerents. Tradition was drawn upon, but there was innovation too, and the phenomenon of chivalry grew to be a cultural definition of the Middle Ages. More recently the study of chivalry has burgeoned into an enormous area of scholarly research. Excellent books on the subject by, amongst others, Maurice Keen, Richard Barber and Richard Kaeuper have placed the reality, as opposed to the myth, of chivalry in its historical context. Here we will briefly touch upon this vast field; its practical aspects – its restraints and abuses – will come to the fore in the following chapters.

Chivalry was embodied in the person of the knight, the elite soldier of medieval warfare. The stereotypical image of the knight is of an armoured horseman holding fast to values of bravery, mercy and loyalty, one who is ready to lay down his life defending the faith, children and women (especially beautiful women); in fact, when he is described as chivalrous, the adjective is readily understood and sums up the goodness and the nobility of the knight's character. As a stereotypical image, it is deeply flawed. Undoubtedly there were some 'verray parfit gentil knyghts' in the Chaucerian mode, but these were probably given a hard time by their more robust and thick-skinned peers on the military training ground; we do not encounter many such paragons amongst these pages. Huge resources of time, money and equipping were invested in knights not so that they could merely become refined and devout gentlemanly officers, but to render them ruthless killing machines. They were trained not only to possess strength and bravery, but also to develop a calculating intelligence designed to comprehend tactics, strategies, diplomacy, logistics and all matters pertaining to waging effective warfare. Within the constraints of the time, they were trained as professionals just as modern armies train their officer classes. The view of a blundering and gung-ho knight, charging bravely but foolishly and impetuously into battle at the first whiff of blood is a misleading caricature, but one presented by Charles Oman in his influential works on medieval warfare and accepted by many historians into the second half of the twentieth century.

Chivalry emerged from warrior codes into a cultural phenomenon of its own, reflected in art, architecture, the music of the troubadours, religion and literature. From these we are familiar with the ideas of battlefield dubbing and the more elaborate preparations for the ceremony of knighthood, imbued with its mystic, religious overtones. Geoffrey de Charny, a famous knight who died in battle at Poitiers in 1356, describes the process in his *Book of Chivalry*. First the initiate must confess and repent his sins. The day before the ceremony, he takes a long bath, symbolically washing away sin and evil living, and then retires to a bed with freshly laundered linen, this symbolizing peace and reconciliation with God. Other knights come to dress him in new, clean garments, as befits his pristine purity. He is attired with a red tunic to represent the blood he must spill to defend God's faith and the Holy Church, and with black shoes to remind him as he came from earth so he must return to earth, and be ready to die at any time. Then, in a central part of the ceremony, he puts on a white belt to show that he is enveloped in purity and chastity. When this is done, the knights lead him to a chapel to keep vigil all night. In the morning, he hears Mass and has golden spurs lain at his feet to show he no longer desires this most precious of metals. The ceremony concludes with a presentation of a sword and the fraternal kisses of his brother knights. For some knights this ceremony represented the signing of a spiritual contract to serve God and perform good and valiant deeds; for others it was a licence to rape, burn, plunder and kill.

Before such refinements and embellishments allowed chivalry to give a veneer of civilized conduct to warfare in the late eleventh century, combat was a much bloodier undertaking for the warrior classes. The excesses of the Vikings have led to heated scholarly debate about the extent to which they perpetrated atrocities and whether these actually exceeded the norms of contemporary warfare; certainly, 'shock, terror and brutality were employed to the full'.[44] A recent examination of Viking atrocities by Guy Halsall explores the indictments against the Vikings and concludes that they were not alone in designing horrible deaths for their enemies. Even if they had used the 'blood eagle', it was not so different from some European practices. (The disputed, even discredited, 'blood eagle' involved the victim having an eagle traced on his back by a sword, or, alternatively, having his ribcage cut open and his lungs pulled out and spread across his shoulders in imitation of a bloody eagle.) Our discussion of punishment in the High Middle Ages will not leave us surprised to learn of dreadful methods of killing in an earlier age. In seventh-century Europe even the royal great-grandmother Brunechildis did not escape mutilation and being ripped apart by wild horses, just one of many exhibitionist executions throughout the *soi-disant* Dark Ages. In the pre-chivalric period, political prisoners, whether caught on the battlefield or elsewhere, could expect death from their captors, be they Viking pagans or Christians. The familiar image of Vikings as destroyers of churches and monasteries was not an exclusive trademark then or later; as we have noted above, the movable wealth of the Church attracted armies of all faiths and none. The accusations of Viking barbarity came, naturally, from the helpless religious establishment, but also from the frustration of authorities who could not track down the maritime hit-and-run raiders to carry out reprisals. As Halsall observes, 'The Vikings were not ... deliberately breaking any rules; they were playing to a different rule-book.'[45] Chivalry was, ostensibly at least, to create a new rule book in the wars of Christendom in later medieval Europe.

Chivalry, in conjunction with the Church, did play a part in ending wars as a slave hunt and in sparing some prisoners of war. This is an area that has benefited greatly from the recent researches of Matthew Strickland and John Gillingham, who argue that chivalry was imported into England with the Norman Conquest of 1066. Before chivalry came into widespread practice, the death rates in battle were much higher (they were to rise again in the later Middle Ages). Strickland's study of pre-Conquest England cites many examples of the slaughter. In 655 at the Battle of Winwaed, nearly all thirty commanders in the Mercian army were killed; in 641, the defeated Oswald of Northumbria was dismembered and his head and arms staked; in 686, King Cadwalla of Wessex paused to baptize his royal captives before having them executed. The Celtic fringe preserved the more barbaric habits of warfare for centuries. The tenth-century Sueno Stone in Scotland depicts the headless corpses of prisoners in rows, their hands tied behind their back. In the early eleventh century, Earl Uhtred arranged for the heads of the Scottish defeated in battle to be cleaned and coiffured before the inevitable staking; the women assigned to this task were paid a cow each. In these wars and many in Europe, the general rule was to slay all men capable of fighting, and to enslave the rest, including women and children; any who attempted to impede the dragging away of slaves or who were too vociferous in their beseeching for exceptions put themselves in mortal danger.

Chivalric practices developed side by side with continuing atrocities; the Vikings occasionally adopted policies of ransoming captives while continuing to slaughter and enslave whole communities. During the great siege of Paris in 886, a group of Franks surrendered to the Viking besiegers expecting to ransom their freedom, but they were killed, as was the garrison of St Lo a few years later in 890, despite Viking promises to the contrary. Little clemency was shown to defeated Vikings. In 1066, just weeks before his death at Hastings, Harold of England's crushing defeat of Harald Hardraada's Viking invasion force ended with the Norwegian army being almost totally wiped out; according to the Anglo-Saxon Chronicle, they came in three hundred ships and left in twenty-four.

Wars between Christians became tempered by the Church's condemnation of taking Christian slaves and by the growth of chivalric practices in Europe, especially in France. Knightly codes can be discerned by the mid-ninth century; by the early eleventh century we can observe many examples of chivalrous conventions of warfare in northern France and later in England. As duke of Normandy, William the Bastard was careful to take prisoners alive; as king of England, William the Conqueror compensated Dover for the damage done to it by his troops after surrender and protected the defeated city of Exeter from sack. Nevertheless, this is the same William who, by sword and fire, inflicted the most appalling injuries and sufferings on captured enemies and non-combatants. But the knightly class was increasingly exempt from atrocity. 'This emphasis on capture, as opposed to slaying, stands', writes Strickland, 'in stark contrast to Saxon and Viking

74

conduct in regard to enemy warriors.'[46] Thus the Normans brought with them to England the chivalrous practices of the continent; but this was not the chivalry of *Ivanhoe* and the romanticized images of the Victorian era. In an influential study, John Gillingham has defined chivalry as 'a code in which a key element was the attempt to limit the brutality of conflict by treating prisoners, at any rate when they were men of "gentle" birth, in a relatively humane fashion'. He suggests that 'the compassionate treatment of defeated high-status enemies is a defining characteristic of chivalry – and entirely compatible with very different treatment being meted out to people regarded as low-status'.[47]

Chivalry, then, was little more than an insurance policy for the fighting upper classes, who paid their premiums by the acquisition of the expensive arms, armour and, most of all, warhorses, that signified the elite warrior figure of the knight. This attitude was reflected in post-Conquest England in the disparity, discussed above, between the violent punishment suffered by a lowly criminal, and the humane sanctions imposed lightly (by comparison) upon society's prominent figures. When, in Edward II's reign, enemies of the Crown once again faced execution, the body politic was shocked to its foundations.

The motivation for a code of chivalry was self-preservation. Ransoming made it work. A live (wealthy) prisoner was worth more than a dead one. Large, sometimes huge and ruinous, sums could be extorted from a captive's family to secure the return of a prisoner. The principle applied to the greatest in the land. Richard the Lionheart's release from captivity cost England a staggering 150,000 marks and royal vassalage to Emperor Henry VI; King John II of France, taken prisoner at the battle of Poitiers in 1356, agreed to pay 3 million gold *écus* for his release (a reduction of one-quarter off the original demand and including sixteen other high-profile French prisoners thrown into the bargain). Chivalry could trickle down to bargain-basement levels for the lower orders as ordinary footsoldiers ransomed lesser folk. The prospect of ransom did not ensure the well-being of a captive, as examples from the Hundred Years War reveal. Jean le Gastelier's job in Robert Chesnel's military contingent was to beat the prisoners to extract promises from them of the largest possible ransom. Francois de la Palu imprisoned Henriet Gentian in a dungeon where the captive counted 'eighteen serpents and other reptiles' in his dungeon; furthermore, 'Francois had also sent a letter to the Duke of Bourbon and others amongst Henriet's connections, warning them that if he was not paid promptly he would pull Henriet's teeth out. When they did not respond, he knocked out a few with his hammer and circulated them to show that he meant what he said.'[48]

Ransoming developed into a burgeoning business as warfare opened up this new economic opportunity to be exploited. Orderic Vitalis, our leading source for Anglo-Norman history, informs us of the investment potential of the three-year-long siege (1083–5) of Sainte Suzanne in Maine; large numbers of soldiers were attracted there by the lure of ransoms, many making an 'honourable fortune' in this way, and the whole business proved most profitable. Eventually, the whole process of ransoming accrued legal codes and structures, many cases coming to be settled in the Court of Chivalry. Paul Hyams has neatly summed up this new chivalry in warfare:

> Previously, accepted dogma had held that it was both prudent and legitimate to deal with defeated enemies by killing them, *toute simple*. The newer view preferred to spare noble lives in return for a fat ransom. This was in part a declaration of knightly labour union rules. It was comforting to know as one rode off to battle that you and your genteel peers were not expected to go so far as killing each other, that you merely competed for the twin prizes of knightly valour and earthly swag. Victory now brought applause and enrichment without too direct a risk of death.[49]

The chroniclers testify to the generally satisfactory nature of the chivalric understanding. In a famous example from Orderic Vitalis, we learn of the impressively low mortality rate at the major engagement at Brémule on the Franco-Norman border in 1119, between Henry I of England and Louis VI the Fat of France. Of nine hundred knights involved, only three are reported as killed: 'They were all dressed in mail and spared each other on both sides, out of fear of God and brotherhood in arms; they were more concerned to capture than to kill the fugitives. As Christian soldiers they did not thirst for the blood of their brothers ...'[50]

A century later at the decisive battle of Lincoln, in 1217, only three deaths are recorded; hence the battle became known as the Fair of Lincoln. Only one of these fatalities is a high-ranking knight, the count of Le Perche, and there is concern even at this; the English commander had explicitly ordered his crossbowmen to aim at the chargers of the French knights and not at the knights themselves. Roger of Wendover numbers the prisoners at three hundred. It is worth noting that many of the French who escaped from Lincoln were ultimately the more unfortunate. As they made their hurried retreat back to their stronghold in London, many of them were slain, 'for the inhabitants of the towns through which they passed in their flight, went to meet them with the swords and clubs, and, laying traps for them, killed many'.[51] Non-combatants and townspeople were not recipients of chivalry, so nor were they its exponents.

The chroniclers frequently make a virtue out of a financial necessity by staying quiet on the matter of ransom and instead, like Orderic in the above passage, stress the fraternal ties between the combatants. Money was paramount, but these ties were important nonetheless. At the Battle of Lincoln, Wendover observes that the King's troops only pretended to pursue the fleeing enemy, 'and had it not been for the effect of relationship and blood, not a single one of all of them would have escaped'.[52] The ties were deeper than just those tacitly understood and shared by fighting elites; many knights were more than *com militiones* who shared the same religion and culture, and often language as well, but also familiars who knew each other intimately. Matthew Bennett's article on military masculinity in medieval Europe stresses the experiences that knights shared as boys and squires as they trained in arms together in the schools of combat; this fostered strong male bonding (and what psychologists call primary group cohesion). More close links were forged on the tournament circuit, spectacles of violent display that were also integral to a knight's training, in which opponents could fraternize rather like players from rival football and rugby clubs do today.

It is sometimes said that chivalry came with very real military advantages. The knowledge that a knight's worst fate was likely to be being taken prisoner would have made him more courageous in the fray and less concerned for his own safety. This sense of security was greatly enhanced by his suit of armour that afforded him a high degree of protection in combat. Muslims labelled crusaders as 'Iron Men' because of their chainmail; William the Breton, a keen observer of early thirteenth-century warfare, placed more emphasis on the efficiency of armour than on chivalry as the cause of the dramatic fall in casualties since ancient times, when soldiers were less well protected. Ransoming also seemed to make greater sense in age of castle proliferation; it was easier to exchange a castellan or a lord for a castle than to besiege it. During the wars in England between 1215 and 1217, King John successfully threatened the garrison at Belvoir in Leicestershire with the shameful death of their lord, in John's captivity, if they did not surrender the castle to him. In certain circumstances chivalry could proffer military advantages, but reciprocity simply limited these advantages to occasional opportune moments.

In theory, different types of war dictated different norms of conduct and the laws of war were varied accordingly. Four types of war were recognized: *guerre mortelle*, war to the death, in which a captured enemy could expect either slavery or death; *bellum hostile*, open or public war, in which Christian princes were ranged against each other and knights could plunder and expect to be ransomed; *guerre couverte*, feudal or covered war, in which killing and wounding were acceptable, but not burning or the taking of prisoners and spoil; and truce, a momentary hiatus in hostilities. Siege warfare also developed its own set of laws that were more easily enforced than battlefield rules.

War to the death drew no distinctions between combatants and non-combatants. It tended to be characterized by religious wars, in crusades against Muslims and pagans. However, bloody as these wars were, they did not exclude financial incentives and, in the Holy Land, ransoming was common. Amongst Christians, mortal war was rare, but not that rare. As Robert Stacey observes, 'Only in exceptional circumstances would knights agree to fight under such conditions. It was too dangerous for all involved and not very profitable either, since ransoms were disallowed.'[53] As the next chapter demonstrates, the carnage of many medieval battles highlights the frequent exceptions to restraint amongst Christians; that the lower orders had the same religion as Christian knights meant very little except in the avoidance of slavery. The French, rather optimistically, flew the red banner of no quarter at Crécy and Poitiers, two of their worst defeats in the Hundred Years War. Civil wars, as between Simon de Montfort and Henry III in mid-thirteenth-century England, could also see the unfurling of the red flag; but it was popular rebellion especially, such as Flanders fought against the French in the early fourteenth century, and peasant revolts, such as the Jacquerie, that tended to produce the greatest bloodshed.

Knights much preferred to fight under the rules of engagement for *bellum hostile*, when 'spoil and plunder were the order of the day'. Despite the strictures of the Peace of God designed to protect peasants, women, children, the elderly and the clergy from looting, 'in practice, however, neither soldiers nor the lawyers and judges who adjudicated the resulting disputes over plunder paid the slightest attention to such immunities'.[54] As chivalry developed into a cultural and literary phenomenon, the vision of the ideal knight came increasingly into conflict with the reality of the battlefield knight, exposing contradictory views held by society that on the one hand praised all the finer aspects of chivalry, but on the other condemned the all too frequent deviations from its ideals, principally in vanity, self-indulgence and incontinent bloodlust. As Richard Kaeuper has shown in his recent book, this contemporary issue gave rise to a debate in which both knights and clergy engaged in seeking reforms to bridge 'the yawning gap' between knightly practice 'and the impossibly high ideals expressed for it in one major text after another'.[55] Princes did lay down their own rules to curtail what one medieval writer called 'evil enterprises', which he listed as 'pillage, robbery, murder, sacrilege, violation and raping of women, arson and imprisonment';[56] clearly he did not share the soldier's attraction towards war. Frederick Barbarossa, Richard I, Henry V and Richard II are just three monarchs who issued ordinances of restraint; in 1385 Richard II stipulated the death penalty for profanity against the Eucharist and its vessels, and for robbery from churches, clergy, women and civilians in general. Evil enterprises, flight from battle and pledge-breaking were also punished by naming and shaming, one particularly dreaded device being to hang a knight's coat of arms upside down at tournaments or at court, or tying them to a horse's tail.

Chivalry certainly did not always ensure guaranteed safety for knightly prisoners, as we are about to see; but its socially exclusive application explains why, in the 'golden' age of chivalry, warfare was still marked by appalling and widespread atrocities. Theory and practice failed to match each other. The laws of war were, in theory, designed to afford protection to non-combatants as expressed in the Peace of God; in practice, the laws were reserved for the ruling classes.

Urban militias, peasant levies and national call-ups often meant that non-combatants were turned temporarily into belligerents, and with little or no choice in the matter; these were particularly vulnerable to slaughter on the battlefield, especially when the bloodlust of battle-enraged knights could not be sated on enemy *milites*. Caught up in the wars of their masters, chivalry was an alien concept to them.

Chivalry, for what it was worth (and that was never very much), saved the life of many a knight; the poor bloody infantry and everyone else could expect little from it. Through its acceptance of moral hazard (the business term is applicable here), chivalry offered knights the insurance and security to wage war with regard to their own class and safety but with none to the rest. Thus, as Maurice Keen has perceptively observed, the impact of chivalry was not to limit the horrors of war, but 'rather to help make those horrors endemic'.[57] The atrocities in this book (Charlemagne at Verden excepting) all occur in chivalry's bloody 'golden' age. Most are carried out under royal command; and the king was the greatest, most chivalrous knight of all in his realm. Gallant and honourable knights charging at each other with lances on the field of battle was only one, very small part of medieval warfare; it was too important, too all-encompassing for such civilized and restricted practices. As the chroniclers tell us repeatedly, wars were waged with terrible violence 'by fire and sword', or sometimes 'by sword and fire', directed with devastating consequences against non-combatants and those who tried to escape the path of the Mars juggernaut.[58] This book has adopted the lesser-used phrase for its title, 'by sword and fire', to give prominence to the sword: the sword is the abiding symbol of chivalry, yet it was responsible for most of the horrors of medieval warfare. By stressing the dominance of the sword, I hope to show how deliberate military policy set the precedent for the atrocities in war.

3

BATTLES

Hastings, Bouvines, Crécy, Agincourt – the Middle Ages seem crowded with famous battles; indeed, for a long while medieval warfare was studied almost exclusively through the battles fought in this period. In fact, full pitched battles were relatively rare; campaigns and sieges were far more prevalent and characterized the warfare of the time. A recent, highly authoritative book on warfare in the Middle Ages, written by a team of experts covering all the major topics and themes, actually has no chapter or even sections on battles. This is perhaps a revision too far and distorts the rarity of full-scale engagements; skirmishes, combats and substantial military encounters far out-number the Hastings and Agincourts in the medieval world.

The paradox of medieval battles was that they were at the same time both too risky and too indecisive. Thus while some commanders actively adopted a battle-seeking strategy, most pursued a policy of battle avoidance relying instead on campaigns and sieges to win the war. When battle was engaged, a commander had only limited control of his forces once they had been committed. Despite battlefield organization into tactical units *(conrois* and the larger *batailles)* with banners, heraldic devices and surcoats to aid recognition, the din and confusion of the combat, the spread of the fighting, communication difficulties, exigencies and unexpected events, surprise tactics by the enemy – all these led to intense confusion and meant that great dependence had to be placed on the training, experience and good sense of a commander's soldiers and the initiative of his captains. After the dust of battle had settled, it was still not easy to discern what really took place on the field of combat; Wellington's choreographical allusion – that one might as well write the history of a ball as of a battle – was even more applicable to the Middle Ages than to the nineteenth century. Even with a battle as renowned as Crécy, we have half a dozen contesting theories as to the disposition of the troops. Sometimes, as with the major battle of Bannockburn in Scotland, not even the actual place of battle can be positively identified.

The outcome of battle was nearly always uncertain. Despite this, many generals actually sought to take their chances with the fortunes of war in a major engagement. When William the Conqueror landed his army in England in 1066 he wanted to entice the English into battle; with Harold and his main forces defeated at Hastings – and better still, with the king killed in battle – the kingdom was more easily subjugated. The chronicler William of Poitiers noted that William had, in effect, conquered all of England in a day. Harold also wanted a decisive battle (like the one fought a few weeks earlier in his crushing defeat of the Danes at Stamford Bridge) and in this he was adhering to a very Anglo-Saxon strategy: the absence of substantial fortifications in pre-Conquest England meant that battles rather than sieges largely determined the result of wars. Duke William's desire for a conclusive early battle was driven by two overwhelming factors: he was unlikely to be in a position to assemble and maintain such a huge invasion force again; and he knew that the scarcity of castles in England meant not only that battle would settle the outcome of his expedition, but also that this was to his advantage. The chronicler Orderic Vitalis offers a succinct analysis of the Duke's conquest of England: 'The fortifications that the French call "castles" were very rare in the English regions and hence, although the English were warlike and bold, they were weaker in resisting their enemies.'[1] By the end of the Middle Ages, commanders in England reverted to this form of warfare: long periods of peace had led to the desuetude and hence disrepair of fortifications, forcing the armies to contest in the field rather than at sieges. (It was a different story in the north, which witnessed a number of sieges during the wars; border warfare had ensured the upkeep of strongholds.)

Battle-seeking strategies are clearly evident in certain campaigns on the continent, as in the little-known wars between the Salians and the Saxons fought in late eleventh- and early twelfth-century Germany. When disputing territory in the relatively uncastellated region between East Saxony and Thuringia, the antagonists Henry IV and Henry V clashed in a series of major engagements; the 'war was decided not by capturing strongpoints but by winning battles'.[2] Simon de Montfort's success during the Albigensian Crusade was in large part owed to his determination to force events in the field. In 1211 he concentrated his small army in the weakened fortifications of Castlenaudary, situated south-west of Toulouse in southern France, which was soon besieged by his opponent, Count Raymond VI of Toulouse. De Montfort's men took the initiative, sallying forth to engage the enemy and rout them. De Montfort reprised this tactic at nearby Muret in 1213 with even greater success. Battle was risky, but fortune frequently favoured the brave.

Despite the dominance of the castle in medieval warfare, sieges were not always a commander's first choice. In southern Italy, Charles of Anjou conducted his military campaign based on battles; his victories at Benevento (1266) and Tagliacozzo (1268) gave him Sicily. A provocative book on the wars of Edward III by Clifford Rogers claims that Edward, contrary to long-held opinion, was an active battle seeker. Rogers puts forward the controversial case that Edward and later his son the Black Prince, better known for their famous hit-and-run *chevauchées* (fast-moving ravaging expeditions), had learned from his early wars with the Scots (as when he forced them to fight at Berwick in 1333) that tactical superiority on the battlefield was the most efficacious way to achieve his ends; his sieges of Tournai in 1340 and Calais in 1347 were undertaken with the design to provoke the French into battle.

The examples of Charles of Anjou and William the Conqueror reveal how high the stakes of battle could be; a single battle could determine the future of an entire country. Philip Augustus's spectacular victory at Bouvines in 1214 secured France under the Capetians from imperial domination, while Henry Tudor's triumph in central England at Bosworth in 1485 meant a new dynasty on the throne of England and 120 years of Tudor rule. R. C. Smail, a leading authority on crusading warfare, declared that the defeat of the Latin army at Hattin in 1187 decided the fate of the kingdom of Jerusalem. And, as with the judicial trial by combat, success in battle also conveyed to the victor the blessing of God's judgement; Fulk le Réquin attributed his victory over his brother at Brissac in 1167 to God's grace. Conversely, of course, defeat on the battlefield could incur the highest price, even for kings: Harold was killed at Hastings; Richard III at Bosworth; and, in

1213, Peter II of Aragon at Muret. Even when monarchs or princes were not specifically targeted for death, as Philip Augustus was at Bouvines, their capture meant not only the collapse of their army, but a huge political and financial cost. The Battle of Lewes in 1264 delivered King Henry III and England (temporarily) to Simon de Montfort and the baronial rebels.

Captivity was something of an occupational hazard for French monarchs, for whom a king's ransom was more than a figure of speech: Louis IX was taken prisoner on the Seventh Crusade (1248); John II of France was captured after the defeat at Poitiers in 1356; and Francis I was seized at the battle of Pavia in 1525. Little wonder, then, that in the late medieval period the French kings Charles V, Charles VIII and Louis XI ordered their armies to avoid engaging the enemy on the battlefield. After all, the French had suffered battlefield defeats for over sixty years, losing major engagements at Crécy, Poitiers, Nájera and Agincourt – but they still won the war. Lest this seem somewhat pusillanimous, it should be remembered that Richard the Lionheart, one of the greatest military commanders of the Middle Ages, fought only two or three pitched battles during his lifetime of active and dedicated belligerence. Richard's father, Henry II, was a renowned war commander, likened to Charlemagne by the chronicler Jordan of Fantosme; yet he never led his forces onto the battlefield once.

Another pressing reason for avoiding battle existed when a commander was uncertain of the loyalty of either his troops or his allies. At Bosworth in 1485, Richard III's forces outnumbered Henry Tudor's by a margin as great as two to one; however, at a crucial juncture in the battle, the defection of Lord Stanley from the royalist cause to the Tudor one ensured defeat for Richard, and the King was killed by Stanley's men. This fear of treachery was an ever-present anxiety for generals. When campaigning in Normandy in 1117–18 against a background of baronial unrest, Henry I was unwilling to commit his men to lengthy operations because of the very real danger of split loyalties. At Hastings in 1066, the Anglo-Saxon Chronicle reports that Harold was supported only by 'those men that *wished* to stand by him'.[3] Attempts at securing allegiances were prudently made before a planned or expected outbreak of conflict. Blandishments, privileges, promises of land and booty all played their role in this, as did the sanctions, punishments and threats discussed in chapter one. A politically inept king was therefore likely to be a militarily inept one, too. Both failings are perfectly encapsulated in King John, whose reign was punctuated by a spectacular procession of both political and military disasters. Rarely had a monarch inspired less confidence: not only did a high proportion of his magnates wisely not trust him on a personal level; they were also so alarmed at his incompetence they could see little self-interest in serving him faithfully. There was a high price to pay for John, both financially and militarily, as he came increasingly to rely on overseas troops.

In 1216 he was faced with his greatest threat: a French invasion of England led by Prince Louis. Rather than meet the invaders in battle and drive them back into the sea, John declined battle and instead permitted the French army to establish itself in the country and hence gain vital momentum. Roger of Wendover records events: 'As King John was surrounded with foreign mercenaries and knights from the continental provinces, he did not venture to attack Louis on his landing, lest in the battle they might all leave him and go over to the side of Louis; he therefore chose to retreat for a time, rather than to give battle on an uncertainty.'[4] The French went on to occupy one-third of the country. They were driven out after John's death following two substantial battles in 1217, those of Lincoln and the naval engagement off the south-eastern coast at Sandwich.

BATTLES IN MEDIEVAL WARFARE

Whether sought or not, battles were a feature of medieval warfare. Contemporaries were keen to write about them, often with great vigour and zeal. Then, as now, they represented the climactic drama of knightly combat, with all its chivalric glory and heroics. The role of the knight in battle is a matter for much scholarly debate. Revisionist historians in the eighties and nineties played down the role of heavy cavalry, emphasizing instead the central part played by infantry, long neglected by historians not least because most chroniclers concentrated instead on the prowess of their patrons and princes. More recently, John France has led the counter-revisionist charge, convincingly arguing that some commentators have gone too far in drastically reducing the importance of cavalry; its great strength, he asserts, always lay in its mobility. Certainly, despite the fuss made over an alleged 'Military Revolution' in the late Middle Ages, the mounted warrior remained an essential component of armies throughout the period: when Charles VIII invaded Italy in 1494, half of his army comprised heavy cavalry. The enormous expense of such a move tends to reveal the high premium still set on knights.

The truth, as usual, lies somewhere between the two extremes; infantry and cavalry were both vital elements within an army. The history of medieval warfare notches up plenty of victories for both over the other. Heavy cavalry decided the day at Hastings in 1066; at Jaffa in 1192 it took less than a dozen knights to see off the Muslim enemy; and it was Muslim heavy cavalry (spahis) that led to the mass surrender of the French at Nicopolis in Bulgaria in 1396. The Military Revolution thesis is supported by the increasing frequency of infantry battles over cavalry as the Middle Ages moved into the fourteenth and fifteenth centuries: Courtrai, 1302; Crécy, 1346; and Murten in Switzerland in 1476, when Charles the Bold's cavalry could not prevent his forces from being massacred by Swiss pikemen. But infantry was defeating cavalry much earlier. In 1176, long before any 'revolution', Frederick's imperial cavalry were defeated by the infantry of the Lombard League at Legnano, near Milan. A decade later, in 1188, an encounter at Gisors in Normandy saw English foot soldiers beat off two charges by French cavalry, considered Europe's elite. The *History of William Marshal* records how the French 'launched into the press' and were met by Angevin infantry 'who did not evade this onslaught' and who 'received them with their pikes'. Apparently, not one foot soldier was lost.[5]

Even more instructive, perhaps, are early twelfth-century engagements like Brémule, fought in 1119, when Henry I dismounted his knights and combined them with his infantry to defeat French cavalry. William of Tyre reports that during the Second Crusade in the late 1140s, German knights followed their custom of dismounting to fight. Sources tell of Frankish cavalry fighting on foot as far back as 891 at Dyle in Belgium. The point here is that knights were flexible; they were formidable, professional fighting machines who could adapt to fight just as well either on foot or on horseback.

The debate over infantry or cavalry supremacy is a misleading one.

Very few battles were purely foot-versus-horse affairs; rarely did one arm exclusively defeat another. In the vast majority of battles, as in those highlighted above, it was the tactical deployment and ability of the cavalry, infantry and archers combined that settled a battle (if, indeed, the battle had a clear outcome). The different forces had established roles, but these could be changed according to circumstances. Heavy cavalry was designed to launch a shock charge that would break up infantry and enemy cavalry formations, or, as at Hastings, it would feign flight to draw the infantry out; but as mentioned above, they could just as easily fight defensively on foot. Archers and missile men similarly used a barrage to achieve the same effect, softening the target up for cavalry; of course, they were also used to break up cavalry charges. Infantry provided a shield wall for cavalry; but they also were used offensively, especially when following up after mounted charges. And knights would even advance on foot (something the French still did not quite have the knack of by 1415, as Agincourt shows). There were many other varying and diverse factors that determined the outcome of an engagement: leadership, morale, use of terrain, training and discipline, to name some of the most salient.

The last of these – discipline – merits attention here, as command structures, and breakdowns of these structures, often influence our understanding of atrocities committed in warfare. Effectiveness in combat situations often depends on a disciplined force operating under strict orders. Although there is an element of truth in the concept of medieval armies composed contrastingly of nervous peasants, ever on the point of fleeing into the distance, and knights sometimes straining at the bit to get at the enemy, the view fostered by Charles Oman that knights were Hooray Henry amateurs piling into the fray in a disorganized mess at the first smell of blood is a parody that sadly remains potent to this day. In a recent essay on military lust for glory, Nobel Prize winner Steven Weinberg writes of 'foolishness on a scale that even medieval knights might find implausible'.[6] Keeping formation was vital for cavalry; a successful charge depended on the enormous weight of a mounted force moving in serried ranks. Commanders and writers alike recognized the importance of this. A youthful Edward III, fighting on his Weardale campaign in 1327, informed his men that he would kill anyone who advanced before being ordered to do so. Joinville offers an example from the early thirteenth century: during

St Louis's first crusade in Egypt, Gautier d'Autrèche broke ranks against strict orders and was mortally wounded; neither writer nor king expressed any sympathy for him.

Naturally, spur-of-the-moment bravery had its place in battle. On his march south to Jaffa in the Holy Land in 1191, Richard the Lionheart's crusading army was sorely tried by Saladin's forces shadowing them. Richard had issued firm instructions that, despite the severe provocations of the Muslims, his men were to maintain tight formation at all costs. The Hospitallers, bearing the brunt of the Muslim assault in the rearguard, were incurring more casualties and losing more horses than anyone else, mainly to archery. Unable to wait for the designated signal to counter-attack, two of the Order, one of whom was the Marshal, cracked under the strain and charged. They were immediately followed by the rest of the Hospitaller cavalry. Seeing this, Richard also committed his knights. Had he not done so, disaster would have ensued. However, the surprise of the counter-attack and, crucially, its size, resulted in a tremendous victory for the crusaders. Richard himself famously led from the front as an inspiration to his troops. (Such bravado had its limits; Richard died conducting a siege in 1199.)

Orders were not merely verbal affairs and hence more easily misinterpreted; they were regularly written down in careful detail. Roger of Howden records Richard's draconian navy regulations for the maintenance of discipline during the voyage to the Holy Land:

> Any man who kills another shall be bound to the dead man and, if at sea, be thrown overboard, if on land, buried with him. If it be proved by lawful witnesses that any man has drawn his knife against another, his hand shall be cut off. If any man shall punch another without drawing blood he shall be plunged in the sea three times. Abusive or blasphemous language shall be punished by fines according to the number of offences. A convicted thief shall be shaved like a champion, tarred and feathered and put ashore at the first opportunity.[7]

Such ordinances were not exclusive to Richard. Any soldier in the crusading army found guilty of gambling was to be whipped naked for three days through the army camp. (Sailors got off more lightly, being plunged into the sea first thing in the morning instead.) Ordinances for conduct in war were common throughout the Middle Ages: Richard II issued his in 1385 at Durham; Henry V his at Harfleur in 1415. These afforded protection to non-combatants and religious, and restricted ravaging. In Henry's case, the desire was to win over the population of Normandy as his loyal and trusting subjects. But not all such directives were so considerate. Twenty years later, Sir John Fastolf was giving orders for extreme, unrestrained warfare, *guerre mortelle*, in a vicious effort to suppress French rebels. Massacres and savagery were just as likely to be officially sanctioned as to be the result of a collapse in discipline.

Loss of discipline on the battlefield could precipitate a rout. This was the most dangerous part of any battle, when the killing fields were the domain of cavalry mopping up scattered infantry, and foot soldiers following up despatching the wounded and worthless. Here is William of Poitiers's account of the aftermath of Hastings. The English

> turned to flight and made off as soon as they got the chance, some on looted horses, many on foot; some along the roads, many across country. Those who struggled but on rising lacked the strength to flee lay in their own blood. The sheer will to survive gave strength to others. Many left their corpses in the depths of the forests, many collapsed in the path of their pursuers along the way. The Normans ... pursued them keenly slaughtering the guilty fugitives and bringing matters to a fitting end, while the hooves of the horses exacted punishment from the dead as they were ridden over.[8]

We have seen how chivalry afforded substantial protection to the knight; it was the poor bloody infantry who tended to get it in the neck. But this was not always the case: the nature of the war being fought, the attitudes of the enemy, class hatred, religious beliefs, ethnic and national identity – all could seriously affect the casualty rate. Philippe Contamine examines the relative degree of risk in his classic book *War in the Middle Ages*. In the West, he notes, inter-communal warfare, even when involving the nobility, could be particularly deadly; in such cases, it was rare to take captives for ransom. The great chronicler Froissart writes disapprovingly of the unchivalrous Frisians in their conflict against English, French and Lowland troops in 1396:

they refuse to surrender, preferring to die as free Frisians; they do not take prisoners for ransom; as for the few prisoners they do seize, these are not exchanged for their own men taken captive; the Frisians leave 'to die one after another in prison'; and 'if they think none of their own men are prisoners, they will certainly put all their prisoners to death'. Little wonder, then, as Froissart claims, that 'it is a general rule that the greatest losses occur on the side of the vanquished'.[9]

Detailed casualty rates are usually hard to ascertain, especially when they are high, and corroboration of sources is relatively rare. Thus the dead at the Scottish Battle of Dunbar in 1296 have been numbered by four contemporary chronicles at 30,000, 22,000 and 10,000 (two agree on the lowest figure). Once again, it is the nobility amongst the fallen who are newsworthy, and for this reason their mortality rates are better known. The combination of chivalric codes and armour usually kept their death rate down, so when nearly forty English knights were killed at Bannockburn in 1314 it was considered a rare and major event. The mortality rate for both knights and common soldiers was increasing by the early fourteenth century. At the French defeat at Poitiers (1356), nineteen leading members of the nobility were killed, along with over 2,000 men-at-arms; the slaughter at Agincourt saw the deaths of nearly one hundred leading nobility (including three dukes), 1,500 knights, and perhaps 4,000 gentlemen, all on the French side. This amounts in both cases to a loss rate for French cavalry of approximately forty per cent. Compare this to Brémule in 1119, where Orderic Vitalis recorded only three knights being killed out of 900 who fought in the battle. Overall, it has been estimated for the medieval period that defeated armies lost between twenty and fifty per cent of their men.

Surveying the aftermath at Waterloo, Wellington referred to the human cost of war, saying 'that next to a battle lost, the greatest misery is a battle gained'. Medieval chroniclers were not always so reflective, as the graphic passage below demonstrates. It comes from an Arab writer walking across the battlefield of Hattin in 1187, where Saladin had just crushed a crusading army. It could easily be a description of any scene at the end of a battle in the Middle Ages.

The dead were scattered over the mountains and valleys. . . . Hattin shrugged off their carcasses, and the perfume of victory was thick with the stench of them. I passed by them and saw the limbs of the fallen cast naked on the field of battle, scattered in pieces over the site of the encounter, lacerated and disjointed, with heads cracked open, throats split, spines broken, necks shattered, feet in pieces, noses mutilated, extremities torn off, members dismembered, parts shredded, eyes gouged out, stomachs disembowelled, hair coloured with blood, midriffs slashed, fingers sliced off, chests shattered, the ribs broken, the joints dislocated ... throats slit, bodies cut in half, lips shrivelled, foreheads and ribs pierced ... faces lifeless ... wounds gaping, life's last breath exhaled. ... rivers of blood ran freely. ... O sweet rivers of victory! O sweet heart's comforter![10]

As we shall see below, this was not the worst of the carnage; even this horrific shedding of blood did not satisfy the victors.

MASSACRES OF PRISONERS

The focus of this book is how the excesses of war affected non combatants: women, children, those in holy orders, peasants and prisoners of war. The laws of war, such as they were, afforded protection to these groups; the practice of war frequently did not. *Jus ad bellum*, a just cause for war, was either too often ignored or too disproportionately embraced for over consideration of *jus in bello*, the justification of actions in war. The effective waging of total war in the twentieth century is both condemned and justified for putting non-combatants in the front line, giving us Dresden and Hiroshima. But the Middle Ages were not so different: economic targets were no less important than military ones; displays of power and terror could and did affect the resolve of enemies. In truth, with the possible exception of the age of battles in the Late Modern period, non-combatants were always the most vulnerable victims in time of war. Unlike most sieges and practically all ravaging expeditions, medieval battles represented war in its 'purest' form: no women, no children, and priests only present on the periphery, praying that their God would bring victory and hence bestow His blessings on their side's cause. The field of battle itself was filled with nothing but combatants, soldiers whose sole

purpose was to destroy the opposing army. When a soldier surrendered, or was captured and disarmed, his status immediately
changed to that of a non-combatant. This was a clear delineation that,
in theory, secured the prisoner's life. But the messy and bloody reality
of medieval warfare meant that surrender or capture was rarely a cast-
iron guarantee of safety. Battlefield confusion and the fog of war would
always mean that some men who had thrown away their arms would
be cut down; the bloodlust of the victors could also mean lack of
restraint or unwillingness to take prisoners when the heat of battle
had not yet fully subsided. In the majority of the massacres discussed
below, combat had come to a definite end. All have this in common:
the killing of prisoners was a deliberate and calculated act, carried out
on the explicit orders of the victorious army's commander. With one
exception, the commanders were all kings.

Verden, 782

We start with an episode that falls outside our high age of chivalry
and which did not follow on immediately from a battle, but instead
followed a revolt. It is included here for three reasons. First, it concerns
the emperor Charlemagne, that great paradigm of chivalrous virtue
whom all Christendom looked up to and venerated as the epitome of
chivalry. Just as Charlemagne looked back to the great days of the
Roman Empire for his inspiration, so medieval princes looked back to
Charlemagne's *imperium* as a golden age to be emulated; acclaim for
Charles the Great was universal throughout the medieval period. Secondly, it demonstrates the bitterness and savagery that always characterized religious and frontier wars. Charlemagne's actions at Verden
make an interesting comparison with those renowned symbols of personal chivalry Richard the Lionheart and Saladin four centuries later
in the frontier territories of the Holy Land. Thirdly, the response of
contemporaries to what happened at Verden is a revealing one.

By the time Charlemagne was crowned with the revived title of Holy
Roman Emperor in Rome by Pope Leo III on Christmas Day 800, he
had extended the boundaries of his Frankish kingdom to such an
extent that the monk Alcuin (in effect Charlemagne's minister of edu-
cation after their meeting in 781) had already labelled the King's territories a Christian empire two years earlier. Of his many campaigns to

subjugate peoples and regions coterminous with his ever expanding Frankish state, the expeditions against the Saxons from 772 and 804 were some of the most viciously fought. Einhard, Charlemagne's contemporary biographer, wrote: 'No war ever undertaken by the Frankish people was more prolonged, more full of atrocities or more demanding of effort ... The Saxons, like almost all the peoples living in Germany, are ferocious by nature.' Einhard is also quick to emphasize the spiritual dimensions of the conflict: the Saxons 'are much given to devil worship and they are hostile to our religion. They think it no dishonour to violate and transgress the laws of God and man.'[11]

Charlemagne had three main aims in Saxony: annexation, conversion and, ultimately, possession of Frisia. The religious element of these wars was expressed in 772, when Charlemagne completely obliterated the Irminsul, described in sources as both a shrine and an idol that served as the Saxons' main sanctuary of their pagan cult. This was a symbolic action to intimidate the heathen Saxons; it was more a political act than a religious one. Even the man who was to become the inaugural *imperator* of the Holy Roman Empire, an institution that survived until the Charlemagne-imitating Napoleon ironically dissolved it, put temporal concerns before spiritual ones: he placed his Saxony operations on hold as he mobilized to assist both Christian and Muslim leaders who had requested help in Spain. This led to the famous defeat of his rearguard at the pass of Roncevaux in 778. It was here that Roland's brave, though perhaps unnecessary, death in battle later became immortalized in *The Song of Roland*, the most celebrated and influential of the Old French epics that recounted the valiant deeds of chivalrous heroes who inspired courtly culture and battlefield bravery for centuries. This glorious defeat served only to enhance futher Charlemagne's reign as one of virtuous chivalry. The fact that the great Christian king had, very much like that Iberian icon of knighthood El Cid, helped Muslim allies, is often glossed over. It serves as a salutary reminder that religious enmity was – and still is – at best only ever a partial excuse for the justification of wartime atrocities. Political and military considerations must always come first when seeking explanations. This is equally true for Verden.

The Saxon wars were so protracted because whenever knocked down the Saxons refused to stay there; whenever Charlemagne thought he had brought them to heel they would rebel. This was tiresome enough, but the utter defeat of a Frankish force in Lower Saxony at Mount Suntel in 782, when four counts, some twenty nobles and most of their troops were annihilated by Saxons under Widukind, elicited an overwhelming response from Charlemagne. He assembled a huge army, entered Lower Saxony and cowed the Saxon nobility into submission without a fight. He ordered them to identify and round up all those who had fought with Widukind. The Saxon chiefs did so and handed them over to Charlemagne at Verden on the banks of the river Aller. Some were enslaved; the rest – as many as 4,500 – were beheaded in a single day. The scale of the slaughter and its manner are truly horrific. (As so often when dealing with figures derived from medieval sources, it is important to allow for the distinct possibility – and frequent certainty of – number inflation and the symbolism of a given figure; but even if the 4,500 accepted by many historians is too high, it nevertheless still denotes a wholesale massacre of frightening proportions.)

We have explored the various gruesome punishments meted out by rulers to political and military opponents, but it is hard to imagine Charlemagne inflicting such retribution on a similar number of Christian enemies. The clash of faiths certainly added an increased element of brutality to Charlemagne's response. It has been argued that, just prior to Verden, exasperated at the resilient obduracy of the Saxons, two leading clergy – Abbot Sturm of Fulda and Lul, archbishop of Mainz and disciple of his predecessor St Boniface – had successfully urged Charlemagne to adopt even harsher measures to be employed in the war against the pagans. However, it is interesting to note that there were dissenting voices within the Church, taken aback at the enormity of the massacre: Alcuin, for example, warned that violence begot only violence. Einhard and Notker the Stammerer, encomiastic biographers of Charlemagne, pass silently over the whole episode, as if ashamed to associate the King with such a shocking event. Indeed, lest Verden sully the saintly image of Charlemagne, the massacre has in some quarters been passed off as myth. (Not so with SS leader Heinrich Himmler, who established a monument to the executed Saxons.)

Charlemagne had other well-practised options at Verden. He might have executed a number of the more important rebels, taken others hostage, sold yet more into slavery and, in a well-established policy, dispersed the rest around his territories in a form of internal exile. Einhard informs us that during the Saxon wars Charlemagne 'transported some ten thousand men ... and dispersed them in small groups, with their wives and children, in various parts of Gaul and Germany'.[12] At Verden, frustrated at yet another uprising and encouraged by the exhortations of some bloodthirsty churchmen, he may have decided these measures were no longer sufficient. This may also have justified for him his undoubted desire for vengeance after the severe and embarrassing defeat at Suntel. This was not a petty motive but a practical measure: the defeat had exposed a huge weakness in the Franks' seeming ability to project their power; as such, a counteracting show of force was necessary to disabuse the Saxons of any such dangerous notions. Additionally, by killing so many who had taken up arms against him, he was also performing a simple exercise in numbers: now there would be a few thousand less Saxons to fight against Carolingian expansion. However, the fact that the Saxons had so readily submitted before Charlemagne's army and acquiesced to his demands for handing over the combatants reveals that the show of force had already proven to be efficacious. The massacre seems to have been the result of a combination of the personal and the political, both inextricably intertwined in the figure of a medieval king: revenge for a humiliating and costly military reverse, and a display of practical terror to cow the enemy. It is remarkable how so stark and spectacular a lesson could be so transient. The following year, the Saxons took up arms again. They would not be subjugated for another two decades.

Waterford, 1170

Britain's troubled relations with Ireland have been punctuated by atrocities up until the end of the twentieth century. An atrocity also marks the beginning of England's colonization of Ireland, announcing the onset of a long line of brutality that has marked Anglo-Irish conflict, especially during the centuries of frontier conquests. Internal warfare in Ireland was a savage affair with quarter in short supply; when English knights arrived in force from England in 1170, they accommodatingly left behind many of their chivalric ideals. Instead, they brought with them a violent superiority complex, fostered by the propaganda of twelfth-century English writers, that conveniently justified their civilizing mission against the benighted barbarians on the Celtic fringe.

Exactly eight centuries before 'the Troubles' in Northern Ireland began, English soldiers were invited over to Ireland by King Dermot of Leinster to aid him in his wars there. Mercenaries made their way across the Irish Sea, but intervention became organized and serious only with Strongbow's private expedition there in 1169. Strongbow – Richard FitzGilbert, Earl of Pembroke – agreed to send troops to Dermot on condition that the Irish king marry his daughter Aoife to him and so placed him in line for succession. Strongbow's fortunes had declined precipitously and he saw in the Irish expedition an opportunity to restore his political and financial position. The Normans had carved out kingdoms for themselves in England and Sicily; in Ireland their English successors could perhaps do so again. In 1169, Strongbow sent out an advanced force to prepare the way for his campaign the next year. This expeditionary force included impoverished adventurers looking, as many landless knights and younger sons did, to make money from war, whether in the form of booty, from military patronage, or from advantageous marriage. Gerald of Wales describes this contingent as comprising eleven knights and seventy archers; in Gerald's estimation, foremost amongst these was his cousin Raymond FitzWilliam, known as Raymond le Gros.

On arrival, they set in at Baginbun (originally known as Dun Domhnaill), four miles from Waterford, and constructed a flimsy, makeshift timber-and-earth fort surrounded by a ditch. This was completed rapidly as the men of Waterford soon bore down on them. Gerald puts their figure at 3,000, drawn up in three companies, while the author of *The Song of Dermot and the Earl* says between 3,000 and 4,000, against no more than 100 English. Whatever the truth of the figures, the English were heavily outnumbered. They made a sally, hoping that the combination of their heavily armoured shock charge and archery would drive the Irish off. But numbers got the better of them and they were driven back into their camp. Here they rallied and counter-attacked with such success that they put the Irish to flight, only ending their killing spree when they 'were worn out by striking'.[13] It was a remarkable victory for such a small force, demonstrating the effectiveness of even just a few professional knights and archers. The contemporary chronicler Gervase of Canterbury notes that the

Irish always found it impossible to beat numerically inferior but tactically superior English troops, who were braver and more skilful.

One of the most important spoils of this triumph was the capture of seventy leading figures from the Irish side. These were shackled in fetters and brought inside the camp. The English then debated what to do with the captives. Raymond le Gros took the view that they should be ransomed; Gerald argues that the English would have received a vast sum of money for them, or even the town of Waterford itself. Hervey of Montmorency insisted that they be killed; it was his counsel that was taken. Although they agree on the number of prisoners executed, Gerald and *The Song of Dermot* diverge as to how this was done. Gerald claims that they were thrown from the cliff top. *The Song of Dermot* offers a more gruesome alternative. The writer of this Old French epic says they were beheaded and their torsos then cast off the cliff. This source also asserts that their executioner was Alice of Abervenny (Abergavenny?), whose lover had been killed by the Irish in the battle. However, *The Song of Dermot* somewhat contradicts itself by also saying that the knights were responsible. Indeed, it is highly unlikely that a female camp follower would have the strength and stamina necessary to wield an axe to decapitate seventy men and then throw their bodies into the sea. If this version holds any truth, it is possible that Alice may have killed one or two as a token revenge.

The Song of Dermot explains clearly why the Normans carried out this mass execution: it was to display their ferocity and to terrorize the enemy:

> Of the Irish there were taken
> Quite as many as seventy.
> But the noble knights
> Had them beheaded.
> To a wench they gave
> An axe of tempered steel
> And she beheaded them all
> And then threw their bodies over a cliff.
> . . .
> In order to disgrace the Irish
> The knights did this
> And the Irish of the district

Were discomfited in this way.
To their country they returned
Outdone and discomfited.[14]

Gerald of Wales's account in his *Conquest of Ireland* offers an altogether more interesting explanation in the form of the fascinating three-page debate between Raymond and Hervey. This provides an invaluable insight into the military and moral dilemma between mercy and ruthlessness; between the dictates of humanity and the expediencies of war. Raymond's speech attempts in a reasoned way to marry mercy with practical consideration. He starts by reaffirming his hardy credentials, claiming that he would not insist on sparing his enemies, clearly defining separately the non-combatant status of the prisoners by identifying them as 'vanquished opponents'. They deserve clemency because 'they are not thieves, seditious, traitors or robbers', rather 'they have been defeated by us while they are defending their country', which is 'assuredly an honourable avocation!' Raymond argues that mercy to these fellow 'human beings' would offer a better example to the Irish than cruelty, torture and death, which would 'bring infamy and shame upon us, and would considerably damage our reputations'. He then appeals to his comrades' more unsentimental side, arguing that the deaths of the captives affords no real military purpose, whereas 'their ransom must be considered far more advantageous to us ... because it will augment the soldiers' pay and give an example of noble conduct'. This last reason is an eminently sensible tacit warning appealing to self-interest: if we do not kill their men when they are captive, perhaps they will not kill us if we fall into their hands. Such considerations were a very real restraint on wartime excesses, as we shall see later. He then ends with an impassioned description of the soldier's ferocious role in battle, and his humane behaviour after it. (This exceptional conclusion to his speech is quoted at the end of this book.)

Hervey's response is more utilitarian, direct and traditional in terms of military attitudes, but its simplicity should not detract from its practicality. He mocks Raymond's faint-hearted stance: 'As if any foreign country is to be conquered by acts of mercy rather than by fire and slaughter!' He makes his own case forcefully. Enemy races did not submit to clemency but '... rather bowed their necks in submission under the compulsion of armed might and terror bred of cruel treatment. While peoples are still proud and rebellious they must be subdued by all possible means and clemency must take a back seat.' He accuses Raymond of 'criminal compassion' and being 'bent on increasing the number of enemies'. He moves on to raise the question of practical personal safety more explicitly than Raymond: 'We have now within our camp a greater number of our enemy than of our own people.' Thus they were not only surrounded by danger on all sides outside the camp, but also within it. 'What happens if these men free themselves . . . and make a sudden rush to seize our arms?' Playing on his men's fears, he adds that had they been the ones caught, the Irish would not have given them any quarter. He concludes with the classic medieval military rationale that lies behind the majority of atrocities committed in war during the Middle Ages; he urges that the prisoners be executed so 'that the deaths of these men may inspire fear in others, and as a result of the example we make of them this lawless and rebellious people may shrink from engaging our forces in the future.'

Unsurprisingly, Hervey won the argument: the experienced warriors listening to him understood full well the dreadful underlying principle of the application of terror. The message sent out by the executions was unequivocal; that the 'discomfited' Irish understood it is confirmed by the author of *The Song of Dermot and the Earl*.

The absolute accuracy of the exchange and its undoubted fabrications with classical allusions to Julius Caesar and Alexander the Great has to be questioned; what matters is that it reveals the medieval mindset not to be one of unremitting and universal advocacy of violence. Both sides of the debate offer sensible and practical thinking. That Raymond lost it does not automatically weaken his contention that self-preservation merits clemency: on occasion the same case was made successfully in other medieval conflicts. That Hervey won it merely reflects the established military orthodoxy of the time. Gerald makes clear his own position: 'The victors, acting on bad advice, misused their good fortune by displaying deplorable and inhuman brutality.'[15] It has been suggested that Gerald of Wales harboured a grudge against Hervey, and was using his actions at Waterford to incriminate him. More usually it was the case that politically neutral or friendly commentators were far more accommodating of such extreme action; the sheer ruthlessness of military commanders like Henry V and Richard the Lionheart and countless others rarely did their reputations as champions of chivalry any harm. We cannot know what might have happened had Raymond's advice been taken; but Hervey's counsel did the English no harm: by 1171, Strongbow was King of Leinster. Such was his success that Henry II of England felt compelled to launch a major expedition to Ireland during 1171-2 to subdue him, forcing all to submit before the Crown.

Hattin, 1187, and Acre, 1191

Once again, we are taking examples from the expanding frontiers of Christendom where the clash of cultures and, as at Verden, religion, might be expected to add intensity and bitterness to wars of conquest. From the time of the West's conquest of Jerusalem in 1099 on the First Crusade, when chroniclers gleefully reported the crusaders wading knee-deep in the blood of the massacred Muslim inhabitants of the city, the crusades are notorious for their free falls into savagery, with religious fanaticism being the main culprit behind the excesses of wars – crusade or jihad – fought in the name of God. Hence there is to this day a widely held belief that religion is the cause of so many of the world's conflicts, as can be seen today in the Shia–Sunni Muslim civil war in Iraq. But the reality is that politics uses religion more than religion uses politics, even as far back as the Age of Faith in the medieval world. Religious fundamentalism is an insufficient explanation for two notorious, but in many ways representative, atrocities from the Third Crusade. The terrible events at Hattin and Acre involve two figures regarded as epitomizing the very essence of chivalry: Richard the Lionheart and Saladin.

The Latins' victory in the First Crusade was one of the most outstanding military campaigns of the entire Middle Ages. But it was not a victory that could be easily sustained. Manpower shortages and a resurgent Islamic enemy put enormous pressures on the crusading states; despite the formation of the military orders, the famous Knights Templar and Hospitaller, the northern city of Edessa was lost in 1144. This prompted the Second Crusade of 1146-8, under the leadership of the French king, Louis VII, and the first Hohenstaufen German emperor, Conrad III. While the crusade brought in a temporary influx of much needed men, held together only by the discipline of the

Templars, it ended ignominiously at Damascus with very little to show for the huge enterprise.

The crusader states were left exposed and when Saladin arrived on the scene and largely united the Muslims under his sultanate by 1186, they were left ever more vulnerable. As much by diplomatic skills as by military ones, Saladin made substantial inroads into the Latin states, isolated castle garrisons often surrendering without resistance to him, relying on his reputation as a merciful victor. In 1187, having lost some momentum during a serious illness, Saladin invaded the Latin states and based his strategy on seeking a major engagement with the crusaders. He had a number of reasons for such a strategy: it was difficult to maintain his forces in the field for long periods of time; the crusaders had been weakened by losses earlier in May that year, the military orders suffering particularly heavily, and Saladin would have wished to capitalize on this; and the crusaders' defence-in-depth strategy, in which they relied on the impressive strength of their castles, made a decisive victory difficult for Saladin. To draw the crusaders out, at the beginning of July Saladin besieged and took the town of Tiberias in eastern Galilee, leaving its citadel holding out. Usually, besieging armies felt vulnerable to the possibility of being caught between a relief army and the garrison; but this was what Saladin wanted the crusaders to hope for, as he deployed his forces for the trap. The leaders of the crusading forces debated fiercely over what to do. Count Raymond of Tripoli, whose wife was in the citadel at Tiberias, actually advised against a relief army, as he astutely reasoned that this was exactly what Saladin wanted. However, he was goaded for lack of vigour and his loyalty was questioned. The hawks won the day and the crusaders took the bait. A relief army under King Guy of Jerusalem quickly made its way to the beleaguered town.

Guy had emptied his fortress garrisons to make up his field army. He had need to. Despite generous estimates of his army allowing him 1,200 knights, perhaps 4,000 lighter cavalry and some 15,000 infantry, he was facing a Muslim army that outnumbered his by three to two. The army approached Tiberias in traditional battle order: Count Raymond took charge of the vanguard; Balian of Ibelin led the Hospitallers and Templars in the rearguard; and at the centre was the notorious Reynald of Châtillon with King Guy and the Holy Cross, that most sacred of relics on which it was believed Christ had been crucified.

Before they could reach Lake Tiberias and its essential waters, on the 3 and 4 July Saladin engaged them between the hills known as the Horns of Hattin.

The battle was to prove one of the most decisive of the whole crusading period. During the night, Saladin's army harried the crusaders' camp. In a letter after the battle, Saladin wrote that he 'kindled fire against him [the enemy], giving off sparks, a reminder of what God has prepared for them in the next world. He then met them in battle, when the fires of thirst had tormented them'.[16] Short of water as they were, the smoke would have exacerbated the already telling thirst of men and horses alike, thereby weakening and demoralizing them before the battle was fully engaged. Although six knights and some sergeants deserted to Saladin, the effect on the infantry was, as we shall see in a moment, more crucial. Saladin's army was well supplied with water from the lake, which a train of camels carried to reservoirs created for his men. The constant rain of arrows pouring onto the crusaders served to dispirit them further. On 4 July, the vanguard attempted to spearhead the way to the lake, which was quickly blocked. The whole army became severely pressed. In the centre division, King Guy was met with desperate requests for help by both the van- and rearguards.

Known for his vacillation, Guy first decided to help Raymond, who calculated that the force of the two divisions combined might be enough to break through the Muslim ranks and thereby reach the vital waters of the lake. But Guy changed his mind, and made the fateful decision to instead move back to help Balian and the military orders. Whether on his own initiative or commanded by the King, Raymond led a downhill cavalry charge in a drastic attempt to break enemy lines. The Muslims in his path simply moved to one side and let his knights through, launching a fierce missile assault on them as they passed. They then closed the gap behind the crusaders, leaving them entirely cut off from the main army and unable, through losses and fatigue, to launch an uphill assault. Raymond had little choice but to make good his escape as best he could; with a dozen knights he fled the scene of battle. For this action, his name was traduced by many chroniclers, who branded him a traitor.

Having fought his way back to the rearguard, Guy ordered his men to go on the offensive. When repeated cavalry charges exhausted the knights' horses, and Muslim archery had taken its toll on their chargers, they continued to attack on foot. Some infantry joined the dismounted knights, but most took refuge on one of the Horns, rejecting the King's pleas to protect the Holy Cross; they replied to the King that they were dying of thirst and would not fight. As the crusaders retreated uphill the Cross was lost. With Muslim forces concentrated on King Guy's position, Balian escaped with some of the rearguard. Exhausted, surrounded and parched with thirst, the remaining crusaders threw down their arms and surrendered.

It was a crushing defeat. Despite the escape of Raymond and Balian, almost the entire leadership of the crusader kingdom was captured, including Reynald of Châtillon, the Masters of the Templars and Hospitallers, and the King himself. The infantry, as usual, suffered the heaviest losses, though large numbers still managed to escape. Despite the intensity and ferocity of the fighting, relatively few knights had been killed in combat – a testament to their armour, which had earned them the name of 'men of iron' from the Muslims. But the real bloodbath was yet to come.

The first casualties would have been the captured Turcopoles: as apostates from Islam they would have been slaughtered on the spot. The leading crusaders were another matter. Saladin had King Guy and Reynald brought to his tent. The King was offered some sweetened water: in Arabic custom the captive was safe if his captors gave him either food or drink. Guy passed on the drink to Reynald, at which Saladin said to his interpreter: 'Tell the King, "You are the one giving him a drink. I have not given him any drink".'[17] For Saladin had sworn some time before to kill Reynald. Reynald had been a thorn in Saladin's side for a long while. Castellan of the powerful and famous fortress at Kerak, he ignored truces to prey on Muslim trade routes and embarrassed Saladin in a number of ways: in 1186, he captured the Sultan's sister in a caravan that passed provocatively close to Reynald's stronghold; in 1182, he had set out to attack Mecca, which severely dented Saladin's prestige as Protector of Islam's Holy Places; and in most of their encounters, the ruthless adventurer had got the better of him. According to Ibn Shaddad, at Hattin Reynald was offered the chance to convert to Islam. Reynald refused: he had between 1160 and 1176 spent seventeen years as a Muslim captive, during which time he had come to utterly despise his enemy. Instead, according to one Latin chronicler, he now displayed his customary fiery arrogance and defiance. At this, Saladin took a sword and struck Reynald on the shoulder, severing his arm. Guards then dragged him from the tent and beheaded him. Saladin dipped his fingers in Reynald's blood and sprinkled it on his own head in an acknowledgement that vengeance had been taken. This done, he reassured King Guy, shaking in fear at what had befallen Reynald, that his safety was assured. Reynald's head was later dragged through Damascus. Saladin had just cause to execute Reynald, but this was not his only motive: not only did he wish revenge on him for the setbacks he had caused the Sultan; he was also removing once and for all an effective and therefore dangerous enemy.

Enemy prisoners were so abundant witnesses record seeing up to thirty at a time being led by their captor on a single rope. This excess of supply over demand drastically slashed their sale values as slaves, with the new going rate down to 3 dinars; one captive was even exchanged for just a shoe. However, one group of prisoners held their price: the Templars and Hospitallers. Saladin now changed his mind over the fate of these fighting monks of the military orders, numbering nearly 240 in total. Rather than be held captive or sold into slavery, they were to be killed. His command for execution was sent out, Saladin compensating anyone holding a Templar or Hospitaller with 50 dinars per man. The prisoners were brought before Saladin. Only conversion to Islam would save their lives; despite the ideological fervour of the orders, a few did so. The grisly task was left to amateur executioners. Imad ad-Din reports graphically and gleefully what happened. Saladin

> ordered that they should be beheaded, choosing to have them dead rather than in prison. With him was a whole band of scholars and sufis and a certain number of devout men and ascetics; each begged to be allowed to kill one of them, and drew his sword and rolled back his sleeve. Saladin, his face joyful, was sitting on his dais; the unbelievers showed black despair. . . . There were some who slashed and cut cleanly, and were thanked for it; some who refused and failed to act, and others took their places. I saw there the man who laughed scornfully and slaughtered . . . how much praise he won, the eternal rewards he secured with the blood he had shed, the pious works added to his account with a neck severed by him![18]

As Saladin wrote in a letter: 'Not one of the Templars survived. It was a day of grace.'[19]

A Latin chronicler offers an alternative version, equally religious in its appeal, in which the knights are willing Christian martyrs who 'joyfully offered their neck to the smiter's sword'.[20] A Templar zealot called Nicholas, possibly half-crazed with fear of his imminent death, had actually recruited other knights to take the Templars' tonsure, thereby sealing their fate, too, but as martyrs. There was then a rush to be the first executed, Nicholas 'obtaining the glory of martyrdom first'.[21] As a last insult, the victims were left unburied.

Both accounts emphasize the religious dimension of the slaughter, with both victims and executioners alternatively acting for the glory of God; Saladin explained away his actions as a way of purifying the land of the infidel. But there are problems with focusing on just this aspect. For a start, crusading indulgences took care of the Christians' spiritual needs in death; a tonsure was not prerequisite for a martyr's death. And the role of 'holy men' in the massacre is clearly designed to gloss the atrocity with a spiritual motive, while at the same establishing Saladin as a holy warrior. It is not easy to determine Saladin's explicit motives for taking the Templars and Hospitallers prisoner, only to kill them two days later. One modern historian has said that Saladin had no choice: as monks, the knights of the military orders would not become apostates (although some actually did); and as part of the orders, they would not receive ransoms. Yet this does not mean they had to be killed: imprisonment, slavery and exchange were other options. In 1157 Bertrand of Blancfort, Grand Master of the Temple, was captured by Muslim forces, but released two years later. In 1179, another Grand Master, Odo of Saint-Amaund, was seized by Saladin but died in prison; his body was exchanged for a Muslim leader held by the crusaders. And at Hattin, the Grand Master was spared again: Gerard of Rideford was released within the year (as was the King). Political, financial and military considerations took precedence over religious ones.

Propaganda on both sides depicted the pagans and infidels as dogs condemned to Hell. Yet both sides were perfectly capable of arranging amicable truces and agreements that suited each other. The famous civility between Saladin and Richard the Lionheart was reciprocated at various levels throughout the Holy Land. Balian of Ibelin, who led the rearguard at Hattin, was a personal friend of Saladin. Even the implacable Reynald of Châtillon was party to treaties made with the Muslims when it suited him. Count Raymond of Tripoli's period of captivity (eight years in Aleppo) brought him to a greater understanding of Islam and he came to respect his captors. But it went further than truces: Muslims would ally with Christians against other Muslims, just as Christians would ally with Muslims against other Christians. In just one relevant example, only two years before Hattin, Raymond of Tripoli had entered an alliance with Saladin against no less a person than the king of Jerusalem, Guy of Lusignan. Two months before the battle, Raymond had briefly even given Saladin permission to lead the Muslim army through his territory so that the Sultan could attack the King. In most respects, holy war was waged in the Middle East little differently from how it was waged in the West: ever-changing alliances reflected the potential for political gain; principles were displayed from time to time, but they rarely superseded pragmatic opportunities.

As noted above, for some historians Saladin's magnanimity, rather than his severity, had proved to be a military asset: he could be trusted to treat his prisoners mercifully, so encouraging swift capitulation to him. But like any medieval military commander, Saladin was no stranger to ruthless measures in war, frequently killing captives, whether military or civilian, and even after promises of quarter had been given. His actions in 1179 at Bait al-Ahzan, just north of the Sea of Galilee, are instructive. Here, when the crusaders' castle was about to fall, the Christians asked for quarter; none was granted. This did not mean that all the garrison was killed – perhaps half was taken prisoner – but that no guaranteed protection was afforded to the defeated defenders. An Arab chronicler reports that although many crusaders were killed indiscriminately, Saladin gave direct and specific orders that the garrison's crossbowmen were to be executed. This was a testament to the crossbowmen's efficacy: the casualties they inflicted earned them the particular enmity of the Muslims. Capture and slavery would equally have neutralized these men, so the killing of them seems to be sending a warning message to demoralize others who would replace them. It is also a possibility that their deaths would help sate the Muslim troops' thirst for revenge for their fallen comrades; mercy may have gone down badly with the victorious troops.

These are the likeliest reasons for the executions at Hattin: revenge on the crusaders' most effective fighting men, who were harsh, brutal and unrelenting in their war against the Muslims; and a lesson not only to the military orders, but also a warning to anyone thinking of joining them, with the intent of hindering recruitment. In this, Saladin was following precedent: Templars who were seized after storming a breach at Ascalon in 1153 were decapitated; their heads were sent as trophies to Cairo, while their bodies were left behind so that the garrison could decorate the walls with them as a ghastly gesture of defiance. In his account of Hattin, the author of *The Rare and Excellent History of Saladin* does not mention the offer of conversion to the Templars and Hospitallers; instead he baldly states that Saladin made a deliberate choice to have them executed: 'As for the officers of the Hospitallers and the Templars, the Sultan chose to put them to death and killed them without exception.'[22] Saladin was aware that manpower shortages were an overriding concern for the crusaders; with some sixty Templars having been killed at the encounter at Sephorie two months before Hattin, and another 230 now, Saladin had dealt a severe blow to the strength of the military orders while encouraging his own men with the crushing of their fiercest opponents. A Latin chronicler's explanation for the massacre is the most likely one: Saladin 'decided to have them utterly exterminated because he knew they surpassed all others in battle'.[23] Unlike Grand Masters, to Saladin the knights were worth more dead than alive.

After Hattin, the crusader kingdom all but imploded. By the year's end only the coastal towns of Tripoli, Antioch and Tyre and a few castles held out. The body blow came in early October with the loss of Jersualem, the ripest fruit of Hattin, Saladin's greatest victory. The Sultan was triumphant while Latin Christendom stood in dismay at the loss of their Holy City. It was the rallying cry for the Third Crusade.

The great set piece of the Third Crusade was the siege of Acre, 1189–91. The city, the chief port for the kingdom of Jersualem, was initially besieged by King Guy of Lusignan, despite his promise to Saladin that he would not take up arms against him on his release. Throughout the long investiture, Saladin remained camped nearby with his army, unable to shift the crusaders or to breach their siege lines. The stalemate was broken by the arrival of reinforcements under King Philip II of

France and Richard the Lionheart, leaders of the Third Crusade, in April and June 1191. Saladin's repeated attacks with his field forces were successfully rebuffed and the defenders of Acre were left isolated. Prolonged artillery barrages and mining operations brought the siege to an end in mid-July. Fearing an imminent storming of the city and being put to the sword, the garrison came to terms and surrendered on the understanding that they would be spared. Two thousand six hundred were beheaded.

In a chapter on battles, the dramatic details of this epic siege must be passed over; but as a chapter on massacres of prisoners, and hence non-combatants, Acre requires discussion. For the fate of the Muslim prisoners was not determined at the moment when the city fell, but over a month after the siege had finished. Also, what happened at Acre is the most notorious episode of the Third Crusade and is considered one of the blackest episodes of the whole crusading era. Yet it must be seen in part in the light of what happened at the Battle of Hattin, four years earlier.

On 20 August, nearly six weeks after the city's fall, Richard marched out his Muslim prisoners some distance beyond the city walls to a plain. Baha al-Din, Saladin's panegyrist who wrote an immensely detailed account of the siege, described what happened next. Richard

> dealt treacherously towards the Muslim prisoners. He had made terms with them and had received the surrender of the city on condition that they would be guaranteed their lives come what may and that, if the Sultan delivered what was agreed, he would free them together with their possessions, children and womenfolk, but that, if the Sultan refused to do so, he would reduce them to slavery and captivity. The accursed man deceived them and revealed what was hidden in his heart. ... He and all his Frankish forces ... came to the wells beneath tell al-Ayyadiyya ... and then moved into the middle of the plain. ... The enemy then brought out the Muslim prisoners for whom God had decreed martyrdom, about 3,000 bound in ropes. Then as one man they charged them and with stabbings and blows with the sword they slew them in cold blood, while the Muslim advance guard watched, not knowing what to do because they were at some distance from them.[24]

The scale of the massacre is one to compare with Verden. For Muslims, it was a day of infamy that resonated in their history. When Acre fell to the Muslims in 1291, they meted out the same treatment to the crusading garrison, a chronicler justifying the ensuing massacre as revenge for the Christians' actions exactly one hundred years earlier:

> Almighty God permitted the Muslims to conquer Acre on the same day and at the same hour as that on which the Franks had taken it: they ... promised to spare the lives of the Muslims and then treacherously killed them. ... The Sultan gave his word to the Franks and then had them slaughtered as the Franks had done to the Muslims. Thus Almighty God was revenged on their descendants.[25]

The terms of Acre's surrender in 1191 were that all inhabitants of the city were to be spared in exchange for 1,500 prisoners, a huge ransom of 200,000 dinars and the return of the Holy Cross; finer details were to be hammered out in negotiations with Saladin. (The chronicler Roger of Howden claims that many of the Muslims were freed after having been baptized into the Christian faith; but conversions were stopped by Kings Philip and Richard as many of those freed returned to Saladin's army.) Saladin, beset with financial pressures of his own after years of campaigning, struggled to meet swiftly the conditions stipulated; however, he offered a first instalment of all the prisoners, the Holy Cross and half of the money to be delivered on 11 August. When the agreed day arrived, Saladin started to prevaricate, insisting on new terms: all Muslim prisoners should be released and Richard should accept hostages until payment was made in full; failing that, Richard should offer hostages to Saladin until the rest of the money was forthcoming. This was rejected and Saladin then repudiated the initial agreement. As John Gillingam, the leading authority on Richard I, says: 'Neither side trusted the other and so both were looking for guarantees which the other would not give.'[26] Discussions and skirmishes – and even exchanges of gifts – continued until the day of execution.

Saladin deliberately placed Richard in a difficult position, exploiting the situation to hamper the progression of the crusade. Chroniclers wrote at the time: 'King Richard knew for sure and realized without doubt that in truth Saladin was only putting him off'; and Saladin 'sent the king frequent gifts and messengers, gaining time with deceitful and crafty words. . . . He aimed at keeping the king hanging on for a long time through his myriad subtleties and ambiguities.'[27] Richard's forces were poised to march south; the longer they were at Acre the more time Saladin had to prepare for the expedition, and the more resources the crusaders would be forced to work their way through. These resources would have been depleted even faster by the need to feed all the prisoners. Saladin had devastated the region around Acre, so food supplies were already constricted. Having won a momentous victory at Acre, the morale of the crusaders was high; but empty stomachs would quickly sour the triumphant mood, especially if food were to be shared with their Muslim enemies. The continuator of William of Tyre's chronicle actually explains Richard's actions at Acre as a morale-boosting gesture: when Saladin failed to materialize with the Holy Cross on the day set for exchange, the crusaders were so upset and distressed Richard took pity and calmed them by ordering the execution of the prisoners.

Then there was the very real problem of guarding such a large number of prisoners. Richard needed most of his soldiers for the campaign; he could not afford to leave sufficient men behind merely to ensure effective guard duty. The Templars no doubt told Richard the tales of large bodies of prisoners overwhelming their guards during the Second Crusade; this was also the concern of the English in Wexford, and one of Hervey of Montmorency's arguments for killing the Irish prisoners there. An Arab chronicler gave this as one of the explanations for the executions: 'The King of England had decided to march on Ascalon and take it, and he did not want to leave behind him in the city a large number of enemy soldiers.'[28]

These considerations were substantial enough for Richard to forego the enormous ransom, the value of which was decreasing by the day with the financial cost of feeding and guarding the prisoners, and the heavy strategic cost of lost momentum. He had the possible option of releasing the prisoners on payment of half the ransom − still a significant amount; but as Gillingham notes, this would have meant loss of face, as he would have been seen to have been outmanoeuvred by Saladin. Richard had weighed everything up: his decision was not made rashly, vindictively or in the heat of a temper as some historians claim in the rush to condemn him. Richard had actually convened a meeting to discuss what should be done: as the contemporary writer Ambroise tells us, the matter was 'examined at a council where the great men gathered and decided that they would kill most of the Saracens and keep the others, those of high birth, in order to redeem some of their own hostages'; they 'decided not to waste time waiting any longer for anything, but that the hostages should be beheaded'.[29] Coldly calculating the current stalemate, and having failed to obtain political and financial gain from the situation (through prisoner exchanges and ransom), Richard took his final decision based on military priorities – the need to move on – and used the occasion to capitalize further militarily with a message of terror for Muslim resistance.

The executions – as was the way of the spectacle of violence in the medieval world – were carried out 'near enough to the Saracens that they could see them well'.[30] The demonstration was designed to terrify the enemy and undermine his will to resist the crusading King. It had considerable effect. Latin and Arab chroniclers attest to how Saladin, fearing another Acre, vacated and destroyed Ascalon, the next city on the crusaders' campaign list: he knew it would be difficult for any garrison there to hold steadfast knowing what had happened to their comrades when they defended Acre. Town after town capitulated to Richard without a fight: if Saladin had not saved Acre, he would be unlikely to save them. Jacques de Vitry, bishop of Acre from 1216 to 1228, calmly recognized the obvious practicality of such a slaughter: 'the king of England did more to injure and weaken the enemy by slaying many thousands of them'.[31] Richard had made a vicious virtue out of harsh necessity.

Rationalization of such brutality explains much. But one should not ignore the basic human instinct for revenge, especially at a time of war. The desire for vengeance can be an irrational emotion, but occasions like Hattin and Acre could be used to disguise it under a cloak of logic. Of course, more often than not acts of vengeance were performed to be seen exactly as that; failure to exact revenge would be regarded as a sign of weakness. When Richard wrote to the abbot of Clairvaux declaring his victory, his tone was matter-of-fact and businesslike. Of the prisoners and Saladin's acceptance of terms, he said: 'But the time-limit expired, and, as the pact which he had agreed was entirely made void, we quite properly had the

Saracens that we had in custody – about 2,600 of them – put to death'.[32] Any analysis of strategy and deeper explanations were left to the chroniclers; both Arab and Latin ones raise the matter of revenge. The author of *The Itinerary of the Pilgrims and the Deeds of King Richard* says that the crusaders were only too willing to carry out the executions: 'Men-at-arms leapt forward readily and fulfilled his [Richard's] orders without delay. They did this with glad mind and with the assent of divine grace, to take revenge for the deaths of the Christians whom the Turks had killed with shots from their bows and crossbows.'[33]

Baha al-Din also acknowledges this possibility: 'It was said they killed them in revenge for their men who had been killed.' (This may be a specific reference to six noble crusaders captured and killed during the siege.) The siege had lasted nearly two years and cost the crusaders huge casualties. Many leading figures of western Christendom had perished here, and it is likely that it was not just the men-at-arms and ordinary sergeants who wanted the Muslims to pay a heavy price for the lives lost. Nor should we forget that the massacre at Hattin would have loomed very large in the crusaders' deliberations. (Baha al-Din may also have been referring to this episode.) The crusaders would have wanted retribution for this atrocity and calls would have come loudest from the Templars: Richard worked extremely closely with the Templars while on crusade, developing intimate ties with them. And at Acre they had lost another Grand Master in combat with the Muslims.

Taken together, Hattin and Acre show how the cycle of violent vengeance was easy to perpetuate. Indeed, for a time after Acre, Saladin routinely put prisoners to death, even permitting some to be cut into pieces to satiate his soldiers' desire for revenge. That each massacre did little to harm the chivalric reputations of Richard and Saladin reveals the priorities of contemporary writers. Much was overlooked in the wake of military success: after Hattin, Saladin went on to take Jerusalem; after Acre, Richard regained hugely important areas of territory that contributed enormously to allowing the Latin kingdom in the Holy Land to exist for another century. Even in defeat, there would have been few dissenting voices. It was the way of war and accepted as such. The friendship of Richard and Saladin grew even stronger after Acre.

Agincourt, 1415

Agincourt vies with Hastings as the most famous battle of the Middle Ages in the English-speaking world. Despite its having comparably minimal historical impact beyond the battle itself, it is even more celebrated in the annals of English history. No doubt this elevated position is due to its being a remarkable victory: a hopelessly out-numbered band of plucky Englishmen under a brave and chivalrous king utterly destroying an overwhelming force of France's best soldiers in a supreme feat of martial prowess, marking the superiority of the English fighting man. It is no wonder that Shakespeare's *Henry* V was made into a stirring film designed to stiffen the resolve of a war-weary England facing the might of Hitler's Nazi hordes.

The reality, of course, was somewhat different. The English were not so outnumbered as has been thought until very recently; and Henry's chivalrous reputation has survived relatively intact, despite the horrific slaughter of some of his prisoners taken that day. The massacre associated with this battle has been one of the most closely studied atrocities of the Middle Ages; no doubt the celebrated fame of the victory has meant that this less-than-glorious conclusion to the battle cannot easily be overlooked. There is a general consensus amongst historians (especially anglophones) that the massacre, though regrettable, was understandable given the context of events that day. However, very few accounts of this incident have pieced together all the factors that fully explain why Henry took his fateful decision on St Crispin's Day 1415.

The path to Agincourt lay in the long history of Anglo-French conflict, reignited by Edward III's mid-fourteenth-century claim to the French throne which initiated the Hundred Years War. Under Henry, the war was renewed with vigour. Henry's vacillating demands for the French Crown were but one *casus belli*; another was his demand for satisfaction under the terms of the 1360 Treaty of Brétigny. More opportunistically, he was taking advantage of internal French divisions which weakened his enemy while attempting to bolster his own domes-tic position. There was still much disgruntlement in England that Henry's father, Henry IV, had usurped the throne from Richard II in 1399, a stigma that inevitably fell on the son. In the time-honoured tradition that has survived from Ancient Egypt to today, Henry hoped that waging a victorious war abroad would divert attention from domestic discontent. If any further justification for this cynical move were needed, it came on the day Henry embarked for France from Southampton, when a coup attempt was revealed, resulting in the decapitation of the conspirators. In the process, Henry aspired to establish securely not only his regime but also his reputation as the leading warrior prince of Christendom. In all this, Henry succeeded spectacularly. History loves a winner, and is therefore often willing to treat indulgently – or ignore altogether – the means employed towards victory. One English historian actually describes Henry's butchery of hundreds of his prisoners as a 'peccadillo'.

The quest for personal glory is often cited as the primary motivational factor of the medieval knight. Certainly, at Agincourt, it contributed significantly to the French defeat. The king (as discussed in chapter two) was the foremost knight of all, and thus was expected to win the greatest glory, a process that would serve to enhance his reputation and hence authority. In this respect, Henry immediately had an insurmountable advantage over his French counterpart, Charles VI of France, better known as Charles the Foolish (who must have been a real disappointment to his father, Charles the Wise). Unflattering as this sobriquet was, his other, more accurate one, was Charles the Mad. Charles suffered his first major attack of dementia as a young man in his early twenties: in 1392 he ran amok, slaughtering some of his hunting companions. From that time, he increasingly experienced episodes of distressing insanity. The result was civil war in France and an alluring opportunity for Henry to demonstrate his mastery on the continent to a seemingly leaderless enemy.

Henry provided a striking contrast to the frequently incapacitated French king. Contemporaries portrayed Henry as he wished to be perceived: energetic, thoughtful, just, decisive, devout – and a fearless war leader. Henry, like Richard the Lionheart, was always ready to lead from the front – something which must have impressed the French as their own king was clearly not up to the task (he thought that he was made of glass and would therefore shatter easily). Military prowess was considered an essential element of medieval monarchy, and Henry was going to enhance – and then exploit – his martial reputation for all it was worth. France was to be his theatre of spectacle and the dominant theme of his reign.

After a long period of detailed planning and preparation, Henry embarked for France from Southampton in August 1415. His army was a large one – up to twelve thousand strong, it included the active participation of most of the nobility – and represented the English nation in arms. Henry's first target was Harfleur at the mouth of the Seine. From here, the French could threaten English shipping in the Channel and launch raids on the south coast. For the English, Harfleur not only offered the defensive merits of protecting their maritime interests; more importantly, it meant they could threaten Rouen, the capital of Normandy. One French contemporary considered Harfleur as the key to Normandy; Henry fully appreciated this and invested the town energetically, hoping for its quick capitulation. Unexpectedly, despite the fierce bombardment and mining operations, the town held out for five weeks, much to Henry's deep vexation, surrendering only on 22 September. Henry immediately followed the victory with another propaganda victory: a direct challenge to the heir to the French throne to meet in a duel, a contest between their nations' leading champions which would settle the war without further bloodshed. As expected, the French did not respond to the bearding, not deigning to pick up the gauntlet.

With the first objective taken, if somewhat belatedly, a council of war was convened to decide the next move. The precise aims of the expedition have never been entirely clear to historians; nor do they seem to have been all that apparent to the English, as they debated what their next steps should be. Keith Dockray is convincing in his belief that the whole campaign was, beyond an initial step in recovering the duchy of Normandy, predominantly opportunistic, its eventual shape depending on what the first stages of the incursion achieved.

With a third of the English force either killed, sick, returned home or garrisoning Harfleur, many of Henry's commanders advised the King to return directly home with a limited, but highly respectable, victory under his knightly belt. They were overruled by the belligerent Henry, who insisted that the army undertake a 120-mile march to Calais from where they would only then take ship back to England. His decision has perplexed some historians. Presumably his fleet was still at Harfleur, so why force his exhausted troops, weakened by fighting, casualties, dysentery, cold and hunger, to endure this further pain? In reality, it was to be a show of force and another propaganda exercise: a victorious king making a procession through *his* territory, daring the enemy to move against him (while almost certainly hoping it would not) while simultaneously making his presence known, impressing the inhabitants of Normandy as to who was their true lord and master. Once again, Henry was reinforcing his warrior-king image. His contemporaries fully understood the meaning of this move: Adam Usk likened Henry's actions to that of a brave lion; John Hardyng underscored the king's military machismo even more directly: Henry 'went through France like a man'.[34]

The march might have been expected to take eight or nine days. About fifteen days in, delayed by broken bridges and the search for a crossing over the river Somme, the English were still two days away from Calais. But here, at Agincourt, they came to a complete halt: the French, who had been shadowing Henry's movements while their own forces steadily built up, blocked their way with a larger army, led by the chivalry of France. The opposing forces engaged each other on 25 October.

The fame of the battle of Agincourt has largely rested on a number of myths. A television documentary from 2004, despite the inclusion of some leading medievalists (who were, presumably, selectively ignored), trotted out five leading myths in its first two minutes. It claimed that the 'Age of Chivalry' died at Agincourt. One purpose of this book is to show that the concept of chivalry was limited in military practice and frequently ignored, as it was on many occasions before Agincourt; the battle had little effect on overall concepts and practice of chivalry one way or the other. The film claimed that the longbow was the devastating new weapon of the English; it had been in operation for centuries. It claimed that England and especially France were emerging nation states; but this process had begun much earlier in both countries, thereby permitting both countries to draw on patriotic support. Strangely, it labelled Agincourt as the last major pitched battle of the medieval age; there were to be many, many more. And, in the most persistent myth of all and the one which affords the English victory its mythic status, it stated the long-held belief that the French army comprised up to twenty-five thousand soldiers, outnumbering the English by at least three to one, and perhaps by as much as six to one. Anne Curry, the leading authority on the battle, has very recently calculated the real figures as between eight and nine thousand on the

English side, facing approximately twelve thousand French. She also suggests that the French, too, were likely to have been weary and disheartened.

There are many accounts of the battle from contemporaries, or written shortly afterwards, allowing a reasonably accurate picture of the engagement to emerge. The armies faced each other across a large ploughed field, sodden from days of rain and increasingly churned into a quagmire by thousands of feet and hooves. Henry raised the spirits of his men with battlefield orations as he rode along the ranks, his helmet surmounted by a gold crown. He had deployed his forces in classic formation: three battles (troop formations) of dismounted men-at-arms, with himself at the centre, and his archers on the flanks so that they could shoot obliquely at the advancing French, capturing them in a crossfire. Most archers stood behind sharpened stakes as defence against cavalry; others were positioned in the woods that bordered the field on either side. The French were also drawn up into three battles but, unlike the English, these were in linear form, one behind the other. The van consisted of dismounted knights and archers, including crossbowmen (one French chronicler said that the archers played no part in the whole encounter); cavalry was placed on its left and right flank. The centre was similarly comprised, but without flanking horse; at the rear the heavy cavalry was grouped in force.

The armies stood facing each other for some time in a stand-off. Henry ended the waiting at about eleven o'clock by advancing his army to a relatively narrow part of the field, making a French flanking manoeuvre more difficult, and putting his archers, carrying their stakes with them, within bowshot of the French, now some 250 yards away. The archers loosed their arrows with the desired effect: the French front battle lost its cohesion. First their crossbowmen withdrew from range while the arrow storm provoked a disorganized charge by the flanking cavalry. This was roundly beaten off with the loss of its leader, whose horse had become impaled on a stake. Thomas Elmham, writing perhaps just three years after the battle, offers a graphic description of what unfolded:

> The troops of the French rushed forward against the archers. In the face of a storm of arrows they began to turn back. Their nobility in the front, divided into three groups, advanced [on foot] towards our

banners in the three positions. Our arrows carried and penetrated, and the enemy was worn out under the weight of their armour. Some of our king's trustworthy men pressed down the enemy who penetrated the line with axes and the latter fell down. The living were pushed [from behind] towards death. The living went under the dead. The battle lines piled in. The English rose up against the companies of the French as they came to grips. The French fell before the power of the English. Flight from there was not open to them. They killed them, they captured them and kept them for ransoming . . .[35]

In this way, the first disorganized charge and flight of the French cavalry threw their whole army into disarray. The bulk of the French troops had to force themselves forward by pressing against those in front of them; in full armour, and carrying shortened lances for fighting on foot, they were exhausted just by trying to engage the English across the boggy battlefield. All the while English bodkin arrows penetrated French plate armour and caused tremendous casualties. But momentum and sheer weight of numbers carried the French into the English lines, where there was fierce fighting. In the ensuing mêlée, the Earl of Suffolk and the leading noble, the Duke of York, were killed, the latter most probably from having his helmet smashed into his skull.

Even Henry himself was threatened. A hit squad of eighteen knights had vowed to kill or capture Henry; all died in the attempt. But the Duke of Alençon did reach Henry, striking him on the head and detaching one of the fleurets from his crown. The Duke asked for quarter but was cut down by a knight yielding an axe. Henry, not surprisingly, is praised by English chroniclers for his bravery, standing over wounded nobles and defending them from certain death at the hands of the French. The chronicler Thomas Walsingham depicts him in true heroic fashion: 'The king himself, not so much as a king but as a knight, yet performing the duties of both, flung himself against the enemy. He both inflicted and received cruel wounds, offering an example in his own person to his men by his bravery in scattering the opposing battle lines with a battle axe.'[36] Note how even the King is using an axe when the sword is the true symbol of chivalry. Yet so thick was the mêlée there was hardly room to wield one.

By this stage, the archers had abandoned their bows and set to work on the crush of Frenchmen, many of whom fell and were suffocated under the huge press of soldiers. Packed together with limited mobility, the French were gathered for the slaughter. Many surrendered and were taken prisoner; others attempted to but were cut down in the fray. This was a just war in which such legalized butchery was to be expected and encouraged. The *Deeds of Henry* V, an eyewitness account, recalls the desperate scene:

> Fear and trembling seized them, even of their more nobly born, who that day surrendered themselves more than ten times. No one, however, had time to take them prisoner, but almost all, without distinction of person, were as soon as they were struck down, put to death without respite, either by those who had laid them low or by others following. . . . So great was the undisciplined violence and pressure of the mass of men behind that the living fell on top of the dead, and others falling on top of the living were killed as well, with the result that, in each of the three places where the strong contingents guarding our standards were, such a great heap grew of the slain and those of the lying crushed in between that our men climbed up those heaps, which had risen above a man's height, and butchered their enemies down below with swords, axes and other weapons.[37]

English archers were more numerous than men-at-arms; without equal incentive to take knightly prisoners alive for ransom (though they undoubtedly did so, despite popular opinion to the contrary), but more out of fear of what would happen to them if caught, they were not in a mood to be merciful. The ultimate emergency of life and death on the battlefield put survival at a premium. The chronicle undoubtedly exaggerates the heaps of dead (apparently, corpses cannot be piled high in this way), but the scale of slaughter is expressed. Nevertheless, in a battle fought by so many combatants, hundreds of prisoners were taken and passed down the line to the English rear.

Packed together, the French forces were pushed back onto their second line; the weight of numbers pressing the second division further back as the rout continued. Nearly all the French leaders, most of whom, having led from the front, had been either killed or captured by now; the army commander, Boucicaut, had been taken prisoner. Disorganized and leaderless, the French nevertheless still constituted a substantial force. Their third division had played no significant part in the battle and it was not exhausted by fighting as the English were by now. Although many had fled the field from this division, many also remained.

It was at this juncture that the impending English victory was threatened with defeat. There was a lull in the fighting, which seemed to mark the end of the battle and English success. French survivors, often pulled out from under corpses, were taken captive. The number of prisoners is uncertain, probably between 1,400 and 2,000 men; whatever the actual figure, all sources agree that it was a large number. There is some dispute as to what happened next. There was naturally much French activity on the battlefield's far periphery, where many French remained. At some point a cry had also gone up that the English baggage at the rear was under attack. It is not clear who exactly led this attack, but chroniclers settled on the local lord of Agincourt as its leader; a crown and other precious items were looted. Nor is it clear at what point of the battle the assault on the camp took place; it may even have occurred at the very beginning. Some sources claim that it was this event that precipitated the massacre of prisoners. But given the uncertainty of its timing, another even more pressing development provides a more telling reason.

It was feared that the French third division was regrouping for a major counter-attack; a cavalry charge of some six hundred men-at-arms was about to be launched. This counter-attack was a mortal threat to the English: fatigued and no longer in tight formation on the battlefield, they were extremely vulnerable to a fresh attack. (If the assault on the camp had synchronized with the cavalry charge, the danger was doubled.) At this point of pivotal jeopardy, Henry ordered all but the most important prisoners to be massacred. His knights refused the order. This was partly out of chivalrous and moral concerns, but mainly out of self-interest: the prisoners represented a huge fortune in ransom money, and thus an opportunity for enormous financial profit. A third possible reason for the order being refused is not cited by contemporaries or historians of the battle, but must also be considered: if the English were to be captured afterwards by the

French, either here or before reaching Calais, they would likely suffer the same fate.

Henry was not to be deterred by this act of insubordination. Instead, he relayed his urgent instructions to a squire and two hundred archers; any who refused to carry out the order were themselves to be immediately executed. Not that they would have been as reluctant as the knights to carry out the executions: if defeated, their fate would likely have been the same with or without the killing of the French prisoners. The archers set about their grisly business. Men-at-arms who had surrendered themselves to their captors on guarantee of their safety were massacred. Most of the victims had their throats cut; some were herded into a barn and burned alive. The French chronicler Jean Waurin wrote that the victims were decapitated and inhumanly mutilated.

The accepted explanation for the Agincourt atrocity is straightforward: Henry's immediate concern was that the prisoners, disarmed and dishelmed, but still in their plate armour, might break free, overwhelm their guards, pick up weapons that lay all over the field, and assist the counter-attack – and all this at a time when Henry needed every possible man for the expected renewal of combat in the field. This was a real concern, and one that was faced, as we have seen, by other medieval commanders (although this comparison is not made by Agincourt historians). Some contemporaries from both sides make the danger posed by the prisoners explicitly clear. The *Deeds of Henry V* relates:

[A] shout went up that the enemy's mounted rearguard (incomparable in number and still fresh) were re-establishing their position and line of battle in order to launch an attack on us, few and weary as we were. And immediately, regardless of distinction of person, the prisoners, save for the dukes of Orleans and Bourbon, certain other illustrious men [and] a very few others, were killed by the swords either of their captors or of others following after, lest they should involve us in utter disaster in the fighting that would ensue.[38]

John Hardyng and Thomas Elmham confirm this view, the latter stating: 'Many new battle lines threatened to enter the fray to fight against the weary. .... The English killed the French they had taken prisoner for the sake of protecting the rear.'[39] (Some French sources believe that the knights Henry thought were to attack him were actually leaving the field by flanking to the rear, and blame their manoeuvre for the massacre.)

Historians (especially French ones) have tended to overlook or make insufficient connections between two facts that lend support to this argument at Agincourt. The first was that Henry had already considered the problem of prisoners. The night before the battle, he had actually released all the prisoners he had brought with him on the march from Harfleur and whom he was taking to England for ransom; the French promised to return to their English captors if their army lost the battle. By doing this he was clearly not only freeing up his own men for fighting, but also avoiding the danger of prisoners becoming combatants in the heat of battle. Secondly, the lustre of chivalry was frequently an illusion: prisoners who gave their *parole* often broke it. As cited above, the *Gesta Henrici* reports that some nobles 'surrendered themselves more than ten times'. This can be interpreted in different ways: one is that the prisoner became separated from his captor in the heat of the battle and so gave himself to another English knight for protection; or, just as likely, the prisoner escaped in the confusion only to find it necessary to protect himself soon afterwards by surrendering again. Certainly, a knight's oath was only as sacred as he felt it to be. In the early thirteenth century, France's flower of chivalry and answer to England's renowned William Marshal was William des Barres; on at least two occasions he broke his *parole* to escape being held prisoner. What is truly remarkable after Agincourt is that the men Henry had released on the eve of battle held true to their word and fulfilled their promise by later returning to him.

So concern for the security of the French prisoners and keeping them as non-combatants was a genuine problem and one that Henry had already considered. But this explanation can serve only up to a point. It poses real logistical difficulties. Christopher Allmand, in his magisterial biography of Henry, raises these difficulties and questions the scale of the slaughter. Would so many men, still in armour, offer no sustained resistance to being murdered? How could Henry afford the men for the task? Was it because they had too few arrows left to shoot at the cavalry? (If so, one could also ask why the men-at-arms were given the initial orders.) The number killed is also difficult to ascertain: Henry returned to England with well in excess of a thousand prisoners, so how many were actually slain at Agincourt? (Allmand may have forgotten the Harfleur prisoners who presented themselves after the battle.) Most relevant of all, with up to two thousand prisoners, how would Henry have expected them all to be killed in the short time before the imminent cavalry charge, by a number perhaps one-tenth their size? As John Keegan has noted, the mechanics of such a gruesome task would have entailed a lengthy process. He judiciously infers that the number of victims was in the low hundreds, if that.

The impracticalities of this battlefield slaughter – so unlike the post-battle massacres of Acre, Hattin and Wexford – pose the question of what the most substantive reasons behind Henry's orders were. Again, we must turn to the lesson of terror in medieval warfare. Henry was using terror for two ends. First, he was demonstrating to the prisoners what their fate would be should they have thoughts of escaping to help the counter-attack; he wanted them cowed into submission and away from the battlefield. Secondly, and more importantly, he ensured that the French third division could see the executions: he was warning them that not only would their charge put his other prisoners their comrades – in deadly peril; but also that they could expect the same treatment if they, too, fell into English hands. As a matter of clear-headed urgency, he even sent a herald to the French to relay this message explicitly to them. Some of the sources openly attribute the killings to this purpose. Titus Livius writes that the English

> feared that they might have to fight another battle against both the prisoners and the enemy. So they put many to death, including many rich and noble men. Meanwhile, the most prudent king sent heralds to the French of the new army asking whether they would come to fight or would leave the field, informing them that if they did not withdraw, or if they came to battle, all of the prisoners and any of them who might be captured, would all be killed by the sword with no mercy. He informed them of this. They, fearing the English and fearing for themselves, departed with great sadness at their shame.[40]

The Pseudo Elmham and *Brut* chronicles corroborate this, the latter writing: 'Afterwards, news came to the king that there was a new battle of Frenchmen drawn up ready to steal upon them and come towards them. Immediately the king had it proclaimed that every man should kill the prisoners he had taken. . . . When they [the French] saw that our men were killing their prisoners, they withdrew, and broke up their battle line and their whole army.'[41]

That Henry immediately brought the massacre to an end when he saw the French retreat is confirmed by a French chronicler. Both sources quoted above attest that it was at this stage that victory was finally claimed and celebrated. Henry's brutal tactic had worked; victory vindicated his ruthless actions.

The crucial explanation for the killings lies in the fact that, for Henry, the battle was not conclusively over: enemy activity convinced him that victory could easily be turned into defeat. At this juncture, his prisoners, though technically non-combatants, were, as conventional opinion rightly points out, potentially a real threat to Henry; but what is overlooked is that they also constituted a powerful weapon for him. In threatening to kill them, and in being seen to carry out his threat, Henry, being a highly capable, hard-hearted military commander, was turning a weakness into a strength. The power of this weapon was too great for the enemy and ensured Henry's complete triumph at Agincourt.

As arguably the most famous battlefield massacre of the Middle Ages, it is perhaps surprising that by no means all contemporary accounts include the episode in their versions, and that protestations against what happened were muted, even on the French side. One might have expected writers from the defeated nation to have comprehensively discredited Henry for his actions, and poured opprobrium on him; the scale of the defeat and the killings – whether on the battlefield or after it – were lamented as an epochal tragedy, but the massacre was passed over without condemnation. The Monk of St Denis, writing the earliest French account of the battle, possibly offers a brief exception with 'O eternal dishonour!' (although this may actually refer to the shame of knights being killed by common soldiers in battle), but he was far more concerned with the national loss of face: 'Most galling of all was the thought that the defeat would make France feeble and the laughing stock of other countries.'[42] The lack of outcry reflects contemporaries' realistic acknowledgement of the precedence of military necessity in a kill-or-be-killed situation. Medieval writers on war and chivalry such as Bouvet and Christine de Pisan might have decried slaying of prisoners, but the exigencies of battle required decisive and ruthless commanders. There is an almost discernible tacit understanding in the sources that the French may have done the same in a similar situation. After all, before the battle they had unfurled the *oriflamme*, the sacred blood-red war banner that the French carried into battle at a time of national crisis as a symbol of France and of *guerre mortelle*: seeing this, their enemy could expect no quarter. In practice, the *oriflamme* did not preclude the taking of prisoners; nevertheless, it was a sign of intent and, crucially, that nothing, not even mercy, would stand in the way of complete victory. Henry did not need such a symbol: his relentless ambition and hard-hearted generalship meant, as we shall see again later at Rouen, that he approached every military challenge with his own psychological *oriflamme*.

There is an even more pertinent explanation for the sources' lack of censure: the judgement of God. No one was prepared to take issue with the divinely guided outcome of the battle. In this, all the sources – both English and French – concur: Henry had won against the odds because God had favoured his just cause. Henry certainly recognized thanks were due; as Thomas Walsingham observed: 'The king, ascribing all these good outcomes to God, as he ought, gave ceaseless thanks to Him who had bestowed an unexpected victory and had subjected savage enemies.'[43] This echoes the *Deeds of Henry V*: '...far be it from our people to ascribe the triumph to their own glory and strength; rather let it be ascribed to God alone, from Whom is every victory.... To God alone be the honour and the glory, for ever and ever, Amen.'[44]

French sources are no more reticent in accepting the will of God, the Monk of St Denis noting that Henry owed his victory to 'the special grace of God', and thus he was being used as a divine instrument in bringing low the French in all their 'insolence and pride'.[45] One French source relates how Henry explained his victory to his noble captives in terms of celestial intervention and moral rectitude: the French had only themselves to blame for their defeat as they were over-proud, sinful rapists and despoilers of churches and people. Another interprets the calamity in similar terms: in France, 'men of worth said that it was divine punishment and that God wanted to bring down the pride of many'.[46] The idea that Henry had punished the French for their sins was widely accepted; therefore, criticism of his battlefield massacre was perforce muted: no one was going to pick an argument with God. It was clearly a case of might makes right.

Historians generally agree that the pious Henry firmly believed that he was doing God's will; when he returned home to England, his triumphal procession being received ecstatically by huge crowds, he did so as God's favoured and humble servant. Yet it is easy – and probably necessary – to cast a cynical eye over this heavenly justification for victory, and even to question how completely contemporaries accepted it. English propagandists expressed complete faith in the justness of their cause, so why, as Walsingham reveals above, should the victory be 'unexpected'? And why also explain the victory in terms of English prowess? Similarly, God's final and decisive judgement did not prevent the French from analysing what had gone wrong at Agincourt: tactics, poor discipline, morale and political disunity were all proffered as contributing determining factors. Apologists would rationalize defeat in any number of ways. As seen above, the Monk of St Denis's main concern was that the defeat made France a 'laughing stock', and not that God had rejected his country. Medieval writers were also acutely aware of how risky a business battle was, and how the wheel of fortune was forever spinning. Writing in the fourteenth century, John of Trokelowe observed, '. . . the fates of battles are unknown. For the sword consumes now these and now those . . . with fortune turning its wheel.'[47]

The religious angle was useful for both victor and vanquished. For the latter, a ruler might exculpate himself by blaming instead the sins of his people and nobility; likewise, subjects could concentrate moral failings in the person of their prince. In either case, God's will precluded culpability on the grounds of military or political incompetence, matters that were harder to rectify than the cleansing afforded by a quick confession and repentance. For the victors, the display of practical powers was elevated even further by the display of spiritual ones. Then, as now, political capital was to be made from enjoying a special relationship with God. Who could stand against you if God were clearly on your side? Rebelling against Henry was now tantamount to rebelling against God. As Anne Curry has observed, Henry exploited God's unambiguously bestowed favour to the full: 'Victory was God's will and . . . Henry was God's chosen warrior. This was the line that Henry himself encouraged. . . . His prayers were answered. His steadfastness, his willingness to kill in God's name, had been rewarded.'[48]

So Henry escaped the Agincourt massacre with his chivalric reputation not sullied, but enormously enhanced. The prisoners killed were undeniably non-combatants who had surrendered; they had been accepted as prisoners and so, in accordance with the practice of the time they had been promised their safety. Henry breached this agreement in the most spectacular and egregious way possible, slaughtering tens — and possibly hundreds — of France's chivalry, all Christian brothers in arms. Yet he escaped censure: the religious and practical legitimacy of victory combined with the accepted acknowledgement of the military imperative ensured that Henry did not require any exoneration for his brutality; instead he was exalted amongst the greatest princes of Christendom.

For all that, and for all the consensus of the sources, there is a tantalizing indication that the massacre was nevertheless considered to be a disreputable, or at least an objectionable, act. Why, otherwise, did most of the earliest English sources recounting the killings omit to lay the order of execution at the feet of the King? The *Deeds of Henry V*, Thomas Elmham and Titus Livius all make an intentional omission of the royal command (although the last does relate how Henry sent his herald with a minatory message of no quarter), while the *Brut* chronicler and French sources specifically name the King as the author of the order. It can be argued that, like Walsingham (who does not refer to the massacre at all), those ignoring the King's role considered the incident of little importance or significance, and that later English chroniclers latched on to the event for political reasons, establishing an anti-Lancastrian (i.e. anti-Henrician) stance in the new Yorkist age. But on the same lines, political motivation may well have prompted silence in the first place; and the fact that later writers felt they could latch on to the massacre meant they perceived something incriminating in it. Chronicles such as the *Deeds of Henry V*, in this case composed by the royal chaplain (possibly John Stevens), were designed to glorify the writers' patrons to a wide audience; the *Deeds* was meant to elevate Henry's reputation throughout Europe, something that may well have been hindered by unequivocally identifying him as a killer of knightly prisoners.

No one is certain how many died in this famous battle, whether as combatants or as prisoners. The many highly inflated figures have to be dismissed; just as English sources exaggerated the size of the French army so as to make the victory all the more impressive, so they would overstate the enemy's casualties. (And, as seen earlier, medieval sources were frequently disconcertingly wayward when dealing with army sizes.) French casualties may have been as high as over five thousand, but that still seems very high; sources indicate that English casualties were as low as in the thirties, though they may well have exceeded a hundred deaths. All agree that the disparity was huge (this often being the case in decisive medieval battles). The mortality rate of Agincourt is regarded as one of its most salient features. Another is the killing of a large number of prisoners who might have been ransomed, which many historians consider a unique and distinctive event. But it is hard to portray the Agincourt massacre as unique: such an assertion sits uneasily within the norms of the brutality of medieval warfare, whether before Agincourt or after.

Henry's actions at the battle were not so alien to contemporaries: in France during just one month of his reign (January 1420), the English massacred a large force of Armagnacs who had been retreating under safe conduct, while the Bastard of Alençon slaughtered his numerous English prisoners at La Rochelle. In 1373 at Derval, it was the sheer want of compassion and compromise that led to both sides slaying their prisoners: neither of the forces' commanders could concur on the terms of surrender. The French who survived the carnage of the historic engagement at Agincourt (including the following day's despatching of wounded soldiers still lying on the battlefield) were the lucky ones, even if their lives were spared only to be incarcerated in England until death or ransom: the French commander Boucicaut died in captivity in 1421; the Duke of Orleans was not released from the Tower of London until 1440. Rather, Agincourt owes its notoriety to a number of specific aspects: it was a major and decisive battle; the scale of victory/defeat ensured it has received detailed study by historians; the attraction of Henry V and his iconic personal role, illuminated further still by Shakespeare, has spread its fame more widely; and, crucially, it is well represented in contemporary sources.

Agincourt was a sensational and renowned victory which nevertheless produced nothing in the way of geopolitical and strategic success in the same vein as acquiring Harfleur. Henry had to return to France later in his reign to accomplish his greater objective of winning

Normandy. However, there were tangible results in the number of important prisoners taken and the financial value they represented. More important were the intangible benefits: France's loss, either through death or imprisonment, of so many of its leading nobility; greater domestic political stability for Henry in England; and Henry's embellished reputation as a foremost warrior prince and a leading figure of chivalry. Henry's ruthless conduct at Agincourt had secured all this for him. The massacre was not a one-off incident, but all as one in his pitiless mindset. We shall see this mindset applied again at the siege of Rouen.

Towton, 1461, and Tewkesbury, 1471

The case of Agincourt exposes the fine line between battlefield exigency and calculated murder; between the rout of absolute victory and the cold-blooded slaying of the captured and vanquished. Soldiers fleeing the field of combat habitually dropped their weapons and discarded their armour so that they could run all the faster. The need for speed was made even more urgent by the practice of using cavalry – 'prickers' – to mop up the enemy in flight. But despite these open signs of ceasing hostilities – throwing away weapons, removing armour and panicked retreat from the field – the soldier running away was still considered fair game for killing. Surrender ostensibly guaranteed personal safety, but in a rout it was fraught with danger: those pursuing might not be inclined to stop and deal with the taking of prisoners while allowing others, some of whom might be of high rank, the time to make good their escape. A rout was the background to the credits of a victory already won; in such cases, unlike the not-quite-finished encounter at Agincourt, the taking of prisoners would not offer any immediate military advantage in the field. Chasing the enemy from the place of battle ensured high-adrenalin activity: the rush of battle and the bloodlust of mortal combat meant that many soldiers were still operating in killing mode. The lull at Agincourt gave time for the combatants to recover from the immediate psychological and physical crisis of battle; that, together with the prisoners already having been corralled, makes the massacre here a cold-blooded one, and not the hot-blooded decimation of a defeated enemy being routed.

This fine line has recently been revealed in an analysis of the Battle of Towton in 1461, the bloodiest battle ever fought on English soil, which ended with an infamous rout. When in the mid 1990s a funding body asked me to assess and evaluate a proposal for an archaeological excavation of the grave pits for this battle, I was happy to lend my approval, expecting some rich findings to result from the dig. All expectations were exceeded, resulting in an important book and a television documentary. The analysis of skeletons from the burial pits has led to speculation that the rout was not the cause of most of the deaths, but a post-battle execution of prisoners. Fought in south Yorkshire on 29 March 1461, the battle proved to be the decisive engagement during the first phase of the Wars of the Roses. At the beginning of the month, the nineteen-year-old Edward of York had proclaimed himself King Edward IV. He took the war north to confront the Lancastrians, meeting them at Towton. There are no detailed, reliable sources for the battle; but from what evidence there is it is clear that the numbers involved were exceptionally large, as were the casualties: the total for the latter is often given as an excessive twenty-eight thousand; the lowest contemporary total is nine thousand. All concur that the battle was an especially murderous one, one source observing of the soldiers that 'so great was the slaughter that the dead carcasses hindered them as they fought'.[49]

The armies clashed in the midst of heavy, driving snow. A change of wind direction curtailed the flight of Lancastrian arrows, while carrying the Yorkist ones further, a disadvantage which forced the Lancastrians onto the attack (as English archers forced the French to do at Agincourt). In the long, intense mêlée that followed, the Yorkists were on the point of being driven from the field, but lack of Lancastrian follow-up support granted Edward the opportunity to brace his men for a counter-surge which broke the Lancastrian line. From that moment, a closely contested battle was transformed into one-sided slaughter. Those that could headed for York to take refuge behind its walls. Some fled across Bloody Meadow, well-named for the carnage that chased at their heels. Others made their way to the river Cock, where steep gradients, rendered slippery with snow, caused many fatally to lose their footing. These fared no better: frantically looking for a place to ford the river, they proved easy targets for the cavalry preying on the banks. Those wading across the river were quickly picked off by archers; many met their end not at the hands of the enemy but from drowning in the freezing waters of the river. Such was the butchery here that locals later recalled a scene of so many corpses falling on each other that they actually dammed the river – in what became known as the 'Bridge of Bodies'. Those making it to York were pursued and many were cut down in its streets, long after the battle itself was over. One chronicler informs us that forty-two Lancastrian knights were rounded up and executed. Decapitation was the usual means of despatch in the Wars of the Roses.

The grave pits record the wounds inflicted on the soldiers' skeletons: the majority of possible fatal wounds appeared on heads, necks or shoulders, with the blows coming from behind. The preponderance of such blows, especially to the head (one skull received eight blows on the battlefield), would indicate that the victims were without helmets, like the massacred prisoners at Agincourt, adding to the conjecture that these soldiers had been executed. Philip of Commines writes that Edward informed him that after a victorious battle the King would mount his horse and order his men to spare the commoners and instead kill the lords. This draws attention to a relatively new departure in concepts of military chivalry that was witnessed most notably in England in the late Middle Ages: the higher orders were not only no longer secure in their presumption of safety if taken prisoner; they were actively targeted for killing, as happened at Towton.

Despite Edward's apparent concern for the ordinary soldier, this unfortunately did not translate into battle conditions that were any less deadly for them, as the enormous casualty rate at Towton shows. Here, even if the rank and file were not despatched as non-combatant prisoners, they were massacred in droves as they threw away their weapons and attempted to flee the battlefield. Many of the wounds found on the skeletons might be similar to those found on executed victims, but they are also indicative of trauma suffered by men being pursued in a rout.

The increased risk for knights and nobility is reaffirmed at another battle in the Wars of the Roses: that of Tewkesbury in Gloucestershire, fought a decade later on 4 May 1471. Once again, Edward IV defeated the Lancastrians, this time finally securing his throne. Once again, there was a rout of the vanquished. During this last phase of the battle, Prince Edward of Lancaster, the contender for the throne, was killed. Accounts tell of how he requested quarter in vain; the Crowland chronicler, considered the most reliable, claims that he and other Lancastrian leaders were deliberately struck down and eliminated at the first opportunity. Others, including the Duke of Somerset, escaped the initial carnage and took refuge in the abbey church of Tewkesbury, claiming protection of sanctuary. Initially, while still feeling magnanimous under the euphoria of such a decisive battle, Edward pardoned those inside. However, he soon shrugged off his clemency and, two days after the battle, he had his troops enter the church and drag the Lancastrians outside. They were summarily executed. Amongst those decapitated were the Duke of Somerset and a notable religious figure, John Langstrother, Prior of the Order of St John. Warkworth's Chronicle relates how these and others

> were taken and beheaded afterwards, where the king had pardoned them in the abbey church of Tewkesbury. . . . A priest had turned out at his mass and the sacrament in his hands, when King Edward came with his sword into the church. [The priest] required him by virtue of the sacrament that he should pardon all. . . . They might have gone and saved their lives; however, on Monday after, they were beheaded notwithstanding the king's pardon.[50]

Killings of sanctuary refugees also took place in the church of Didbrook, ten miles from Tewkesbury. Edward's apologists asserted the dubious claim that Tewkesbury had never been officially declared as a sanctuary; they hoped to mitigate Edward's dismissal of religious norms and the fact that his soldiers had actually killed some Lancastrians within the church itself. It was, of course, just self-justifying spin to cover the cynical brutality of the act. It has been argued that Edward was well within his rights to command the deaths of his prisoners: these men were guilty of treason against the King; some had even been pardoned before for the very same crime. But the whole point of the Wars of the Roses was that those fighting against the 'king' did not recognize him as their rightful monarch. As ever, might makes right.

The fog of war was commonly exploited to shroud questionable acts that would later be recounted as the consequence of glorious victory. At Tewkesbury, Edward, Prince of Wales, met his end. It is uncertain how he died, although contemporary sources suggest he was struck down while he was fleeing the battle and crying for assistance from his brother-in-law, the perennial turncoat George, duke of Clarence, who was fighting on the King's side. Edward's death meant, at a stroke, the end of the Lancastrian line and an immediate diminution of the threat to Edward IV's throne. This lessening threat was diminished even further by the post-battle executions.

We see similar motivations at the Battle of Shrewsbury on 21 July 1403. Here, the usurper king Henry IV was facing a rebel army headed by Sir Henry Percy, the earl of Northumberland (more famously known as 'Hotspur'). Once again, the very throne of England was the goal; with such high stakes, any vestiges of chivalric notions were discarded even before the battle had begun. As Alistair Dunn has noted, 'at Shrewsbury, the objective of each side was nothing short of the annihilation of the enemy, and, if possible, that of as many of his kin and supporters as could be ridden down and slain'.[51] High rank and eminence did not guarantee safety on that bloody day. On the loyalist side, Sir Walter Blount, the King's standard bearer, and Earl of Stafford and his knightly retinue were all cut down. Inflicting such losses only made matters worse for the rebels when they lost. The illustrious Thomas Percy, earl of Worcester, pleaded for his life, but was immediately beheaded. When asked what should be the fate of the rebel prisoners, the loyalist general Sir John Stanley instructed his troops: 'Burn and slay! Burn and slay!' The arrow stuck in his throat at the time did not predispose him towards clemency; but nor did the significant losses incurred by the royal army. Once again – a repeated theme of this book – the role of vengeance in medieval military atrocity should not be underplayed. Nearly fifteen hundred bodies were found in the rebel burial pit. The closeness in time of battlefield slaughter and contiguous execution of prisoners while the dust of combat was still settling may serve to blur the distinction between the two, separate events. The bloodlust of battle could still be coldly directed towards killing after the fighting had ceased.

CONCLUSIONS

The killing of high-ranking prisoners was still the exception to the norm in medieval warfare, but had become increasingly less so in

England since the disastrous reign of Edward II, from whose time, as we have seen, political motivation and justification were merged with the military context. Before Edward's reign, harsh punishment meted out to defeated enemies of note was frequently measured in shaming, but not mortal, acts. William the Lion, king of Scotland, when captured at Alnwick in 1174, suffered the familiar fate of being tied to a horse's tail and dragged along. When Prince Louis, son and heir to Philip II of France, was defeated by the English loyalist forces in 1217, he was compelled to sign the Treaty of Lambeth in nothing but his woollen underwear. (Louis compromised on this act of penitence, wearing a mantle over his embarrassment.) Prison and shackles were offensive enough to one's honour, but King John was judged by contemporaries to have been vindictively abusive in his treatment of prisoners caught at Mirebeau, near Poitiers, in 1202. These he manacled and paraded on carts on the way to prison; this was considered especially humiliating as it suggested connotations with the executioner's tumbrel for hangings. (As previously discussed, noble prisoners considered hanging as the most degrading form of death, associated as it was with the punishment appropriate for common criminals.) The fact that twenty-two of John's captives were to die under the severe conditions in which they were held added injury to insult, prompting many leading figures in France and Normandy to defect to the French. When John looked for much-needed allies in 1203 and 1204, too few were forthcoming to help him save his duchy of Normandy: his treatment of prisoners captured in war had alienated a critical contingent of support and had therefore been massively counter-productive.

As we have seen, it was much simpler dealing with the rank and file, the 'plebs' as chroniclers sometimes called them: these were commonly despatched without consciences being much troubled. Especially vulnerable were crossbowmen and archers, testimony to their deadly efficiency and the thirst for vengeance for fallen comrades. Saladin, as discussed above, was not lenient to crossbowmen; in 1153, Count Henry of Anjou (soon to be Henry II) gave quarter to the knights of Crowmarsh Castle, but executed its sixty archers; King John spared the garrison at Rochester in 1215, but hanged its crossbowmen; Henry III saw that over three hundred archers were beheaded in the civil war in 1264. Even in the early period of high chivalry, when knights had even less to fear from their often familiar opponents and battles often witnessed only a handful of their deaths, the infantry were customarily cut down in droves, as happened at Dol in 1173. At Tinchebray, Normandy, in 1106, Henry lost just two knights, while over two hundred infantry were killed.

This picture does, however, require a little clarification. It is commonplace to believe that soldiers of the lower orders were massacred simply because they had no value in ransom. This is not true, as we shall see in a later chapter. However, in certain situations and in certain places, circumstances dictated that it was either not practicable or not militarily sensible to allow the infantry to live. An example of the former might be a fast-moving campaign where the captors could not hang around for ransoms, or for it not to be expedient for relatives to follow the army with release money or goods, especially if the soldiers caught were fighting far from their homes. In cold economic terms, guarding prisoners might also mean an encumbrance to the pursuit of booty. Examples of the latter have been discussed at Agincourt, Acre and Wexford, where the weight of numbers proved deeply problematic. The number of deaths of infantry also reflects military reality: the foot soldier rarely had armoured protection equivalent to that of the knight; and, by definition, he lacked a horse to facilitate his quick escape from the battlefield.

When foot soldiers escaped death at the hands of their captors, they may not have avoided terrible punishment. Roger of Wendover describes one stock treatment meted out to them. During the Albigensian Crusade in 1228, the Count of Toulouse ambushed a French force and took, so Wendover believes, as many as two thousand prisoners. 'After they had all been stripped to the skin, the count ordered the eyes of some to be torn out, the ears and noses of others to be slit, and the feet and hands of others to be cut off; after thus shamefully mutilating them, he sent them to their homes, a deformed spectacle to their fellow Frenchmen.'[52] Such actions, like mass killings, were practical demonstrations that served as a warning to the enemy, to deflate their morale, hinder recruitment and simply to reduce by physical means the manpower available for fighting. However, as the Middle Ages moved into its later stages, mutilations were not quite so common, as *guerre mortelle* increased in frequency and fewer prisoners of any rank were taken quite so readily. In his war against Ghent in 1451–3, Philip the Good, duke of Burgundy, explicitly ordered the slaying of all prisoners; as rebels, they deserved nothing else. In the fifteenth and sixteenth centuries, German and Swiss mercenaries, the backbone of many a national army, were notorious for not taking prisoners. Thus a Swiss battle order of March 1476 instructed that there were to be no prisoners, as all enemy soldiers, regardless of rank, were to be killed; the result was the annihilation of some six thousand Italians. Where possible, physical elimination of the enemy on such a scale was an eminently practical measure, a savage exercise in pure numbers.

Mass killing could even be endorsed and presented as a public good, especially when it came to the universally hated mercenaries, not noted for their own merciful tendencies. Mercenaries on the losing side could expect little clemency; none was given to the Flemings in England in 1174, nor to those at Bouvines in 1214, where their ferocious last stand was a desperate acknowledgement of their expected fate. When Philip Augustus moved against *routiers* (bands of mercenary brigands) in 1182, he was lauded for his ruthlessness. He was also enthusiastically assisted by civilian local defence associations which grouped together to hang five hundred *routiers* at one mass execution. Of course, kings continued to employ mercenaries in their armies in great numbers (Philip Augustus as much as anyone) and their leaders – such as Cadoc, Mercadier and John Hawkwood – were rewarded with land, honour and titles. War was the most upwardly mobile profession throughout the medieval period.

The treatment dished out to the 'plebs', the rough *rustici*, in turn did not predispose them to politely doff their caps at their social betters on the battlefield. Outbreaks of peasant revolt were common, and sometimes on a scale large enough to threaten the social order: the Jacquerie in fourteenth-century France, the Peasants' Revolt in England (1381) and another in Germany (1524–5). When Flemish townsmen and peasants defeated the cream of French chivalry at Courtrai in 1302, they could have reaped a fortune in ransom; instead, following orders to 'kill all that has spurs on', they slew somewhere between forty and fifty per cent of French knights, including their illustrious leader, Count Robert of Artois. At the naval battle of Sandwich in 1217, defeated French knights dived into the Channel rather than surrender to English sergeants; only with great effort did English knights prevent these sergeants from executing on the spot thirty-two

French knights taken when their ship was boarded. Much has been made by historians of the slaughter of notable prisoners at Agincourt, an action carried out by the lower-class archers; but Crécy, that other signal victory for the English in the Hundred Years War, was also marred by massacre. Froissart describes what happens when non-knightly soldiers roam the battlefield when the main combat is over:

> Among the English there were pillagers and irregulars, Welsh and Cornishmen armed with long knives, who went out after the French and, when they found any in difficulty, whether they were counts, barons, knights or squires, they killed them without mercy. Because of this, many were slaughtered that evening, regardless of their rank. . . . The King of England was afterwards very angry that none had been taken for ransom, for the number of dead lords was very great.[53]

A scene from Bouvines in 1214 nicely encapsulates the social divide on the battlefield. The Count of Boulogne, one of the allied commanders against Philip II of France, is trapped under his horse. Animated by the competitive and lucrative business of ransoming, half a dozen French knights engage in a heated dispute in the midst of combat over who shall claim the Count as his prisoner. Meanwhile, hovering about the Count is a lowly youth with no prospect of receiving any share of future ransom. Knife in hand, he sets about the unfortunate victim, alternatively prodding him with his weapon and trying to remove his armour to deliver the fatal blow. All the time, the Count is screaming for any one of the knights to take him prisoner and thus ensure his safety.

Poor discipline could, and on occasion did, contribute to massacres of prisoners; but for all the examples of military disorder in the medieval period, there are counter-examples of commands being strictly enforced, even after battle, when soldiers' bloodlust was still high and the pursuit of booty was paramount. Following the great French victory at Bouvines in 1214, late in the day trumpets were sounded to recall the French from chasing down the enemy and seizing plunder. King Philip gave the order, as he was concerned that there were insufficient men left to guard his huge trawl of prisoners, many of whom were of great political value; he feared elements of the defeated enemy might regroup and attempt their rescue. In another time and place, like Agincourt, these prisoners might not have been so lucky as to live. In fact, discipline was frequently an essential element of massacre: at Waterford, the prisoners were executed only after deliberation, despite leading dissenting voices; at Agincourt, the massacre was carried out only when the archers and sergeants proved more disciplined than the insubordinate knights. Forgoing the immediate profits of war required substantial restraint but was possible owing to the unrelenting pressure of the imperative of war. Geoffrey de Charny's mid-fourteenth-century *Book of Chivalry* was alive to the dangers of placing personal financial gain before collective military victory:

> It often occurs that through . . . those who chase after plunder before the battle is over, that which is thought to be already won can be lost again and lives and reputation as well. It can also happen in relation to such people who are very eager for booty that when there is action on the battlefield, there are a number of men who pay more attention to prisoners and other profit, and when they have seized them and other winnings, they are more anxious to safeguard their captives and their booty than to help bring the battle to a good conclusion.[54]

Henry V was clear that this was not going to be the case at Agincourt. Financial motivations were not in themselves damaging – in fact, they conferred significant military advantages in recruiting and motivating troops – but it was often deemed necessary to suppress them for the greater military and political good. In the cases studied in this chapter, valuable prisoners were executed and their ransom forfeited so that a greater military objective may be achieved. For as much as gain was a great motivator for one's own troops, fear was often an even greater demotivator for enemy ones.

For ruthlessly effective commanders, fear was considered one of the most powerful weapons. Much as students of history are accustomed to the chivalric bravado of medieval chronicles and *chansons de geste*, writings from the Middle Ages did not shy away from the terror their own soldiers faced in war. In 1104 in the Holy Land, Ralph of Caen relates how Archbishop Bernard was amongst the crusaders put to flight by the Muslims: 'His heart was heavy with fear. He called out to his fleeing companions. ... Many crusaders turned a deaf ear and galloped on, so hard of hearing did their terror make them. Nor did anyone have sympathy for his friends, so much was he taken up with his own fear.'[55]

Gilles de Muisit describes the fear of the French in the aftermath of their defeat at Courtrai in 1302: 'They were so terrified that many of them could not eat.'[56] In 1327, foreign knights faced a barrage from English archers at York, Jean le Bel recalling, 'Never did men live in such fear, and in so great danger of their lives, without any hope of ever getting home again, as we did then.'[57] Suger informs us of the panic that struck the French at the siege of Chambly in 1102: 'The army was so frightened that some of the men hardly hoped to survive. ... In their state of unbearable fear ... some were getting ready for flight. ... Thrown into terror by the sudden need to escape, everyone rushed together, each paying no heed to the others.'[58]

The fear of facing certain death as a prisoner is portrayed by Joinville's vivid account of his time as a captive of the Muslims in Egypt in 1250. He and his men witnessed daily executions of prisoners, usually by beheading. Those who refused to convert to Islam and those who fell ill, like Joinville's priest, were summarily despatched. Joinville's group of prisoners were expecting at any moment to be dragged from their prison room and treated likewise. One day, some thirty Saracens entered with swords drawn and axes at the ready.

> I asked Baudouin d'Ibelin, who was well acquainted with their language, what these men were saying. He told me that they were saying that they had come to cut off our heads. At once a great number of people crowded round to confess their sins to a monk of the Holy Trinity. ... I for my part, unable to recall any sins I had committed, spent the time thinking that the more I tried to defend myself, or to get out of this predicament, the worse it would be for me. So I crossed myself and knelt at the feet of one of the Saracens who was holding an axe. ...[59]

A fellow knight confessed himself to Joinville who absolved him. Immediately afterwards, however, such had been his fear, Joinville could not remember a word of what he had been told. The crusaders were not killed, but led to the hold of another ship, where they were packed in tightly, expecting to be taken out and killed one by one. They spent a night of terror, squalor and misery before the threat of execution passed.

Fear could lead to armies crumbling or being weakened through desertion, even by their leaders: Stephen of Blois abandoned the First Crusade and Joinville witnessed important nobles flee the Battle of Mansurah in 1250. This made morbid and catastrophic anticipation a powerful component of a general's armoury. In 1337, the knight Jean de Beaumont is reported as saying that when 'in the tavern drinking strong wines', knights are brave enough to take on the most formidable opponent, 'but when we are ... on our trotting charges, our bucklers round our necks and our lances lowered, and the great cold is freezing us altogether and our limbs are crushed before and behind, and our enemies are approaching us, then we should wish to be in a cellar so large that we might never be seen by any means'.[60] Such dread was heightened when it was known that an enemy was particularly ferocious. Some French nobles attempted to persuade Philip the Fair in 1304 to cease the war with the Flemish because they did not take prisoners.

Vengeance was a factor in Charlemagne's treatment of the Saxons and Richard the Lionheart's slaughter of the Muslims at Acre; but the desire to create fear was just as important. The wish to project fear was a paramount – and effective – objective at Agincourt, Hattin and Wexford. In the localized and claustrophobic atmosphere of siege warfare, it was an even more potent and devastating weapon, as we shall see in the next chapter.

Torture of captives. The livery of the soldier is that of William Marshal, considered by many contemporaries and historians as the epitome of chivalry.
(Matthew Paris manuscript, 13th century.)

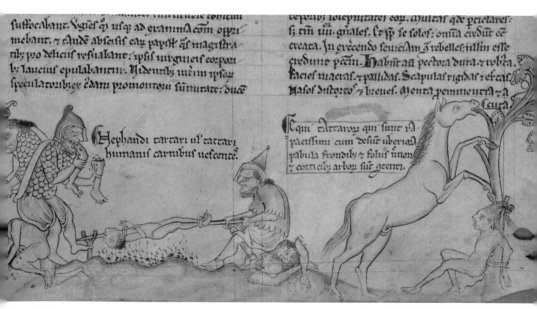

Turkish soldiers torturing, killing and eating prisoners. Although such depictions were designed to demonize the enemy, they frequently had their foundations in reality.
(Matthew Paris manuscript, 13th century.)

The execution of Hugh Despenser in 1326. Public executions served as a deterrent by the authorities while also meeting popular demand for the visible enforcement of justice and punishment. Many executions, such as the one here, involved mutilation and torture of the condemned man before death. (French School, 15th century.)

Massacre of prisoners, believed to be at the battle of Agincourt, 1415. Henry V's chivalrous reputation survived unscathed despite his order for the execution of French prisoners. This action, based on ruthless military reasoning, has shocked modern commentators more than Henry's contemporaries. (English School, 15th century.)

Crusaders hurl the heads of Muslim soldiers over the defences at Nicaea in 1097. Atrocities committed on both sides were not limited to the Crusades: medieval armies regularly employed such acts of psychological warfare so as to undermine the morale and resistance of the enemy. (French School, 13th century.)

Richard the Lionheart orders the beheading of over 2,500 Muslims prisoners at Acre in 1191. Richard's decision was based on a combination of factors: maintaining face, revenge and, most importantly of all, military imperative. (French School, 15th century.)

A mother and child escape their house which is being burnt. Scorched-earth policies deprived an enemy of resources and were also used as a punitive measure against troublesome regions. (Bayeux Tapestry, 11th century.)

Soldiers kill non-combatants and sack a town. Non-combatants were frequently targeted with the intention of terrorizing a population into submission while undermining the econom base of the enemy. The victim on the left being run through with a sword is a priest.
(French School, 15th century.)

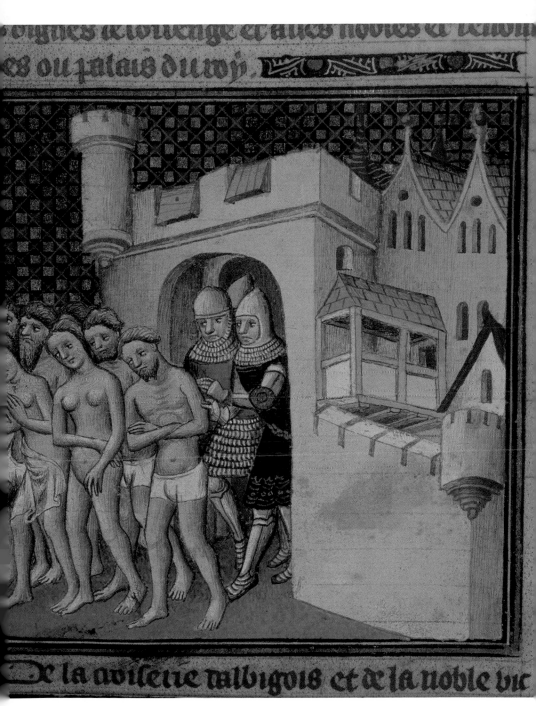

The expulsion of inhabitants from Carcassonne in 1209 during the Albigensian Crusade. Unlike the massacre at Béziers a few weeks earlier, the Crusade leaders prevented any slaughter here – not on humanitarian grounds, but primarily for strategic and financial reasons. (French School, 15th century.)

Massacre of the Innocents. Depictions of biblical horrors often coloured monastic reporting of contemporary atrocities. However, many monks were well informed and had local knowledge of the savage reality of warfare. (Psalter, German, 13th century.)

4

SIEGES

Sieges provide history with some of the great set pieces of war in the Middle Ages, and with some of its worst atrocities. The immediate and localized event of the siege; the large proportion of non-combatants commonly involved, swelling further the already significant number of soldiers engaged in the operation; the crucial importance of the siege to the success or failure of a campaign; the frequently astonishing amount of money, resources and time invested in sieges; and the particularly savage but finely developed laws for siege warfare: all these combined to increase the magnitude of the dreadful consequences for the defeated when a castle's or town's defences were breached by storm.

Medieval warfare quite literally centred on sieges. The English won all the major battles in the Hundred Years War – Crécy, Poitiers, Nájera and Agincourt – but were still ultimately defeated because they lost their strongholds in numerous sieges. Wars were fought for the control of land, and land was controlled by castles. The popular image of the castle standing strong and alone, dominating the local, rural landscape, tells only part of its story. Castles were mostly constructed in towns and cities, which themselves were usually walled, thus creating further layers of defence. The very fact that population densities reflected concentrations of wealth, economic production and central administration made them paramount targets of military campaigning. Where castles were built in isolation, as in frontier regions and in the Holy Land, towns would frequently and quickly spring up around them. The obvious effect of this military–civilian symbiosis was the inevitable and direct involvement of non-combatants in the wars of the time. Even when castles stood separately from settlements, as Château Gaillard still does high above Andelys on the Seine, they were the first place of refuge sought out by the surrounding communities when rumours of approaching armies spread, or the smoke from enemy depredations was seen in the distance. Stone walls and a garrison afforded greater security than an open village, and it was a lord's most fundamental duty to protect his subjects. But castles were far from being purely defensive architecture; their proliferation in marches and border territories is testament to their offensive intent as forward bases for military incursions.

Whether in a defensive or offensive role, the primary function of a castle was to subjugate an area and assert the authority of its lord over it. The ability to do this depended less on the walls and towers, but on the garrison within; without sufficient manpower, architecture counted for nothing. For this reason garrisons would contain mounted soldiers. Cavalry played a necessary role in sorties from castles under siege; but in the lifetime of a castle, these were very rare events – if they occurred at all – and they certainly would not justify the expense of maintaining mounts and knights. It was the cavalry force that gave a castle its operational range. As renowned castellologist R. Allen Brown explains it, 'the mounted elements of the garrison could swiftly respond to danger and command the surrounding countryside, riding out at will to protect or enforce the loyalty of neighbouring districts, or to launch attacks on marauding hostile forces, or to devastate the lands of their enemies'.[1]

The range of such activities has been calculated as a radius of up to ten miles, a distance that would permit cavalry to leave and be back at their castle within the hours of daylight. In the Midlands of England during 1174, knights from Leicester rode to Northampton to plunder the town. This military capability made the taking of castles, or at least their containment, a priority for commanders in the field who did not wish to be ambushed or to have their supply lines broken. Even more seriously, an unconquered castle was both a potent symbol of resistance and, more practically, one that could receive large numbers of reinforcements who could then operate in the area from a secure base. Field armies regularly comprised men taken from castle garrisons en route. Whether for defence or attack, the size of a garrison was a barometer of the political environment at any moment in time.

However, such talk of garrisons and their military functions risks oversimplification. Although many sieges saw castles defended purely by soldiers, the fact is that most included non-combatants. Here the term 'non-combatant' has less clarity of definition than it does in battle situations. Inhabitants of a besieged town would find themselves assisting in the defence in one way or another, either voluntarily or coerced to do so. Many cities, as in the Italian states, had strictly enforced regulations that dictated organized roles for its citizens in officially designated quarters of the city. In a siege situation, any assistance − be it providing water and food for the men on the ramparts, dowsing fires or just engaging in what economic activity was possible − was deemed to be furthering the military effort of resistance and prolonging the defence. For a besieger, there was no way of knowing who amongst the besieged had helped the defenders, and who had not. The safe rule of thumb adopted by most besieging commanders was to assume that those beyond the walls were hostile; if they were friendly, why had they not turned on the garrison and opened their gates to him? (Naturally, he would attempt to exploit the fears of the non-combatants to do just this.) The confusion of the battlefield at least had the merit of providing a distinct and identifiable enemy combatant; siege situations, although easier to delineate, allowed stone walls to obscure who was actually doing the fighting. That many of those actively manning the ramparts were non-combatants only inclined the besieging commander further to consider all within the walls as collectively responsible for whatever would befall them. Simon de Montfort, leader of the Albigensian Crusade, was killed in 1218 at the siege of Toulouse by women operating a stone-throwing machine.

It is no surprise, then, to learn that when a fortified place was taken by storm, the result could be horrific, with little or no distinction made as to who among the defeated would go under the sword. Yet the many tragic occasions that saw sieges ended this way were still relatively few amongst the thousands of sieges during the medieval period; and where storm did occur, we have to try and distinguish between fact and hyperbole. As we shall see with sieges, as with battles, massacre was more likely to be the result of calculation and premeditation than just the bloodlust of combat.

SIEGES IN MEDIEVAL WARFARE

The movement of armies on campaign was habitually dictated by the location of castles. Forces moved to and from castles, whether to relieve them from a siege or invest them, to augment their own numbers from garrisons or to install more men into garrisons, to take refuge in them, to collect weapons or to create diversionary tactics. The actions of the rebels and French in the English civil war of 1217 reflects this clearly. Henry de Braybrook, besieged in the Lincolnshire castle of Mountsorrel, sent to the rebels' headquarters in London for help. After a council of war, a large force was sent to raise the siege. The besiegers, learning of the approach of this large relief force, retreated to the defences at Nottingham, and the siege was thereby lifted. The relief army then moved on to Lincoln, where one of their fellow commanders, Gilbert of Gant, having taken the town, was now besieging the royalists in the castle with no success. When the royalist high command learned of this news, it gathered its forces at Newark Castle and set out to raise the siege in Lincoln. There, as we shall see later, a rare but major battle was fought, resulting in a rapid flight back to the safety of London. In the majority of theatres of war in the West during this period, chronicles would record the campaigns chiefly as a series of sieges. Their central role in medieval warfare is hard to exaggerate.

Just as battles were avoided, so, on occasion, were sieges. A small garrison within a weak, poorly provisioned castle facing a large, well-equipped army might abandon its position – and was often instructed to do so. However, when undertaken, many sieges followed a distinct pattern. The prevalence of sieges in warfare since ancient times had led to a surprisingly formalized style of combat. The sequence laid out below was far from uncommon, many sieges incorporating most of the stages or tactics described. Throughout, it is well to bear in mind John France's observation: 'Sieges were simply a very specialized form of battle. They did what battle . . . was designed to do – to destroy the basic strength of the enemy and acquire it for your own use.'[2]

One of the first steps taken following any outbreak – or threat – of hostility was the fortification and preparation of strongholds for the possibility of facing a protracted siege. In 1215, with war brewing, King John sent out letters to all the governors of his castles throughout England, ordering them to furnish their castles with provisions and arms and to strengthen their garrisons so that they would be ready to defend them at a day's notice. Castles that were unprepared were prey to sudden attack. In 1221, Count William of Aumale took advantage of Fotheringay's skeleton garrison by applying his scaling ladders to it and taking the castle; Thun l'Evêque near Cambrai was captured in 1339 when it opened its gates one morning to allow its enclosed animals out to graze, permitting the enemy lurking outside to rush in.

Once an enemy force camped outside the walls, negotiations would normally take place in an endeavour to save lives, time and money. If the garrison submitted, it was allowed to vacate the castle unharmed, frequently with its arms and equipment. Truces might be arranged along the lines that, should a relieving force not appear within a stipulated time period, the garrison would hand over possession to the enemy without any bloodshed. This worked in favour of the besieged in Northumberland's Wark Castle in 1173: its castellan Roger of Stuteville had negotiated a forty-day truce and was rewarded by the arrival of a relief force, thereby saving the castle. Bedford Castle surrendered in 1215 when a seven-day truce expired with no sign of help for the garrison. Negotiated settlements were vital lifesavers; the consequences for a vanquished stronghold that had not come to terms were grim.

A shot from a cannon or siege engine would formally open a siege. Assault on a castle's or town's walls came primarily in three forms. Potentially the quickest way was storming. Though the result was often bloody, the losses incurred by the attackers may have been offset by the hazards of a lengthy siege: famine, disease, desertions and the risk of being confronted by a relief army. Escalade – climbing up and over the walls on ladders – was the most hazardous form of all, and for that reason would sometimes occur at night; Robert Bruce took Perth in this manner in 1312. Storming could be ordered at any time during a siege, but particularly when bombardment or mining had taken its toll.

Mangonels, trebuchets, ballistae, belfries and, by the late fourteenth century, cannon were all employed in battering defences, targeting weak spots in the hope of causing a breach. After a fortnight's battering in 1206, the castle of Montauban had suffered so much damage it was unable to defend itself against a successful storming by English troops.

Whereas some sources identify siege machines accurately, others are more prone to error and generalization. Some nineteenth-century translations of these sources do not even attempt to separate the machines listed in the original Latin, and replace whole lines with merely 'siege machines', or name one or two of them, then finishing off with 'and other siege machines'. Basically, siege weaponry falls into the three categories, of assault, artillery and engineering (mining).

The chief assault weapon was the siege tower, or belfry. This was a large wooden tower moved on wheels and brought up to the castle or town walls. This usually necessitated the hazardous task of filling in a section of the surrounding ditch first. The lower levels of the tower provided cover for engineers operating at the base of the wall, while its height was designed for two main purposes. One was to allow a body of troops and archers inside to rain down spears and arrows on the defenders manning the battlements, and within the town or castle yard itself. Medieval writers attest to the efficacy of this manoeuvre. The largest towers could even provide platforms for other siege weapons, such as the mangonel (see below). The primary task of the belfry was to lower a simple wooden bridge or walkway over the space between the tower and the wall to allow the besieging soldiers to storm into the town: a highly precarious, but again effective, way of winning a stronghold. This was ultimately how Jerusalem fell to the crusaders in 1099. The psychological impact of seeing the enemy breach the defences and actually on the battlements was often enough to shatter the resolve of the defenders.

Any glory-seeking urge to be the first on the bridge and, the hope was, the first into an enemy stronghold, was countered by the incredible danger it involved. Siege towers were subjected to a withering and concentrated defensive fire; there was the ever-present danger of falling from a great height; the towers were often unstable and had an unnerving propensity to collapse or topple over; and there was the persistent threat of targeted fire taking hold of these wooden structures (soaked hides and other measures were often insufficient protection against this): all combined to make tower duty understandably unpopular. Belfries were a prime weapon of a besieging commander. Some even brought them on campaign, as Henry V did in 1415, ready for quick assembly, but most were built on site. Such was their importance, relief fleets to the crusaders were sometimes dismantled to provide the wood for them.

Artillery consisted of various missile-throwing machines. The mangonel hurled stones on a relatively low trajectory from a wooden arm shaped like a spoon, the wider end holding the projectile. It operated on the torsion principle, the throwing force relying on the release of twisted rope. Another petrary, or stone-throwing machine, was the much larger trebuchet, which came into more common usage by the end of the twelfth century. This consisted of a huge beam pivoted on an axle: at one end was a heavy counterweight and at the other there was a sling to hold a projectile. Sometimes the counterweight force was substituted for traction, a group of men pulling explosively downwards on ropes attached to the beam. The most powerful trebuchets could launch rocks weighing over a tonne, with devastating effects against many walls. They were the heavy artillery of the pre-gunpowder age. In practice, they were used to chuck anything over the walls at the defenders, including dead animals to spread disease, and the severed heads of captured troops, to demoralize the enemy. These were important machines, reflected in the fact they were given names, such as 'Bad Neighbour' or 'Warwolf'. Much controversy and research still surrounds this machine, not least because it is hailed as a medieval innovation, and hence not a device inherited from the wars of antiquity.

Ballistae – and again we have to be careful of interchangeable terms – were large catapult or crossbow-like weapons. A winch or torsion provided the force from which a heavy bolt or other projectile was shot forward. Unlike the machines above, this was an anti-personnel weapon. A chronicler describing the siege of Paris in 885 implausibly claims that seven men were skewered on one ballista bolt like a spit-roast.

Cannon were operating by the early fourteenth century. The earliest depiction of one is in a manuscript of 1326 presented to Edward III. These developed quickly from a vase-shaped chamber device to the more familiar cylindrical shape. Although used on the battlefield, over time they became mainly employed in siege situations, initially alongside, and eventually replacing, the trebuchet. Working on the not entirely accurate biggest-is-best principle, by the mid-fifteenth century cannon like Mad Margot in Ghent (trebuchet sobriquets were transferred to guns) weighed in at over 36,000 pounds. By the fifteenth century, wealthy princes were employing batteries of cannon of a more standard size against towns and castles. For a while, many defences would not hold against them: the end of the Hundred Years War was marked by a series of swift and successful sieges – some sixty between 1449 and 1450 – in which the French made great use of cannon. However, their impact should not be overestimated: the example from France just mentioned may have been as much due to political reasons as to technological ones. Gradually, military engineers and architects rose to this new challenge, designing new defences that were built to counter cannonade. Sieges could remain protracted affairs. It is also worth remembering that all the weapons described above were also frequently employed by the besieged against their attackers.

Mining was another dangerous process, but the most effective of all. A tunnel was dug under a castle or town wall, usually directed against the foundations of a tower. When ready, the wooden timbers supporting the roof of the tunnel were burned, thereby bringing down the tower or section of wall. Medieval chronicles and records refer to the purchase of pig fat for this use at sieges. Defenders attempted to detect mines by placing bowls of water on the battlements; disturbances caused by digging could cause ripples, indicating activity underground. The besieged would sometimes then build countermines, occasionally resulting in subterranean combats. Mining, or sapping, was greatly feared by the besieged. When in 1359 the castellan of Cormicy near Reims was shown the English mine excavated under his tower, he promptly surrendered. Betran de Born mocked Philip Augustus for taking his engineers everywhere with him, decrying how unchivalrous it all was; yet Philip was one of the most successful military commanders of the Middle Ages, with a reputation earned almost entirely by his castle-breaking prowess.

Subterfuge and treachery were other commonly employed methods in taking castles. Louis VIII bribed the English-held port of La Rochelle into submission in 1224. Circa 1342, Bertrand du Guesclin and his men took Fougères from the English by posing as woodcutters bringing firewood. This episode is sometimes related with du Guesclin and his men disguised as women, and in this attire gaining access through the castle gates – one of many underhand stratagems often found in contemporary writings; others include burial parties (with a knight in the coffin with weapons) and using delegations of ecclesiastic peacemakers as a cover for rushing gates.

Blockade was the most time-consuming technique of all, and one that could match storming for its awful consequences. Sieges that dragged on for months served to exacerbate the grim mood of the besiegers through deprivation, hunger, exposure to the elements, disease, loss of comrades and absence from home. The bitterness and anger pent up in this way were all the more terrible when they were unleashed. Conditions for the besieged were no better; as we shall see, their enforced incarceration brought on untold miseries. An epic and heroic defence of Rochester Castle in Kent in 1215 ended when the defenders' supplies ran out; having finished off the last of their expensive warhorses for nutrition they were compelled to surrender. Hunger forced Faenza to submit to Frederick II in 1241 after an eight-month siege. As William the Breton observed in the 1220s, 'Famine alone vanquishes the invincible and by itself can take cities.'³

Garrisons could attempt to break sieges and blockades by sorties. Mounted soldiers were obviously favoured for this time of action; besieging forces would sensibly have their own cavalry ready to counter such threats. Full-scale sorties could be spectacularly effective, as Simon de Montfort proved at Muret in 1213. Equally, they could go just as spectacularly awry, as happened at Taillebourg in western France in 1179, Richard I's besieging forces chasing the sortie party back through the town's open gates. Sorties were also made with the more limited objective of gaining provisions from the besiegers, helping them to hold out for longer.

The resources expended at a siege operation were always significant and frequently on a scale that was considered draining to the national economy. Michael Prestwich has detailed the huge amounts of materiel that Henry III diverted to the siege of Kenilworth in Warwickshire in 1266: siege engines constructed in the Forest of Dean and a belfry tower from Gloucester; seventy thousand quarrels from London, Lincoln and elsewhere; three hundred sheaves of arrow from Surrey and Sussex; fourteen carts to transport wine; and, amidst many other items, even a whale to provide meat. 'In all, the requisitions of materials and foodstuffs to support the siege exhausted the revenues of ten counties, whose sheriffs were unable to bring in any cash to the exchequer in 1267.'⁴ In Henry's long reign, this proved to be his second-worst financial year. Such a concentration of effort (sustained in this case over six months), could leave the besiegers thirsting for retribution if the siege was successfully concluded. Such was the exhaustion of both sides at Kenilworth, the garrison were extremely fortunate to be permitted to come to terms and escaped very lightly.

It was not uncommon for sieges to take on epic proportions like Kenilworth. Château Gaillard (1203–4) lasted nearly six months; Crema (1159–60) seven months; Milan (1161–2) ten months; and

Montreuil-Bellay (1149–51) some three years. That sieges could be such gruelling marathons is not just an expression of how much could be at stake in the grand political and military strategies of the time; it also reflects the dilemma of the castellan who was caught between a very hard rock and a very hard place. If he held the castle for a lord then his dangers might be doubled: not coming to early terms with the besieger could lead to harsh imprisonment or death should the castle fall; surrendering too easily could leave him exposed to a charge of treason against his lord and hence execution. In 1453 the Duke of Norfolk declared: 'It hath been seen in many realms and lordships that for the loss of towns or castles without siege, the captains that have lost them have been dead and beheaded, and their goods lost.'[5] Charge of a castle or a town was an onerous personal responsibility, and to surrender it to the enemy without permission (which was commonly given) or without a serious attempt at resistance was a breaking of faith and oath of loyalty. This responsibility was ultimate: in 1356 Lord Greystock was condemned to death because Berwick Castle, commanded by his lieutenant, was taken by the Scots, even though a spirited defence had been mounted; yet at the time Greystock himself was serving the King in France with distinction. (He was pardoned in 1358.) In August 1417, the French garrison at Touques surrendered to Henry V; a leading citizen of the town was later beheaded by the French authorities for this submission, although the Dauphin had not sent assistance (even the messenger was hung for bringing the bad news).

Control of castles and towns, representations of authority over the land, was the ultimate aim of military strategy. As mentioned in the previous chapter, Orderic Vitalis ascribes the Norman conquest of England to the fact that the English lacked castles: 'The fortifications that the French call "castles" were very rare in the English regions and hence, although the English were warlike and bold, they were weaker in resisting their enemies.'[6] William the Conqueror's grip on the country became secure only when he planted castles across the landscape. As symbols of power and intent, castles began their military function even before fighting had begun. Emperor Frederick II (the Hohenstaufen 'stupor mundi') was typical of wealthy rulers in building to impress. He brought enemy Milanese to see his formidable castle at Foggia in south-eastern Italy with the intention that these should return to Milan and report on Frederick's awesome power, thereby persuading the city to submit. Truly, castles were, as William of Newburgh very aptly put it, 'the bones of the kingdom'.[7]

STORM, SACK AND NON-COMBATANTS

In this brief discussion of siege warfare, an obvious but pertinent observation should be made that, for non-belligerents, such combat signified events that were far from the fields of pitched battle where it was only armies that faced and fought each other. Sieges brought the reality of war into people's very homes. This, and the fact that the line between combatants and non-combatants became blurred during sieges, might have produced more refined laws of war to function alongside the highly developed conventions of siege situations. However, if anything, the laws of war were simplified for sieges, and even brutalized. Whereas a soldier might throw down his weapon in the heat of battle and hope to be taken prisoner, non-combatants on the receiving end of a successful storming could expect to be put to the sword with impunity.

This aspect of the laws of siege warfare has not been fully addressed by medieval and military historians, who accept that the wholesale slaughter of a resistant population – men, women and children – was considered justified in contemporaries' eyes on biblical grounds. This justification is said to be found by citing chapter twenty of Deuteronomy, which deals with laws to be observed in war, and verses ten to twenty in particular, which concern the laws governing siege warfare. The confusion arises from verses twelve to fourteen, and verses fifteen to seventeen. The first two, from the King James Version, declare that when an enemy city does not submit, it should be besieged: 'And when the Lord thy God hath delivered it into thine hands, thou shall smite every male thereof with the edge of the sword; *but the women, and the little ones*, and the cattle, and all that is in the city, even all the spoil thereof, shalt thou take unto thyself' (my italics. Deuteronomy 20: 13–14).

Grounds for total slaughter are lifted from the later verses: 'But of the cities of these people which the Lord thy God doth give thee for an inheritance, thou shall save alive nothing that breatheth' (Deuteronomy 20: 16).

However, the next verse clearly specifies these populations as being the Hittites, Canaanites and other biblical groupings; none of which is relevant to the medieval West. Yet this has been extrapolated to permit the slaughter of rebellious townspeople who have defied their divinely appointed lord and master. In other words, in an extremely attenuated interpretation of these verses, a commander can massacre all and sundry only if they are his subjects, but not, as verse fifteen, makes clear, if the towns belong to another nation, when verse fourteen, sparing women and children, applies. Men and men only are to be slain in 'the cities which are very far off from thee, which are not the cities of these nations' (Deuteronomy 20: 15).

As with the laws applying to battle and prisoners, these injunctions were so selectively and individually employed as to be meaningless on many occasions. That these biblical laws were more likely to be inverted than followed – inhabitants of a city besieged by its lord had a greater chance of survival than inhabitants of a different country facing a foreign enemy – serves once again to highlight the limited application of the laws of war in the Middle Ages, and how they always deferred to the military imperative.

Jerusalem, 1099

Few events from the Middle Ages have come to symbolize the carnage that religious extremism engenders as much as the sack of Jerusalem in July 1099. Steven Runciman, the crusades' most famous historian, judged that 'the massacre at Jerusalem profoundly impressed all the world', that it horrified many Christians, and that it 'was this blood-thirsty proof of Christian fanaticism that created the fanaticism of Islam'.[8] H. E. Mayer concurs: 'The Muslim world was profoundly shocked by this Christian barbarity; it was a long time before the memory of the massacre began to fade.'[9] Yet very recent scholarship has questioned the scale of the massacre. Indeed, it is now appropriate to ask whether it was the massacre itself or the fact that it occurred in Jerusalem which was more shocking.

It was a long road to Jerusalem. In March 1095, Alexius I, the

Byzantine emperor, despatched an embassy to Pope Urban II seeking help against the incursions of the Seljuk Turks. The military successes of the Turks had seen them swallow up the greater part of Byzantine territory in the east; they were now directly threatening the imperial capital at Constantinople. Alexius was hoping for professional soldiers; to his great consternation, he received floods of all manner of Europeans inundating his lands, arriving in waves, of whom perhaps only just over ten per cent were knights and nobles. The main force has been calculated as being anything up to sixty thousand strong.

Before even reaching the Middle East, the crusaders began as they meant to go on, with exhibitions of murderous zealotry. In what was to become a traditional start to any new expedition to the Holy Land, they initiated a series of pogroms against the Jews in Europe, whether en route or not. At Mainz in 1096, one of the largest Jewish communities in Europe was wiped out. Latin and Jewish sources offer terrible testament to events there. Albert of Aachen, in a passage reminiscent of events at Masada in the year CE 73, tells of how the crusaders

> killed the Jews, about seven thousand in number, who in vain resisted the force and attack of so many thousands. They killed the women, also, and with their swords pierced tender children of whatever age and sex. The Jews, seeing that their Christian enemies were attacking them and their children, and that they were sparing no age, likewise fell upon one another, brother, children, wives and sisters, and thus they perished at each other's hands. Horrible to say, mothers cut the throats of nursing children with knives and stabbed others, preferring them to perish thus at their own hands rather than to be killed by the weapons of the uncircumcised.[10]

The justification for such indiscriminate murder was laid at the door of the Jews themselves: as the killers of Christ – 'His blood be on us, and on our children' (Matthew 27: 25) – it was all they deserved. However, in Christian theology, mankind was saved by Christ's death and sacrifice; as the Jews therefore played a role in saving mankind, it was at best unsound theology, but in truth mainly cynical opportunism, to claim that they were the victims of their own actions. Early Christians, laying claim to the Jewish Bible as their own, accused Jews of misinterpreting the scriptures, and of rejecting their own messiah and hence God; *The Letter of Barnabas* and other Christian writings portrayed Judaism as a false religion created under the influence of an evil angel.

Religious fervour on the crusade, though manifestly present, was exploited and even largely fabricated as merely a cover for self-interest: the killers of the Jews appropriated their victims' wealth for themselves, partly to line their own pockets, and partly to finance the expensive business of crusading. That these organized crusading groups stampeded over the Church's attempts to protect the Jews – at Mainz in western Germany they attacked Bishop Rothard's hall in which the Jews were sheltering – serves to underline the rapacious greed at the heart of the massacres. As Susan Edington has noted, anti-Semitism 'was never part of papal policy, nor was it approved by respectable commentators'.[11] Which is not to say that there not were plenty of unrespectable commentators glorifying in the slaughter.

Crusaders had a mixture of motives – booty, land and spiritual needs – that were not easily separated from each other. Recently, historians have tended to stress religious motivations over others; but this should be read more as a redressing of the balance that has previously been weighted too heavily, possibly, towards self-interest. But as we have already adumbrated, religion should be counted as just one part of the combustible admixture that drove the crusaders forward. From the start, all were given an overarching holy goal: the liberation of Jerusalem from four centuries of Muslim rule. As *jus ad bellum* it provided supreme and unarguably righteous grounds for colonial expansion, all under the guise of an armed pilgrimage that offered the huge incentive of plenary indulgences (an assured place in Heaven) for those that fell along the way. The central importance of Jerusalem to the Christian religion ensured the inclusion on the crusade of the enormous numbers of accompanying non-combatants, or pilgrims. The sources for the First Crusade focus on the gruelling and draining nature of the expedition to the holiest of cities, in which starvation, unbearable thirst and disease proved as potent enemies as the Turks. It took three years of unimaginable hardship, suffering and loss to reach Jerusalem; taking the city was an explosive climax to a phenomenal and bloody quest.

The official armies were led by Raymond of Toulouse, Godfrey of Bouillion, Hugh of Vermandois, Robert of Normandy, Robert of Flanders, Stephen of Blois and Baldwin of Boulogne. It was this collective force with its core of knights and infantry that won the crusades its spectacular success; smaller groups 'led' by a goat and a goose imbued with the Holy Spirit had, not surprisingly, a much more limited impact. Setting out in late 1096, serendipitously to arrive in a Middle East riven with political disunity, the crusaders successfully besieged Nicaea in May 1097 (only for it to submit to the Greeks instead, thereby depriving the army of valuable loot), following it up with a dramatic victory at the close-run battle of Doryaleum as they crossed Anatolia. Almost as telling as human losses were animal ones: most of the pack animals had died and eighty per cent of knights had lost their mounts by the time the expedition reached the Holy Land. Antioch was placed under siege in October 1097. Exposed to the elements through a bitter winter, the crusaders took nearly eight months to capture the city; when they did, the author of the *Deeds of the Franks* informs us, 'All of the squares of the city were everywhere ... full of the corpses of the dead, so that no one could endure it there for the excessive stench. No one could go along a street of the city except over the bodies of the dead.'[12] The haul of booty was incalculable; but the haul of provisions in a city that had been under siege for so long was minimal. Weakened further by famine and disease, and unable to withstand a siege from a large Muslim army arriving before the city, the crusaders made a sortie that crushed their enemy, adding another spectacular but hard-won victory to their campaign.

The crusading army that had set out for Jerusalem in 1099 had been reduced to about fourteen thousand in strength. It reached the walls of Jerusalem in mid-June and began a fierce siege lasting just over four weeks. The ditch around the walls was filled in at certain places, allowing rams and constructed towers to be brought up to the walls. All the while the crusaders operated under a deadly hail of missiles, including incendiaries in the form of coals, flammable pots and objects covered with pitch and studded with nails. On the morning of 15 July a siege tower allowed the crusaders to fight their way onto the ramparts; the Muslim defence crumbled and the city was sacked. Some fled to the temple, others took temporary refuge in the citadel, the Tower of David.

The Latin accounts of the sack of the city are graphic. Many writers used the *Deeds of the Franks* as a basis for their own accounts, composed by an anonymous eyewitness once thought to be a knight but more recently considered to be a cleric. This explains why there appears to be so much agreement between the sources. Raymond of Aguilers, another observer of and participant in the crusade, adds much further important detail of his own. However, some writers cannot resist further embellishments and heightening of the drama; Robert the Monk in particular enjoys lingering over the gory details. Here is how some of them describe the massacre.

The *Deeds of the Franks* provides history with the famous statement 'there was such a massacre that our men were wading up to their ankles in enemy blood'. The emir of the city surrendered to Count Raymond and was granted his life. His people were not so fortunate. At the Temple, many prisoners were taken; the crusaders 'killed whom they chose'. Many on the temple roof were given Christian banners for protection and spared the immediate slaughter, only to be beheaded the following morning. Such was the stench of putrefying corpses, 'the surviving Saracens dragged the dead ones out in front of the gates and piled them up in mounds as big as houses'.[13]

Fulcher of Chartres writes that 'nowhere was there a place where the Saracens could escape the swordsmen'. Those who had climbed to the top of Solomon's Temple 'were shot to death with arrows', and of those within it, 'about 10,000 were beheaded'. (Albert of Aachen more realistically gives this number as three hundred.) 'If you had been there, your feet would have been stained up to the ankles with the blood of the slain. . . . Not one was allowed to live. They did not spare the women and children.'[14] Raymond of Aguilers exclaims that 'the amount of blood' the crusaders 'shed that day is incredible'; 'piles of heads, hands and feet were to be seen in the streets'. Raymond picks out the events at the Temple as exceeding the 'powers of belief'. Going one better, he describes how the attackers 'rode in blood up to their knees and bridle reins'.[15]

Robert the Monk is the most gratuitous – and disturbing – of all. He is worth quoting at length because his account of the First Crusade proved to be the most popular contemporary account throughout Europe, sating the appetite of the bloodthirsty society described in chapter one. 'In no battle', he writes, were there 'so many opportunities to kill.'

Many thousands of chosen soldiers slashed human bodies from head to abdomen. ... Those who did manage to get away from such butchery and slaughter made their way to the Temple of Solomon. ... Our men ... found a new rush of courage, broke into the temple and put its occupants to a wretched death. So much human blood was spilt there that the bodies of the slain were revolving on the floor on a current of blood; arms and hands which had been cut off floated on the blood and found their way to other bodies so that nobody could work out which body the arm had come from which was attached to another headless body. Even the soldiers who were carrying out the massacre could hardly bear the vapours rising from the warm blood. Once they had finished this indescribable slaughter their spirits became a little gentler; they kept some of the young people, male and female, alive to serve them.

Describing the killings at the Temple of Solomon the next day, Robert displays his sadistic humour: 'A very large number of Turks had in fact climbed up there, and would have been all too grateful to flee if they could have grown wings and flown away; funnily enough nature failed to provide wings, giving instead a miserable exit from their wretched lives. ... They flung themselves to the ground, finding death on the soil which provides all things needed to sustain life.' Yet even Robert does not claim that the massacre was total: 'The Christians did not kill everyone, but kept many to serve them.'[16]

The most obvious discrepancy from the texts is Fulcher of Chartres's claim that all the inhabitants of Jerusalem were put to the sword without exception. This extreme version has tended to dominate the modern perceptions of the scale of the massacre. Ibn al-Athir believed over seventy thousand were killed in Jerusalem; a modern historian has put the figure between twenty and thirty thousand, which is still very excessive. Jerusalem had evacuated many of its citizens before the siege and its garrison of experienced soldiers was not large. Evidence exists to mitigate the scale of the massacre: Ibn al-Athir allows that only the men were killed, women and children being taken into captivity, and that a promise to spare some of the garrison was honoured; many Muslim survivors from Jerusalem turned up in Damascus; and a Jewish source states that so many prisoners were taken the ransom price had to be lowered.

Allowing for these reservations, it is clear that Jerusalem still witnessed scenes of widespread slaughter. Storming was a violent climax to any siege; and although the investiture of Jerusalem was relatively brief, it came at the end of a campaign that lasted nearly three years and which was full of hardships and deprivations that exceeded even the harsh conditions of warfare in Europe. Ever present had been fear of a strange and alien enemy; disease which weakness made even more deadly and which claimed as many lives as combat; excruciating hunger which led some to resort to cannibalism; and, constantly referred to by the chroniclers, the agonizing thirst, which one source says finished off hundreds of crusaders on one occasion alone. Jerusalem offered a chance to avenge these deprivations and torments with the winning of the crusade's ultimate goal. The need for revenge was also prevalent in an army that had been depleted to just over ten thousand by the end of the expedition; an attrition rate approaching seventy per cent has been calculated for the crusaders' losses over the three years. Robert the Monk believes that by the time of the siege of Jerusalem, Duke Godfrey was no longer interested in the spoils of war, 'instead, as the head of his Franks he was desperate to make the enemy pay for the blood of the servants of God which had been spilt for Jerusalem, and wanted revenge for the insults [hardships] they had heaped on the pilgrims'.[17]

In the bloodlust of combat, with adrenalin still coursing through their bodies, many crusaders, like other soldiers in their position, were more than ready to kill an enemy who only moments before had been trying to kill them. But killing and revenge were not the only things on their minds as they stormed the city: all were in pursuit of booty, a practical and financial reward to complement the spiritual one, a monetary recompense for their suffering and an opportunity, finally, to make a profit. The *Deeds of the Franks* tells how 'the army scattered through the city and took possession of the gold and silver, the horses and mules, and the houses filled with goods of all kinds'.[18] Fulcher of Chartres is explicit on this point: 'After this great massacre', the crusaders 'entered the homes of the citizens, seizing whatever they found in them. *It was done systematically*, so that whoever had entered the home first ... was to have and to hold the house. ... Since they mutually agreed to maintain this rule, many poor men became rich'[19] (my italics).

Killing the inhabitants removed an obstacle to plunder: there could be no protests or physical attempts to stop the soldiers and it removed the possibility of any later claims or exemptions that might be sought after the dust of combat had settled. Fulcher also offers another explanation why killing assisted the pursuit of booty:

> It was an extraordinary thing to see our squires and poorer people split the bellies of those dead Saracens, so that they might pick out besants [gold coins] from their intestines, which they had swallowed down their horrible gullets while alive. After several days, they made a great heap of their bodies and burned them to ashes, and in these ashes they found the gold more easily.[20]

As with revenge, the correlation between atrocity and financial gain is overwhelmingly strong. At Marrat the previous year, the poorer crusaders tortured and murdered prisoners in order to terrify others in to revealing where valuables were hidden. (The question of rape is not raised by the chroniclers, but it is easy to envisage situations where family members were also killed if they intervened or even pleaded for a wife, daughter or mother.)

What made the sack of Jerusalem special was not the massacre carried out there – Antioch and Marrat shared a similar experience during the crusade – but that it took place in Jerusalem, Christianity's most hallowed city (in medieval maps it was positioned at the centre of the world), and one also holy to the other two great monotheistic religions. The chroniclers reflect this salient fact and, as clerics, they can play up the religious angle of the massacre to the point of hyperbole. Thus Raymond of Aguilers' description of crusaders riding up to their bridles in blood is in fact a biblical allusion, an apocalyptic and millenarian reference to the Book of Revelation. The propensity of some crusade writers to exaggerate the quantity of blood spilled in massacres has been addressed in a very brief but highly instructive paper by David Hay. He shows that distance from an event served to promote an author's extravagant and bloodthirsty rendition of it, while writers from an ideological perspective opened the taps to a bloodbath even further. For the latter, 'massacres were not to be abhorred but were instead divinely ordained rites of purification, and consequently these writers sought to convey the impression that non-Christian populations were completely annihilated; hence Fulcher relates how Jerusalem was "restored to its pristine dignity" and cleansed of the contagion of its pagan inhabitants by the triumphant crusaders.'[21]

It is worth adding that Muslim thinking on purification through blood-shedding was similar, as we have seen at Hattin. Furthermore, as with battles, victory was a sign of God's approval; the more complete the victory, the greater this approbation; and nothing was more complete than the total annihilation of an enemy in a thorough massacre. Hay proposes that a proper interpretation of the sources reveals that it was normally just the male population that was massacred. This is an important corrective up to a point, and explains some of the differences in reports of the scale of the massacre at Jerusalem. However, even those who wrote disapprovingly of such killings, as Albert of Aachen does above in describing the anti-Jewish pogrom at Mainz, point out that women and children were victims, as they too commonly were in Christian versus Christian wars in the West. Very few massacres were complete – the practicalities of mass killings made such events rare – and many perpetrators did single out just the men; but women and children were all too easily, in modern parlance, part of the collateral damage. Even when not directly targeted, as they sometimes were, they could just as readily be killed by a deliberate policy of inaction, as will be seen in the next section. The laws of war that afforded women and children more protection were not always put into practice and were flouted with impunity on many occasions.

Whereas the looting at Jerusalem was systematic, the butchery was not. The *Deeds of the Franks* coldly captures the arbitrary nature of brutality when not predetermined: the crusaders 'killed whom they chose, and whom they chose they saved alive'.[22] Peter Tudebode writes: 'Our men grabbed a large number of males and females ... killing some, and sparing others as the notion struck them.'[23] For some men, this decision – the notion to act one way or the other – would be rational; for others, more disturbingly, the action might be random and capricious. We are not aware of any orders that specifically commanded the killing of the entire population at Jerusalem. The killings, therefore, were not ostensibly the result of military instructions in pursuit of strategic ends, which would seem to make it a rare example among the cases studied in this book.

Or it would but for a tragic postscript to events at Jerusalem. The sack has simplistically been seen by many as a manifestation of the murdering fanaticism of the crusading hordes, giving vent to their bloodlust as they poured into the city. However, it seems that there were actually two massacres in the city – or even three, if the killings of the prisoners on the roof of the Dome the day after the city fell are treated separately. According to Albert of Aachen, three days after taking the city, a council held by the leaders decided to kill all the remaining prisoners and hostages, be they men, women or children. Again it is unclear to what extent this was carried out (had some of the survivors we know about been taken out of the city in the intervening period?), but Albert was horrified by the executions that did take place. The reason for these calculated murders is one we have encountered at Wexford, Acre and Agincourt: an Egyptian army making its way directly to Jerusalem raised fears that the prisoners might rise up against the captors, who would be busily engaged in a new round of fighting. That this fear materialized indicates two things: first, there must have been a substantial number of survivors from the first round of killing to cause such concern; and secondly, this new massacre may have been every bit as terrible as the first.

This grim episode in the aftermath of the fall of Jerusalem has been much overlooked in popular histories of the crusade and in some academic ones; consequently, the question not asked is: were all the people of Jerusalem not doomed the moment the city was lost anyway? For if there had been no slaughter when the crusaders broke into the city, there would have been an even bigger massacre three days later, when the remaining survivors were ordered to be put to the sword.

Château Gaillard, 1203–4

One of the defining moments in the centuries of Anglo-French conflict was the English loss of Normandy in 1204. When war broke out between King John and King Philip II of France in 1202, the wealthy duchy of Normandy was the great prize sought by the French. Just as Dover Castle was considered by contemporaries to be the key to England, so Château Gaillard was the great fortress that could open or block the way to Normandy. When Philip's armies set up camp here in September 1203, one of the great set-piece sieges of the Middle Ages was put into motion.

The castle was the personal project of Richard I; it was his 'saucy castle', his 'beautiful castle on the rock'. Dominating the region from its site on an imposing crag high above the river Seine, and the heart of an integrated defence complex at Andelys, it represented state-of-the-art architectural engineering; it was so well designed that Richard I boasted it could be defended even if the walls were made of butter. The money he lavished on it came to more than the expenditure on all his castles in England throughout his entire reign. No wonder it was considered impregnable. But for Philip to annex Normandy, he had first to conquer Château Gaillard.

The epic six-month siege that ensued received little detailed attention from chroniclers, with only a few mentioning it little more than in passing. Our main record for events here comes from the distinctly pro-French sources penned by William the Breton, Philip's royal chaplain. It has to be said that his chronicle and, even more blatantly, his epic poem the *Philippidos*, make no attempt to disguise his partiality; yet as an eyewitness who had a clear understanding of the nature of war, his vivid account of events at Château Gaillard is an invaluable insight into the reality of medieval siege warfare.

The castle was in the charge of Roger of Lacy, constable of Chester, a veteran soldier widely acknowledged for his martial ability. With no landed interests in Normandy, he was loyal to the English Crown, on which his fortunes depended. His defence of the castle under siege was dogged and determined, resisting the huge concentration of French forces that blockaded him in for half a year. At one stage, the siege was nearly lifted by a spectacular combined river and land relief attack led by William Marshal, but poor co-ordination, a misreading of the tides and the determined resistance of the French saw it end in failure. Soon afterwards, the fortified island by the town of Petit-Andely fell to a daring French commando operation; left unprotected, the inhabitants of the town fled to the castle for refuge, only to be expelled later. The French tightened the blockade: excavating lines of circumvallation and contravallation (for defence and attack), and, building a siege camp, they literally dug in for the duration.

By February 1204, with the garrison of nearly two hundred men not having succumbed to hunger, Philip made ready to storm the castle. Moat-filling, siege engines and sappers were all brought into action as intense fighting resumed. When a tower on the curtain wall was brought down, Lacy ordered his men to torch the outer ward before retreating across a drawbridge to the castle's middle ward. The French poured into the outer ward and some sergeants immediately investigated for any weak spot the new line of defence might expose. They soon found one. A new building had recently been added here, comprising an upper storey of a chapel and a lower one of latrines. (William the Breton condemns this arrangement for being 'against religion'; it is possible that the upper level was in fact a storehouse).

There are two versions of what happened next. The most likely is that a Frenchman by the name of Peter Bogis stood on the shoulders of a comrade and was able to make an entrance through an unguarded window of the chapel; the understandably more popular rendering is that he gained access by crawling up a latrine chute. From here a rope was lowered and troops were pulled up. Panicking in the noise and confusion that followed, the garrison withdrew one last time to the strongest part of the castle: the keep in the inner bailey. The heart of the castle was enclosed by a wall of seventeen D-shaped towers, convex buttresses eight feet thick. But even these could not withstand for ever the single-minded and unrelenting assault of Philip's war machine. A combination of further mining and bombardment from a huge stone-thrower finally brought a section of the wall down. French soldiers scrambled up the tumbled masonry and stormed the breach in force. The English still fought desperately and bravely on, but were quickly overwhelmed by sheer weight of numbers. Philip Augustus had taken Richard's beautiful and powerful castle. Normandy fell soon afterwards.

Roger of Wendover's account has Lacy and his men ride out from the keep in a gallant last sortie, only to be overcome after having inflicted great losses on the French. However, it is hard to imagine that the garrison's horses would have survived the dinner plate for six months; and the anonymous chronicler of Béthune states that the mounts were indeed eaten and that the garrison still had to surrender through starvation.

What of the garrison? The laws of siege warfare allowed for them to be struck down where they stood. Instead, they were led off in chains. Roger of Lacy met with a different fate. According to Anonymous of Béthune, throughout the siege Lacy had declared that he would never surrender the castle, even if he were to be dragged out by his feet. His heroic defence did indeed end in this dishonourable manner. He, too, was put in shackles, but was then detained honourably as prisoner on parole before being freed when his ransom was paid. The siege of Château Gaillard was a hard-fought contest with many soldiers dying or wounded in combat. Yet the bloodbath that could have ensued with the storming of the castle never occurred. From the soldiers' point of view, the whole engagement seems to subscribe pretty much to the chivalric ideals of medieval warfare. But it was not the soldiers who endured the worst of the siege; it was some of the non-combatants who had fled to the castle for safety who suffered most. In the town hall of Petit-Andely today, there hangs a huge canvas by the nineteenth-century artist Tattegrain. Entitled *Les Bouches Inutiles* (*The Useless Mouths*), it depicts the terrible suffering undergone by these non-combatants. What happened is a grim tale that has received only scant attention from historians.

Roger of Lacy came to regret his decision to allow refugees from the town into his castle. The town's numbers had already been swollen with an influx of people fleeing from the surrounding countryside. The castle was well stocked with provisions for his garrison, but it was woefully inadequate for the needs of somewhere between 1,400 and 2,200 extra people. He reckoned that his supplies would enable him to withstand a siege for a year. His garrison was large enough to defend the relatively small perimeter of the castle so he did not need the encumbrance of non-combatants getting in the way and rapidly depleting his stores. In military terms, they were indeed 'useless mouths'. With the relief army failing to lift the siege, and with a letter from King John that did not offer any fresh help, Lacy had to prepare for a lengthy blockade.

At some point in November, Lacy evicted some five hundred of the oldest and weakest non-combatants from the castle. The French took pity on the feeble and shabby group and opened up their lines to let them through. A few days later the scene was repeated with a similar number, with the French once again allowing the pathetic non-combatants safe passage. The townspeople had already seen their homes occupied by French settlers and a French mercenary garrison; they had nothing left to defend and were now reduced to frightened refugees. King Philip was not present at the siege when this was taking place as he was conducting his campaign elsewhere and attending to matters of state. When he heard what was happening at Château Gaillard he angrily issued orders immediately and categorically forbidding any further egress from the castle. No one, regardless of age, sex or condition, was to be spared the rigours of the siege. No more non-combatants were to be allowed through French lines; they were instead to be driven back into the fortress. Philip wanted the useless mouths in the castle, whittling down the garrison's supplies. The last tranche of non-combatants cast out by Lacy consisted of at least four hundred people, perhaps as many as over a thousand. As they emerged from the castle they thought they were going to rejoin their families and fellow townsfolk away from the dangers of the siege. They could not have been more wrong. William the Breton claims that Lacy knew he was sending these people to their certain death.

They were not met by the opening of the besiegers' lines, but by a hail of arrows and javelins. The French were executing their new orders. The terrified refugees fled back to the castle to find the gates locked and bolted against them. According to William the Breton, their desperate entreaties to be allowed back in were met with the words from the guard in charge of the gate: 'I do not know you; go and search for shelter elsewhere; it is forbidden to open the gates to you.'[24] The garrison then hurled down stones and shot arrows at the people they had previously been protecting to drive them away from the gates. No doubt confused and racked with fear at this brutal turn of events, the wretched crowd had little choice but to seek equidistance from their two forces of assailants. They moved into the no-man's-land between castle and besiegers, finding what little protection they could from the elements and the overhead exchanges of missiles among the shallow fissures and clefts on the steep and barren rock face. Neither the French nor the English relented, leaving the civilians exposed to the wet and cold of three long winter months, to survive, if they were able, as best they could. It was here the real horror of the siege of Château Gaillard was to unfold.

William the Breton expresses revulsion at how the English could condemn their own people to such 'a wretched and miserable existence'.[25] Weakened by cold and hunger, the outcasts had nothing but a few wild herbs (rare in winter) and the waters of the river with which to attempt to sustain themselves. William catalogues their suffering over the twelve weeks of their ordeal. A chicken that wandered onto the slopes was fought over by the strongest and was consumed bones, feathers and all. They feasted on some dogs Lacy sent out to them which they skinned with their bare hands (it is unknown whether this action was prompted by belated pity or by Lacy denying precious scraps to the dogs, which were in all likelihood emaciated anyway). When the meat was gone, they ate the hides. A baby that was delivered was snatched by men who ripped it up and devoured the parts. William wrote that all feelings of shame were suppressed in the fight to survive in a nether-world where many 'neither lived nor died; being unable to hold on to life, they could not quite lose it'.[26] In fact, over half of those in no-man's-land died from exposure and hunger; those that survived only did so because they had water from the Seine to draw on.

Philip returned to Château Gaillard in February 1204. The skeletal survivors, on seeing the corpulent French king, called out for mercy. Philip shows clemency and sees that the wretches are released and fed, much to William the Breton's praise. One among the number was seen still clutching a dog's tail which he refused to discard, saying, 'I shall only part with this tail that has kept me alive for so long when I am full of bread.'[27] However, the suffering was not over even yet. Over half of those who gorged themselves on the food now provided did so with fatal consequences, probably succumbing to acute peptic ulceration and gastro-intestinal bleeding. These terrible scenes were not unique in medieval warfare. At the siege of Calais in 1346–7, Edward III, that most chivalrous and 'perfect' king, allowed one group of refugees to leave the city, but left a further five hundred to die between the town walls and the siege lines. A letter describing the plight of those still left in the city spoke darkly of cannibalism. The siege of Rouen in Normandy during the early fifteenth century was, as will be seen, a copy of that at Château Gaillard. All the commanders involved in besieging these places were using hunger as a weapon, something William recognized when he wrote 'it is cruel hunger that alone conquers the invincible'.[28] Rigord, William's predecessor as royal biographer, disingenuously commentated that Philip intended to take the Château Gaillard by hunger and want in order to spare the blood of men, a distinction lost on the useless mouths. For the English chroniclers Roger of Wendover and Ralph of Coggeshall, it was starvation and not poliorcetics that defeated the castle.

Philip was a master of castle-breaking and never flinched from making the ruthless decisions needed for success. His actions at Château Gaillard were all rational military measures. Obviously, he wanted the non-combatants in the castle to exhaust the garrison's victuals as quickly as possible. With these evicted from the castle, any display of leniency might be perceived by others as a serious weakness; future strongholds resisting Philip would be more ready to send out their useless mouths, too, thereby reinforcing their ability to extend the siege. The longer an investiture took, the greater was the chance of a relief army lifting the siege, counter-attack, and manpower lost to disease and desertion. The plight of the sufferings of their own people in sight of the castle walls would also have applied acute psychological pressure on the garrison, serving to demoralize them, not least because many of them would be related to the local civilians. This pressure was all one way: the laws of war imposed few restraints on a besieging commander in these situations. It was effective, too: events at Château Gaillard frightened the inhabitants of Falaise into persuading their mercenary garrison commander to go over to the French; and when Philip issued the Normandy capital of Rouen with a dire ultimatum, they capitulated, knowing that he was not bluffing.

William the Breton, naturally exploiting the situation, and some modern French historians have condemned Lacy for his callous evictions. After all, these were the people he was obligated to protect under the feudal compact (an unfashionable term these days, but still a potent one). However, most other contemporaries praised Lacy for his stout and loyal defence of the castle, understanding the practical reasoning behind it. Apart from the overarching problem of provisioning, Lacy also carried the enormous responsibility of holding the castle for his lord, King John; we have discussed above the Duke of Norfolk's warning about the possibility of beheading for castle commanders failing in their duty. There was also the very real danger that the non-combatants could turn into belligerents. With the relief attempt having failed, and John's letter suggesting there would be no more help forthcoming, how would Lacy keep up to two thousand hungry people crammed within his walls quiescent? Could the garrison really preserve the food for themselves and not expect trouble?

The sheer weight of their numbers coupled with desperation might have transformed the refugees into insurrectionists who would overwhelm the garrison in their want of food. The garrison might have fended off the French outside for the time being, but it would have been near impossible to quell a large internal rising at the same time. These were real fears, faced by Richard at Acre and by some Greek cities during the Second Crusade (1146–8) when they refused entrance to the French in anticipation of food riots if they were to do so. Once they were outside, it made tactical sense to drive the non-combatants away from the walls: if too close, they increased the threat of a surprise night escalade by the French (something similar happened at Tours in 1189) by providing them with cover. With these considerations, it is not surprising that Lacy's military judgement has been questioned for admitting the refugees into the castle in the first instance. However, this ignores not only his obligation to defend them but, even more pertinently, that the admission took place before the expected relief operation which so nearly succeeded, and before John's letter eventually arrived offering little to hope for in the way of future help. If Lacy can be taken to task for failing the people under his protection, so King John can be for failing to assist Lacy. King Philip used this very argument to persuade Rouen to capitulate: it should accept him as their new lord because their old one, John, was doing nothing to safeguard his people in the city.

Given the efficacy of these ruthless tactics, why did Philip relent? William the Breton would have us believe it was all down to the King's natural soft-heartedness and fellow-feeling: Philip was 'always responsive to supplicants, because he was born to have compassion for unfortunates and to spare them always'.[29] Magnanimous gesture had its place in medieval warfare and politics, but it is doubtful that this was one of those occasions. Much more likely – and more true to form – is that Philip's thoughts were, as ever, taken up with military practicalities. For a start, the siege was taking too long. Success elsewhere had freed Philip to concentrate once more on Château Gaillard and he had returned to the castle to press home the siege more vigorously and decisively. Clearing the refugees out of the way was a necessary preliminary measure for the operations at hand. An even more convincing explanation is that, with the arrival of spring, Philip feared the spread of disease. In their severely enfeebled state and with their immune systems completely run down, the refugees in no-man's-land were particularly susceptible to pestilence which, in turn, might easily spread to his siege camp.

This prospect was a siege commander's ever-present nightmare. Disease could decimate besieging forces. A contemporary account describes how a contagion affected the French entrenchments at the southern French city of Avignon in 1226: 'There arose from the corpses of men and horses which were dying in all directions, a large number of large, black flies, which made their way inside the tents, pavilions and awnings, and affected the provisions and drink, and being unable to drive them away from their cups and plates, caused sudden death amongst them.'[30] It was at this siege that Philip's own son, Louis VIII, died from dysentery. The idea of medieval besieging forces launching rotten meat over the walls of an encircled town is a familiar one, but those outside had just as much reason to dread pestilence. In 1250 at Brescia in Lombardy, a highly infectious epidemic was spreading between the city's animals; these were driven out of the gates so that they would mix with the animals in the besieger's camp.

For some historians, William's account of the useless mouths at Château Gaillard smacks of gratuitous sensationalism. The same offence has been levelled at monks writing about medieval warfare and is easily refuted here. Many medieval chronicles were prone to exaggeration, especially when it came to gruesome details; but this by itself does not negate the essence of what is being related. How could the experience of hundreds of people trapped on a barren rock through winter with no food or shelter be anything but utterly horrific? The most lurid and distressing episode at Château Gaillard reported by William has to be the eating of the newborn baby. This may or may not be a literary device, rich in symbolism; but there was more to cannibalism than mere literary allegory in such situations. The impoverished Tafurs of the First Crusade had a reputation for it, and human flesh was reported as being consumed at Marrat in 1098. Tales of cannibalism emerged from the sieges at Calais and Rouen in the Hundred Years War; worse still, Froissart and others tell of forced cannibalism, inflicted for sadistic reasons, during the fourteenth-century Jacquerie in France. Daniel Baraz has demonstrated how the charge of cannibalism was often made as a way of demonizing an enemy. At Château Gaillard, however, William's attitude was one of deep sympathy to the non-combatants: the real enemy were safe behind the castle's walls; furthermore, he is quite open that it was with the implementation of Philip's direct orders that their ordeal had begun.

Finally, there are touches of realism in William's account that are striking for their modern parallels. The survivors who died after devouring too much food on their release by Philip shared the fate of many starving prisoners liberated from the Nazi concentration camp at Belsen, where food provided by the British troops induced gastro-intestinal bleeding. The man who refused to relinquish his grip on the dog's tail brings to mind the case of the shipwrecked survivors of the whaleship *Essex* in 1820. When rescued from their drifting lifeboat, the two remaining sailors were reluctant to surrender the bones on which they had been gnawing and relying for sustenance. The bones were those of other crewmen.

Béziers, 1209

When the excesses of medieval warfare are considered, the most common association is with the crusades. Their zealous religious motivations certainly provided a dominant element used in propaganda to dehumanize, and hence brutalize, the enemy; but the fact that crusades were fought out on the borders of Christian Europe in unfamiliar territory against peoples of an entirely different culture and society made conditions even riper for atrocity. The savage wars with Muslims in the Middle East and the Iberian Peninsula (the Reconquista) and against pagans on the fringes of eastern and northern Europe bear this out. The Albigensian Crusade of the early thirteenth century was every bit as vicious as the others, yet, being fought in southwestern France, it had none of their frontier antagonisms, and any societal differences were relatively minor in comparison, being merely regional rather than ethnic. It is therefore tempting to emphasize religious differences on the Albigensian Crusade when attempting to explain the quantity of blood it spilt, but this can offer only a partial answer. To understand fully, we must once again examine the part played by the military imperative.

The Albigensian Crusade began in the summer of 1209. It had been declared against Count Raymond VI of Toulouse in the previous year by Pope Innocent III, following the murder of his papal legate, allegedly by a vassal of the Count. The legate had been in southern

France to pressurize secular rulers like Raymond to extirpate the Cathar heresy. The Cathars had developed Bogomil influences from Greece and the Balkans into their dualist religion in which the good God of the spiritual world existed co-eternally in contest with the malign God of the material world. To free their souls from imprisonment in the material, human realm, Cathars aspired to a form of purity indicated by their name and achieved by their *perfecti* elite. This entailed prayers at fixed hours fifteen times through the day and night, and abstention from worldly things such as milk, eggs, meat and sex. It was surprisingly popular. Suppressing the heresy was proving a real headache for the Church, as many noble families and even senior churchmen had relatives who followed Catharism. With its belief in two gods, its denial of the Holy Trinity, and, most damning of all, its renunciation of the Latin Church, it was easy to consider the wayward Christianity of Catharism less as a heretical movement and more as a different religion altogether.

The heretics' power base lay in the city of Albi, situated north-east of Toulouse. With the Spanish engaged in their own campaigns against the Moors, the predominantly, but far from exclusively, French crusading army set out from Lyons at the end of June 1209 and marched south under the leadership of the papal legates Milo and Arnald Amalric, archbishop of Cîteaux. In a little over two weeks it had reached Montpellier, one of a handful of southern cities that remained resolutely orthodox. By this stage, Count Raymond had already submitted to the Church, forcing a change of crusading objective. The new chief enemy was now the young Raymond-Roger Trancavel, Viscount of Béziers, in whose lands the heretics had flourished unchallenged. His two greatest strongholds were the formidable cities of Béziers and his capital at Carcassonne. When Raymond-Roger's negotiations with the crusaders failed – his penitential approach was rejected by the legates – he returned to Carcassonne to hurriedly prepare his defences there. Between his capital and the crusaders lay Béziers. Here he stopped briefly en route to stiffen the resolve of the burgers for the inevitable and imminent siege; this would buy him time to organize a military response, which would include reinforcements for Béziers.

Béziers was a well-fortified and elevated city of some eight to ten thousand people and had a strong garrison. In the few days it had to make itself ready for the investment, it stocked up on plentiful provisions and deepened the ditches around its walls. Its confidence in withstanding a lengthy blockade until either disease and hunger or reinforcements dispersed the besiegers was based on solid, high grounds. So when the crusaders arrived outside its gates on 21 July it rejected the terms offered by its bishop addressing its citizens in the cathedral: the people of Béziers refused to hand over 222 leading heretics named on a list that still exists today in exchange for the city being spared. Nor did the majority Catholics there – not even priests – take up his warning wrapped up in advice to 'quit the city and leave the heretics behind, so as to avoid perishing with them'.[31] William of Tudela reports this in more explicit terms: 'rather than be defeated and killed or imprisoned, their goods and clothing taken from them,' the citizens 'should surrender the town. ... If they refused, they would be stripped of all they had and put to the sword.'[32] Despite the redundant accumulation of threats – what goods were possessions to the dead anyway? – the people of Béziers acknowledged the danger of their situation but then rejected the assurances given for their safety.

Despite religious differences and the concomitant tensions these produced, the heretics (who included some adherents of the less radical Waldensian sect) posed no real dangers to the city. But it was not just a spirit of enlightened liberalism and religious toleration that prompted this, at first hand, admirable defiance; there was more at stake than religious practice. Many of the leading heretics on the list were also leading citizens, which meant they had influence, followers, sympathizers and interests that affected many throughout the city. Secondly, and even more importantly, submitting to the crusading forces would have meant the imposition on the city of a new regime and a feared loss of their hard-earned civic liberties; the city, like a growing number in France during this period, had gained considerable independence and did not wish to relinquish it to outside forces. For all the usual religious justifications propounded by the crusading propagandists, and for all the spiritual indulgences promoted, the Albigensian Crusade was for many little more than a glorified land-grabbing opportunity. Just as the goods of heretics could be expropriated, so could their land. With completely logical and practical reasoning, the Church and the nobles participating in the crusade argued that for heresy to be eradicated, the territory it existed in needed to be under the control of orthodox and actively anti-heretical rulers. That so many heretics were related to the ruling class increased the reluctance of local lords to move against them; even when these lords submitted to the Church, it did not guarantee their enthusiastic repression of Cathars. The people of Béziers were well aware of the importance of this political dimension and it informed their position of resistance.

The scene was therefore set for an epic siege between up to twenty thousand crusaders and an impressively strong city made ready for the oncoming trial of strength. The siege formally began on 22 July – and ended the same day.

All the advantages possessed by the city – the strength of its fortifications, its position, its garrison, its stockpile of provisions, the resolve of its citizens – were totally negated by one act of folly. While the besiegers were having breakfast and setting up camp, a sortie burst out from the city. A French historian has called it a reconnaissance party, but given the war cries and flag-waving reported by one chronicle it was more likely to have been a daring raid, a taking of the initiative while the besiegers' camp was unprepared and still disorganized. It may also have been an act of bravado to raise the morale and fighting spirit of the citizens. A crusader guarding the bridge was cut down and flung into the river below. The cry of 'To arms! To arms!' went up as the crusaders scrambled to meet this unexpected danger.

The contemporary account provided in *The Song of the Cathar Wars* is unconvincing and possibly confused as to what occurred next. According to its author, the sergeants (camp followers, common soldiers and, almost certainly, mercenaries) reacted with an animated fury. Some counter-attacked in force, wielding little but clubs; others jumped down into the ditches and set to work with picks, taking the walls apart stone by stone; while still others began battering and smashing the gates. The assault was so spontaneous the attackers wore nothing but their shirts and trousers, 'with not a pair of shoes between them'. When they forced the defenders off the ramparts, the men, women and children of Béziers fled into the churches for sanctuary. 'It was their only refuge.'[33]

The narrative is somewhat problematic: it is inconceivable that soldiers would make any assault on a city's walls, no matter how extempore, without some minimum form of protection, never mind barefoot; if the ramparts were taken, there would have been some form of escalade, not mentioned here; and picks would not have brought down the walls of Béziers in a day (Peter of les Vaux-de-Cernay says that the city was taken within an hour). Wiliam of Tudela also writes of the gates opening, so it is much more probable that the size and ferocity of the counter-attack in turn surprised the sortie party, which fled back to the castle hotly pursued by the crusaders, who then forced their way in before the gates had been fully closed. As we have seen, Richard I had taken Taillebourg in a similar fashion thirty years earlier. The crusaders poured into the city and sacked it utterly. As Joseph Strayer noted, 'There followed one of the most pitiless massacres of the Middle Ages.'[34]

One German chronicler alleged a few years after the event that the legate Arnald Amalric exhorted the crusaders on to wholesale slaughter with the infamous cry, 'Kill them all; God will know his own!' [35] It seems they tried to do just that. Afterwards, the legate matter-of-factly reported to Pope Innocent III that twenty thousand had been killed and neither age nor sex nor status saved anyone. William of Puylaurens states simply that the people 'fled for refuge to their churches', where the crusaders 'massacred many thousands of them'.[36] Peter of les Vaux-de-Cernay says that the slaughter was not quite total, as 'the crusaders killed almost all the inhabitants from the youngest to the oldest', 'seven thousand' of the 'shameless dogs' meeting their just end in the church of Mary Magdalene.[37] William of Tudela furnishes his readers with the most detail. The citizens

hurriedly took refuge in the high church. The priests put on vestments for a mass of the dead and had the church bells rung as for a funeral. . . . [The crusaders] were in a frenzy, quite unafraid of death, killing everyone they could find and winning enormous wealth. . . . They massacred them at Béziers, killing them all. It was the worst they could do to them. And they killed everyone who fled into church; no cross or altar or crucifix could save them. . . . They killed the clergy too, and the women and children. I doubt if one person came out alive. [The crusaders] burned the town, burned the women and children, old men and young, and the clerks vested and singing mass there inside the church.[38]

Peter's slightly qualified massacre is far more likely than the utter annihilation of the other accounts, for reasons given in the discussion on the sack of Jerusalem above. The rounded figure of twenty thousand is considered a gross exaggeration for a town perhaps less than half that size; however, it should be remembered that its numbers would have been inflated by the influx of refugees from the surrounding areas (one recent respected study puts the number who perished at fifteen thousand). The Church of Mary Magdalene simply did not have the capacity to hold anywhere near seven thousand people. But there can be no doubt not only that the slaughter was extensive even by the standards of the time, and also that the non-combatant victims numbered women, children and priests among their dead. Heretics – the cause of the crusade – were a minority among the dead.

There are both parallels to and differences from the massacre at Jerusalem. The most obvious difference is that the crusaders at Béziers had experienced only the minutest fraction of the hardships of the crusaders in the Holy Land. They had marched through safe territory in France for most of the brief campaign, and the 'siege' had lasted barely twenty-four hours between their arrival at the city and its fall. No wonder the sources make no reference to the deprivations and dangers usually inseparable from besieging a stronghold. There was none of the years of pent-up emotion and vengeance fomented in the hostile deserts of the Middle East. Nor did Béziers have any magical hold on the crusaders' hearts and souls. Religious fervour was still present, of course, but it can hardly compare with that generated by the ultimate pilgrimage.

An obvious similarity, as with all sackings, is the matter of booty. Here we have one contributing explanation for the massacre, but neither the main nor the most interesting one. However, as a factor, it requires a little examination, mainly for the light it sheds on the larger question of population massacres. William of Tudela offers some very useful information in his account of Béziers. He blames the army's rabble for the sack of the city: 'raving, beggarly', 'filthy stinking wretches' and 'wretched' soldiers in one translation; 'ruffians', 'damnable foot soldiers', 'mercenaries' and 'brigands' in others.[39] The legates' report to Rome confirms that it was the lower orders who were first to attack the city. William is making an effort to distance the knightly element of the crusade – the nobility, chivalry and true soldiers of Christ – from the riff-raff responsible for the massacre. This may be a further indication that women, children and priests were victims; had only the male population been killed, the language offers a hint that there would not have been the need for this dissociation to be highlighted. The infantry were certainly the first into the city. Their rapid response precipitated a more general assault, but given the indications of their unpreparedness, it would seem probable that the knights would take even longer to get kitted up for battle. By the time the cavalry entered the city, the killing and looting had gathered its full, horrific momentum.

It is hard to envisage the scenes at Béziers as anything but apocalyptic chaos, a Breughel-style canvas of diabolical anarchy depicting death, fire and misery. Yet when the knights arrived, they immediately imposed some sort of order onto this hellish rampage. They feared they were losing out on the seizing of booty. William of Tudela says of the ordinary soldiers' initial haul of plunder:

> Rich for life they'll be, if they can keep it! But very soon they'll be forced to let it go, for the French knights are going to claim it though it was the foot soldiers that won it. . . . The foot soldiers had settled into the houses they had taken, all of them full of riches and treasure, but when the French discovered this they went nearly mad with rage and drove the soldiers out with clubs, like dogs. . . . The captain and his men expected to enjoy the wealth they had taken and be rich for evermore.[40]

When the barons took their booty from them, the soldiers sent up a cry of 'Burn it! Burn it!' and torched the city so extensively the cathedral collapsed in flames. The part played by the knights begs the question: if they were able to stop the looting, why had they not stopped the indiscriminate slaughter? They were moved to action not by horror at the pleading of the non-belligerents being struck down around them, but by horror at the prospect of not gaining their full and rightful share of the plunder. For the knights, saving the lives of the citizens of Béziers was at best secondary to saving the city's wealth for themselves; at worst, it reflected either a policy of total indifference or even the successful implementation of planned massacre.

The Song of the Cathar Wars informs us that a form of mass execution was part of crusader policy from before the start. The leaders of the crusade, including the clergy, had already taken the 'tactical decision' by which they 'all agreed that at every castle the army approached, a garrison that refused to surrender would be slaughtered wholesale, once the castle had been taken by storm'. The purpose was an intentional strategy of inducing maximum fear: 'They would then meet with no resistance anywhere, as men would be so terrified at what had already happened. ... That is why they massacred them at Béziers, killing them all.' Such ruthlessness proved to be most effective. William vindicates the good sense of the crusaders' terror tactics when he adds that this was how Fanjeaux and Montréal and all the country were easily taken later in the crusade, 'otherwise, I promise you, they could never have stormed them'.[41] William claims that he learned from another source that as far back as the announcement of the crusade, a papal council had called for the utter destruction of all who resisted. The bishop of Béziers also warned the citizens of the fatal consequences of resistance just before the sack started. Certainly the road to Carcassonne was left open to the crusaders, as garrisons deserted their stations when they heard of what had befallen Béziers.

If such a hard and callous plan speeded up the taking of towns, then it fulfilled its purpose. Less time spent on a siege meant less expenditure, less loss of crusading lives, less risk from disease and relief forces and less loss of manpower (many knights were serving on the basis of a forty-day obligation). There is absolutely no indication that William finds the policy anything other than to be expected and sensibly efficient, especially when dealing with heretics. However, his disgust at the common soldiers at Béziers suggests that the killing got out of hand here, claiming the lives not just of the garrison and heretics, but of non-combatant Catholics also. But given the knights' preoccupation with booty over lives, and the later massacres that marked the crusade – five years later at Casseneuil, in 1214, Peter of les Vaux-de-Cernay says that the crusaders 'put to the sword anyone they came across'[42] – the distinction between garrison soldiers and non-combatants was not one that much troubled anyone as they poured into the towns that fell to them, be they lowly common soldiers or the elite of chivalry.

William of Tudela's account claims that it was not the intention to burn Béziers. This has led to some recent suggestions that the crusade leaders, chafing at the booty that went up in flames in Béziers, wanted to take all the enemy strongholds intact, primarily as a way of preserving and maximizing the plunder within. However, the crusade's campaign trail could be tracked by the smoking towns it left in its wake. It is more accurate to say that the crusaders wished to have the towns exhaustively ransacked before the incendiaries went to work. One contemporary source offers an insight into the thinking of the crusaders on what they should do with the places that fell into their hands. After taking the capital Carcassonne, the crusaders held a council which decided not to raze it, because 'if the city were altogether destroyed, there would not be found a nobleman of the army who would undertake the government of the country'.[43] The city became the base of the whole crusade.

A similar policy was followed by military leaders when castles fell into their hands: if the place was useful, they would strengthen and garrison it; if it were thought to be difficult to hold or of no direct strategic value to them, they would destroy it. With towns, there was more to be taken into consideration, as the above quote indicates. Any government needed regional seats of administration; and for these to be of value the areas needed to be economically viable. In many cases, it was more than the infrastructure that required preserving. Where colonists could not be imported to make up for displaced or slaughtered inhabitants, it would be counter productive to slay everyone in a captured town. A depopulated city was one without markets and hence without economic benefits to its ruler. Furthermore, scarcity of labour would serve to raise the cost of labour, a well-known after-effect of the Black Death in the fourteenth century. It could make military sense to kill the garrison, especially as a warning to others; it could also make sense to kill many of the male population as a way of keeping the masses subjugated through fear; but to kill all the population made military sense only on rare occasions, as an exception to the rule or when it was felt a particularly draconian punishment was called for in order to intimidate and inhibit resistance.

Béziers, then, may well have been a planned massacre that rapidly escalated out of control in the unexpected success of the moment. If so, the leadership was unlikely to have been greatly disconcerted, as the victory was so quick and, for them at least, painless. Some booty might have gone up in the flames, but at the same time they had incurred none of the expenses or risks of a lengthy siege. But most of all, the savagery of the sack helped break the resolve of further resistance. Carcassonne was the main prize, and this capitulated after only a fortnight's siege, submitting to harsh terms which nevertheless spared the lives of the inhabitants (even the Cathars among them avoided the stake) and which left the crusaders laden with spectacular spoils of war.

The real financial benefits of Béziers were reaped at Carcassonne. The orderly taking of that city, even after fierce fighting, reveals that medieval armies did not always conform to the popular and largely false image of ill-disciplined rabbles always on the verge of being out of control (which, of course, did happen on occasion). It also suggests that, when coupled with the knights' seeming indifference to the massacre, the carnage at Béziers was the result of a policy that had encouraged the slaughter. Arnald Amalric's infamous cry of 'Kill them all; God will know his own' is today considered apocryphal, but certainly cannot be judged definitively as such. The German chronicler who recorded the phrase did not actually add 'all' (a later addition) and reported the phrase as hearsay. The merciless exhortation allegedly followed questions to the legate as to how the crusaders might distinguish Cathar from Catholic in the chaos of bloodletting, and that the legate demanded the death of everyone lest the former pretended to be the latter. But it is just as likely that if these words were actually spoken, they merely reflected the crusading leadership's agreed policy on massacring those who resisted. Whatever the truth, Béziers had launched the crusade off to a spectacularly good start.

Limoges, 1370

The storm and sack of Limoges in 1370 by Edward the Black Prince is an event that appears to conform to the laws of medieval war siege warfare, even if the extrapolation from Deuteronomy is somewhat forced. Despite this, it certainly shocked many contemporaries for its brutality, and it provides the chronicles of Froissart with one of its most famous passages. Even Froissart, the most celebrated contemporary recorder of chivalrous feats of arms and a writer who tends to romanticize the Black Prince, the epitome of heroic English chivalry at the time, condemns the actions of Edward at Limoges.

In 1369, the Anglo-French Treaty of Brétigny broke down and the Hundred Years War resumed. The terms of the treaty had reflected English successes under Edward III and his son Edward the Black Prince, culminating in the spectacular victory at Poitiers in 1356 and the capture of the French king John. In order to finance his wars in Spain, the Black Prince imposed high taxes on his principality of Aquitaine, provoking the lords of this region to rise in revolt. The Valois offered considerable support in the form of French troops and finance, and rebellion became, in effect, all-out war. Things went badly for the ill-prepared English from the outset and they were forced onto the retreat. Chandos and Audley, leading English commanders and close friends of Edward, fell in the vain effort to save the principality.

Limoges was just one of the many towns and castles that went over to the French at an alarming rate. Its abrupt transference of allegiance was a particular blow for Edward, not least because it had been held for him by Bishop Jean of Cros, a previously faithful adviser and intimate who was godfather to one of the Prince's children. Froissart claims that the Black Prince 'swore on the soul of his father – an oath which he never broke – that he would attend to no other business until he had won the city back and made the traitors pay dearly for their disloyalty'.[44] As the capital of Limousin, Limoges was of central strategic importance and an early objective of the English counter-attack. It was also extremely prosperous; historians have sometimes underestimated its reputation for riches: a medieval equivalent of 'for all the tea in China' was 'for all the wealth of Limoges'. One authority has estimated that the central area of the city under siege consisted of perhaps over three thousand people, including garrison and refugees.

The siege began in mid-September 1370. The Prince took personal control of the operation, even though he was ill with disease and, says Froissart, had to be carried about on a litter. He had with him his leading nobility and just over three thousand men, split equally between cavalry, infantry and archers; but it was his miners, 'rough labourers', who proved the most effective component of his force. These had to operate quickly, as French forces were not far off. They quickly drove their mine to the city walls, and may even have had to fend off a subterranean attack: according to Froissart and the French source *The Chronicals of the First Four Valois*, the garrison commander Jean of Vinemeur 'had a countermine made, and so it came about that the miners encountered one another and attacked each other'.[45] The mine was ready within a week; when it was fired it brought a great section of wall down into the moat. The English stormed through. Froissart describes the sack that followed. The nobles and their men

> burst into the city, followed by pillagers on foot, all in a mood to wreak havoc and do murder, killing indiscriminately, for those were their orders. There were pitiful scenes. Men, women and children flung themselves on their knees before the Prince, crying: 'Have mercy on us, gentle sir!' But he was so inflamed with anger that he would not listen. Neither man nor woman was heeded, but all who could be found were put to the sword, including many who were in no way to blame. . . . Many more than 3,000 persons, men, women and children, were dragged out to have their throats cut.[46]

One contingent of English troops was given instructions to make for the Bishop's palace and seize him. He was brought before the Black Prince, who told him he would have his head cut off. The garrison commander and some of his men put up a valiant resistance before surrendering. 'But there was no respite elsewhere,' reports Froissart. 'The city of Limoges was pillaged and sacked without mercy, then burnt and utterly destroyed.'[47]

Limoges, together with Agincourt and *chevauchées*, has come to symbolize the brutality of the Hundred Years War. Yet as with so many atrocities, the extent of the slaughter has been questioned. Richard Barber has questioned the figure of 3,000; his research puts the figure at about '300, or one in ten of the population', which 'may well have been less than the number of those carrying arms in defence of the city, estimated at about 500'.[48] If this lesser figure is correct it raises an interesting but uncommented on parallel with Roman practice. Legions that were deemed not to have put up a sufficient fight were decimated: every tenth man of their number was killed as a warning to stiffen resolve when fighting the enemy in future. Was Edward consciously acting on this classical precedent? He may have deemed the punishment appropriate, as Limoges had surrendered quietly to the enemy. Whether the death toll was three hundred or the less likely three thousand, Edward was clearly issuing a dire warning to castles and towns in his principality which capitulated too readily.

English accounts play up the carnage, Walsingham writing that the Prince 'killed all those he found there, a few only being spared their lives and taken prisoner', while Chandos Herald claims 'all were killed or taken prisoner'.[49]

As with Agincourt, French sources make little of the massacre, and what little there is proves contradictory. One monk states that people were slaughtered in the churches and monasteries, places sought out for refuge and sanctuary as at Béziers, and *The Chronicle of the First Four Valois* reports that the English 'put many of the citizens to death'.[50] But a chronicle from Limoges itself informs us that 'all those of the city, men, women and clergy, were taken prisoner'.[51] Such was Edward's anger he had Limoges so comprehensively burnt that reconstruction was not completed until the sixteenth century. As Michael Jones has pointed out in his paper 'War and Fourteenth-Century France', the 'systematic destruction of whole towns or even *quartiers* was relatively rare'.[52] So if the fate of the inhabitants in any way matched that of their city, then the slaughter was indeed savage, and many non-combatants surely fell victim to the vengeful onslaught.

That Edward gave orders for no quarter at Limoges and had the city destroyed has been understood by most historians and contemporaries as complying with the laws of war against rebellious cities and judged accordingly. Of the justifications from Deuteronomy this was the most clear-cut, as Limoges was a possession of the Black Prince in his own principality. By going over to the French without a fight, Limoges had committed treason. Chandos Herald judges that 'the good city of Limoges was surrendered by treachery'.[53] Froissart has Edward calling the inhabitants 'traitors' and, even though sympathetic to their eventual plight, writes that 'the Bishop and chief citizens knew that they had acted wrongly and had incurred the Prince's wrath'.[54] A French chronicle makes clear the consequences: the English 'put many of the citizens to death, because they had turned French'.[55] Thus one historian has declared that condemnation of the event stemmed more from 'political opposition than offended sensibilities. If one condemns the Black Prince, then one condemns virtually all medieval siege commanders.'[56]

By the time Froissart was writing about Limoges, it is possible, argues one historian, to detect a growing anti-English bias. Yet his account is palpably both compassionate and perceptive on the strength of the writing alone. He observes of the citizens that 'there was nothing they could do, for they were not masters in their city', and of the English:

> I do not understand how they could have failed to take pity on people who were too unimportant to have committed treason. Yet they paid for it, and paid more dearly than the leaders who had committed it. There is no man so hard-hearted that, if he had been in Limoges on that day, and had remembered God, he would not have wept bitterly at the fearful slaughter which took place.[57]

Thus, as Christopher Allmand has indicated of Limoges, it was 'a technical treason', but no more.[58] Froissart is making the clear point that those responsible for the treason escaped lightly while the innocents were punished harshly and unfairly in a wholly unreasonable act of collective responsibility. Jean of Vinemeur and the men who surrendered while fighting after the storm were taken into honourable captivity when siege laws allowed for them to be struck down where they stood. The Bishop of Limoges did not have his head (or anything else) cut off but was moved to comfortable retirement in Avignon at the request of the Pope. It was a case of one rule for them and another rule for the others. But Deuteronomy does not provide exception clauses for class discrimination. Once again, the interpretation was made to fit the circumstances or, just as frequently, the whims of the moment. This heartless manipulation of the laws to mean whatever the victor wanted them to mean was nothing new. In his authoritative study of the law of arms and the law of treason, Matthew Strickland has astutely observed that 'sovereigns were ostensibly bent on inflicting the death penalty on those whom they regarded as rebels, guilty of withholding their rightful possessions, even if in reality these men were only loyally defending a key fortress for their own sovereign'.[59] As Michael Prestwich has accurately noted, 'Rebellion remained a useful justification for a removal of the chivalric constraints'.[60]

As already discussed in chapter two, clemency had a significant part to play in the symbolism of power politics, as Edward III displayed in the famous episode of the Burghers of Calais. The Black Prince was in no mood for such a display at Limoges and he has been condemned for his lack of pity here. John Barnie has painted a portrait of the Prince as a stern and unforgiving character, who 'waged war with a ruthlessness which terrified his enemies as much as it gladdened his allies'.[61] The Prince's image as an icon of chivalry was built on his involvement in the victories at Crécy, Poitiers and Nájera, but his reputation was built more upon his implacable style of warmongering, as exemplified by his devastating *chevauchées* and his uncompromising stance at Carcassonne in 1355 where, refusing a generous pay-off from the trembling city, he razed the suburbs to the ground. The Walsingham chronicler says that Edward had repeatedly sent messengers to the citizens of Limoges to demand that the city place itself at his mercy and inform them that failure to do so would mean the destruction of the city and its inhabitants. If so, it may have been the very harshness of his reputation that persuaded them to resist, doubting the extent of this mercy. The ordinary townspeople had no real say anyway, as Edward knew; perhaps he hoped that they would rise up against the city's leaders. Ironically the leaders who, by nature of their positions, had most to fear from submission in the form of retributive and judicial executions and hence were not inclined to savour the quality of the Prince's mercy, were the ones who escaped most lightly.

A number of factors in combination may explain the Prince's severity at Limoges. The nature of the treason, his wish to inflict punishment and his style of unrestrained warfare are three, but there are others to consider also. In the most recent study of the Black Prince, David Green hints that honour was at stake: 'The speed with which the principality fell was startling and shaming.'[62] Edward had suffered a humiliating affront to both his power and his reputation, hence retaking Limoges became a matter of honour. He was not predisposed to show leniency to the source of his great humiliation. In more basic – and perhaps more realistic – terms this comes down to a form of vengeance, which may have been fuelled further still (in an aggravating factor usually overlooked) by the loss of three friends: the Bishop to treason, and Audley and Chandos to the French when fighting against the reverses of which Limoges formed part. Nor should his illness be discounted; not because, as some historians think, that it clouded his sense of chivalry, but more because it exacerbated his brutal tendencies and added to this bitterness. Also neglected is the financial angle: the renowned wealth of Limoges obtained in the form of immediate spoils –

liquidated assets – would help finance the Black Prince's campaign to reverse his losses.

Finally, and perhaps most convincingly, it may have been a savage outlet for Edward's deep frustration at his inability – physically and militarily – to save the situation in his disappearing principality. Thus it is hard to disagree with Michael Prestwich that the slaughter at Limoges 'was suggestive of desperation'[63] or with Richard Barber's verdict that 'the very destruction of the city was an admission of weakness, that he [Edward] could not hope to re-establish his authority and had to content himself with trying to overawe his restless subjects'.[64] Just as chroniclers of the sack of Jerusalem reported that those who killed or not did so on a whim – 'as the notion took them' – so personal and petty motivations in vindictive slaughter cannot be easily discounted, even when these motivations are cloaked in the justifications of strained biblical exegesis and military reasoning.

CONCLUSIONS

Sieges prompted the worst excesses of medieval warfare simply because wars centred on the taking and keeping of strongholds. Occasionally, as we shall see in the next chapter, alternative objectives were pursued, but these were very much the exceptions to the rule. Sieges had an importance beyond the immediate geopolitical and military strategies of commanders and kings because, with towns especially, the places under siege usually held concentrations of wealth and hence plunder; and, of course, they always contained people – garrisons or citizens – that could be ransomed. On the larger scale, the spoils from such places as Carcassonne in the Albigensian Crusade could help whole campaigns keep rolling with finances and provisions; on the individual scale, the booty from such places was a huge motivating factor for the common soldier to stay with an army and fight his way into defended places. The prospect of getting rich – or, in the case of the nobility, richer still – was a driving force behind knights and foot soldiers that cannot be underestimated. No one could retire early from soldiering on wages alone, but booty and ransom could transform lives. When Southampton was taken in 1216, the *History of William*

Marshal states that 'such was the booty taken in that town that the poor folk who wished to take advantage and had their minds on profit were all made rich'.[65] In 1097 on the First Crusade, as the Battle of Dorylaeum in central Asia Minor was about to begin, Bohemond of Taranto does not put courage into his men with thoughts of winning honour or, as one might expect, spiritual rewards, but those of winning booty: 'Stand fast together united in the faith of Christ and the victory of the Holy Cross, because today, God willing, you will all be made wealthy.'[66] Recruitment to Charles the Dauphin's army shot up in 1358 when he promised his forces the spoils of Paris.

For all the adrenalin and bloodlust of soldiers storming a town, it is notable how often the ensuing sack was not utter mayhem. As we have discussed above, pillaging could be quite systematic, or even stopped altogether: when, in 1068, William the Conqueror took Exeter in south-western England, he posted guards on the city gates so that his own men could not plunder it. Four centuries later, in 1463, having taken Luxembourg, Philip the Good left his army outside the town while he went to give thanks in the main church; his men had to wait until he was finished for the order that allowed them to loot it. Of course, the prospect of booty could equally lead to a breakdown in discipline and the loss of a battle, as it did on many occasions. This loss of discipline – but not loss of victory – can be seen at Fronsac in 1451, when the lure of booty proved so strong that French soldiers fabricated a crisis to get their hands on it. The English had surrendered the southern French town on terms that guaranteed its protection against plunder. However, in the evening some French troops shouted out war cries and stampeded horses to feign cavalry movements, all to give the impression that hostilities had broken out again. As Maurice Keen relates the story, 'The French soldiers flew to arms, and the town was escaladed, and by the time their officers got onto the scene looting was in full swing, and there was not much they could do except join in. No doubt they were quite willing to do so, but if they had not arrived there might easily have been a massacre.'[67] (Note the difference from Béziers, where officers stopped the looting but not the massacre.)

Many soldiers were after not just money, but also women. The besieging forces anticipated free licence to rape following a storm. This might be actively encouraged by commanders as another way of terrorizing the enemy: submit or we will rape your wives and daughters. Alternatively, demonizing the enemy as rapists – as the Christian West did the Mongols – might encourage a more determined resistance. Sexual atrocity was also a manifestation of sadistic empowerment and revenge, as we have seen in the case discussed in the early part of this book from the Jacquerie, when a knight's pregnant wife and daughter were raped before his eyes, before all three were killed. One of the best contemporary accounts of a city being taken and ransacked comes from Roger of Wendover's detailed narrative of the fall of Lincoln in eastern England in 1217. Roger, who, as I have written elsewhere, is seriously under-utilized as a source on warfare, records what happened when royalist forces defeated the French and baronial rebels there. Note that there is no mention of bloodletting (and, like most writers of the time, Roger was never shy to lay on the gore); instead, what he gives us is perhaps a more typical example of a storm, in which booty and women take precedence:

Of the plunder and pillage of the city

After the battle was thus ended, the king's soldiers found in the city the wagons of the barons and the French, with the packhorses, loaded with baggage, silver vessels, and various kinds of furniture and utensils, all which fell into their hands without opposition. Having then plundered the whole city to the last farthing, they next pillaged the churches throughout the city, and broke open the chests and storerooms with axes and hammers, seizing on the gold and silver in them, clothes of all colours, ornaments, gold rings, goblets and jewels. Nor did the cathedral church escape this destruction, but underwent the same punishment as the rest, for the legate had given orders to knights to treat all the clergy as excommunicated men. . . . This church lost eleven thousand marks of silver. When they had thus seized on every kind of property, so that nothing remained in any corner of the houses, they each returned to their lords as rich men. . . . Many of the women of the city were drowned in the river, for, to avoid shameful offence [rape], they took to small boats with their children, female servants and household property, and perished on their journey; but there was afterwards found in the river by the searchers, goblets of silver, and many other articles of great benefit to the finders.[68]

Roger was a local man, supremely well informed on the war in England and someone was always ready to highlight the sufferings of ordinary people. Yet the only deaths he mentions at Lincoln are accidental; nothing is said of the men whom the women and children left behind; had these been executed, Roger would have told us. (Of the two other sources next closest to events, both in Old French, only one mentions booty, but neither refers to the sack.) The nature of the conflict in England may have mitigated the more fatal excesses of some other wars, as may the fact that the castle still held out, but that the whole city was under anathema stripped away a thick layer of protection. It would seem that an order for no quarter was not given. As so often with the past, we simply do not know. The most famous storms are the ones that gained notoriety by shedding the most blood; but the Middle Ages has its share of other murderous sieges that we know nothing of either because they were not recorded or because their massacres are not mentioned. More often than not, the frequency of sieges, changes of lordship and pillaging of towns have meant that the occasion is marked without much comment; the execution of a garrison or of inhabitants is more noteworthy, but not in every situation. Slaughter following storm was common but, unlike plundering, not the norm; when it happened, it was likely to be a result of either a direct policy determined for the particular siege, or, occasionally, the absence of any set policy at all. Enforced homelessness and impoverishment were often punishment enough, as Enguerrand de Monstrelet makes clear after the orderly and negotiated submission of Harfleur to Henry V in 1415:

> He then had all the nobles and men-at-arms who were in the town made prisoner, and shortly afterwards turned most of them out of the town dressed only in their doublets. . . . Next the greater part of the townsmen were made prisoner and forced to ransom themselves for large sums, then driven from the town with most of the women and children, each as they left being given five sous and part of their clothing. It was a pitiful sight to see the misery of these people as they left their town and belongings behind.[69]

The sparing of a captured place or of non-combatants was as likely to be driven by cynical motives as by humanitarian ones (much as the panegyrical apologists of princes and commanders would have us believe the latter). Carcassonne was needed as an economically viable administrative base for the crusade against the Cathars; Philip Augustus wanted the useless mouths out of the way at Château Gaillard; during his Scottish campaign of 1296, the infamously ruthless Edward I granted terms of life and limb to enemy garrisons, thereby successfully encouraging rapid capitulations on the grounds of clemency (although the citizens of Berwick were not so fortunate). But just as common was the pressure knights placed on their commanders for restraint. Until the later part of the period covered here, this can partially be explained by the fact that the knightly classes were so well known or even inter-related to each other (at Lincoln, many of the vanquished were allowed to escape because of these close connections); however, even more important was the case it made for self-preservation. Just as atrocity often became perpetuated in a spiral of vengeance, so it was hoped that clemency would be reciprocated in kind if roles were reversed at some later stage in the conflict.

Having spent nearly a year besieging Calais, Edward III was not in a merciful mood when the town fell in 1347. Sir Walter Mauny succeeded in changing his mind for purely pragmatic reasons: 'My lord, you may well be mistaken, and you are setting a bad example for us. Suppose one day you sent us to defend one of your fortresses, we should go less cheerfully if you have these people put to death, for then they would do the same to us if they had the chance.'[70] When Rochester castle fell to the ever-vindictive King John in 1215, he wanted to send the garrison to the gallows. He was advised against this move by a persuasive Savari de Mauléon, whose reasons reveal the fears and calculations of soldiers:

My lord king, our war is not yet over, therefore, you ought carefully to consider how the fortunes of war may turn; for if you now order us to hang these men, the barons, our enemies, will perhaps by a similar event take me or other nobles of your army, and, following your example, hang us; therefore do not let this happen, for in such a case no one will fight in your cause.[71]

189

Quarter or no quarter: a strategy of either might be adopted for a whole campaign or just parts of it; it could change between the two on the turn of recent events or the mood of the commander; or the one could misplace the other purely by accident or circumstance. But there can be no denying that cruelty was a constant companion to siege warfare. The extent of massacres was certainly exaggerated on many occasions as chroniclers emphasized the horrible retribution of vengeful princes that awaited their enemies, but they were frequently severe enough to do their job: demoralize enemy garrisons and terrify them into submission. If the soldier did not hesitate to act brutally in siege situations, it might be because he himself could expect to be treated in the same way. Cruelty was not reserved for the intimidation of non-combatants alone. Garrisons were commonly threatened with the worst if they resisted.

These threats were not always carried out, but that was a big risk for a garrison to take. When the Duke of Bourbon arrived before the walls of the Poitevin town of Moléon in 1381, he offered the fortress one chance to surrender; if it did not do so immediately, all would be hung as an example to others who might consider resistance. The garrison did not hesitate to comply. In 1224 Henry III warned the garrison at Bedford that they faced the gallows if they continued to defend the castle. When the castle was stormed, the garrison was beaten and then hung. (The Dunstable annalist puts the figure at over eighty knights and sergeants, though it may have been as 'low' as twenty-four; three were cut down and spared on the intercession of Henry's nobles.) Henry was nipping a potentially serious problem in the bud – Bedford offered a rallying point for discontents – by acting decisively and sending out a message of no compromise to opponents.

Minatory words were backed up with minatory action. William the Conqueror's reputation as a ruthless war leader was built during his time fighting in his duchy of Normandy. In 1049, he took a fort by Alençon in north-western France and, in an act considered savage at the time, the defenders had their hands and feet amputated. As John Gillingham notes, 'William's ferocity persuaded the citizens of Alençon that, if they wished to retain their hands and feet, they had better surrender at once. Equally impressed, the garrison of Domfront also decided to yield.'[72]

Barbaric practices such as these can be seen being applied wherever and whenever Latin armies (or any others for that matter, be they

Muslim, Mongol, Chinese or whomsoever) were engaged in siege warfare; there appear to be no geographical exceptions, only individual ones: England, for example, simply has fewer extreme examples recorded. This is not to say that cruelty was always used, but that it was employed regularly enough to be commonplace. On the First Crusade, crusaders stuck the heads of dead Muslims on poles in front of the garrisons at Nicaea and Antioch; Saladin similarly impaled crusaders' heads at Tiberias during the Third Crusade. At Ascalon in 1153, defenders suspended the corpses of besiegers from the walls. In 1209 on the Albigensian Crusade, Simon de Montfort took the castle of Bram and mutilated its garrison by cutting off the upper lip and nose of each man, and putting out their eyes, except for one whom he left with a single eye to guide them to the next fortress that Montfort planned to besiege (see also chapter two). This was both a warning and a retaliation for similar treatment meted out to his own men. During the Reconquista in the thirteenth century, James I of Aragon catapulted the head of a Muslim captive over the walls of Palma before massacring its inhabitants, while at Lisbon the heads of eighty Muslims were impaled on stakes. At La Roche-Guyon in 1109, Louis VI had the castrated and disembowelled corpses of the garrison (the leader's heart was stuck on a pole) floated on specially constructed rafts down the Seine to Rouen to demonstrate how the king extracted his vengeance. Edward III hung hostages before the eyes of Berwick's citizens in 1333. And in 1344 a secret messenger from the English garrison at Auberoche in Gascony attempted to slip through French lines; he was caught and, while still alive, strapped to a siege machine and catapulted over the walls back into Auberoche.

The Hohenstaufen emperors of Germany seemed to have a particular penchant for cruelty at sieges. At Brescia in 1238, Frederick II tied hostages to his siege machines to try and prevent the besieged from bombarding them. Undeterred, the Brescians created a buffer zone by lowering live imperial prisoners down their walls directly in front of Frederick's battering rams. The investment at Crema in Lombardy in 1159 was particularly horrific, and reveals how a cycle of atrocity fed on itself. Otto of Freising tells us what happened after Frederick Barbarossa's imperial troops killed some of Crema's garrison as they made a sortie: 'It was a pitiable sight when those outside cut off the heads of the slain and played ball with them, tossing them from the right hand into the left, and used them in mocking display. But those in the town, thinking it shameful to dare less, afforded a heart-rending spectacle by tearing limb from limb upon their walls prisoners from our army, without mercy.'[73]

Frederick then ordered other captives to be hung on gallows in view of the town; the besieged did the same with their prisoners on their walls. Frederick then had forty more prisoners hung, including knights and others of high standing. It was said that the defenders carefully scalped a knight and, combing his hair carefully, attached it to his helmet; another had his hands and feet cut off, and was left to crawl in the streets. In a vain attempt to counter the missiles from the town's mangonels destroying his own siege tower, Frederick had hostages tied to it as human shields, 'And so several youths died miserably, struck by the stones, while others, though remaining alive, suffered yet more pitifully, hanging there and expecting a most cruel death and the horror of so dire a fate.'[74] 'In tears', the defenders 'struck the bodies of their comrades. . . . They crushed their chests, their stomachs and their heads, and bone and mushy brain were mixed together. It was a savage, horrid thing to see.'[75] Despite all this, Frederick claimed he was acting 'in all things in accordance with the laws of the war' [76] which further goes to show just how meaningless – and flexible – these laws could be.

In this climate of extreme violence, it is not surprising that non-combatants struggled to evade the excesses of military operations. Their ordeal at a time of siege was highly precarious: blockade brought with it the fear of famine and disease; defeat the prospect of ransom and becoming a destitute refugee; and storming raised the spectre of widespread slaughter. That the last of these presented less of a possibility than the first two does not diminish its threat, as, if it did occur, it could claim as many – or even more – lives in one fell swoop. When towns and cities were besieged, the number of non-combatants exceeded the numbers making up the garrison, and so the miseries of siege warfare fell disproportionately on these citizens – an inversion of battles and a world away from the chivalric image of two knights engaged in single combat on a battlefield.

The fate of the 'useless mouths' at Château Gaillard reflects the agonies of hunger and frightened vulnerability that befell many besieged non-belligerents. Such scenes were repeated throughout the Middle Ages and were probably more common than massacres. We see the same thing happening at Faenza in Italy in 1240–1, at Calais in 1346–7 (where some refugees were allowed through the lines, but another 500 were trapped and left to their fate in front of the town walls), and at Rouen in 1418–19. In each case the commander refusing egress for the useless mouths in no-man's-land – Frederick II, Edward III and Henry V – was regarded as a paragon of chivalric virtue, an exemplar of supreme knighthood. Yet their actions in war, and at sieges in particular, are a world away from the one inhabited by the idealized knight who protects women, the weak and the vulnerable. The victims who died of starvation in these situations were no less the victims of atrocity than those who were put to the sword after a sack; it was just easier to transfer all the responsibility to the enemy, especially to the garrison commander who ejected them, for it was his charge to protect these people.

Let us end this chapter with the plight of the people of Rouen, under siege by Henry V's English forces through the winter of 1418 to January 1419. Henry's blockade was rigorously enforced and the siege viciously prosecuted on both sides. Henry hung his prisoners from gallows. The French, more inventively, hung theirs from their battlements with dogs strung around their necks, or sewed them into sacks with dogs and cast them into the Seine (both common modes of executions for criminals, as discussed in chapter one). Famine and disease broke out in the city and corpses were piled high. The cost of food underwent hyperinflation. John Page, present at the siege, wrote of the inhabitants: 'They ate up dogs, they ate up cats; / They ate up mice, horses and rats.' Cats went for two nobles, a mouse for sixpence, a rat for thirty pennies, while a dog or horse's head went for half a pound. Young girls offered themselves up for bread. There was talk of cannibalism. Like so many of the contemporary writers we have drawn on, Page expresses with real pity and feeling the plight of the citizens; that they represented the enemy in no way mitigates his sympathy for them, or his understanding of how the degrading, dehumanizing effect of hunger was as pernicious as the physical peril:

> They died so fast on every day
> That men could not all of them in earth lay.
> Even if a child should otherwise be dead,
> The mother would not give it bread.

> Nor would a child to its mother give.
> Everyone tried himself to live
> As long as he could last.
> Love and kindness both were past.

As the siege wore on, the garrison leader, Guy le Bouteiller, evicted the useless mouths. Henry refused to let them through his lines and they were left to die in the ditch before the walls. Despite this, Page still considered Henry 'the royallest prince in Christendom'. After all, it was the garrison commander who had sent out these people. Besides, the magnanimous and compassionate Henry even had some food passed to the useless mouths on Christmas Day to celebrate the Nativity. The calculated callousness of medieval commanders in pursuing the military imperative is daunting and unnerving. Would not a quick death by the sword have been more merciful for these wretches? Ironically, that would have been harder to justify. Whether by sword, by fire or by famine, the consequences were equally inevitable, as Page movingly describes:

> There men might see a great pity,
> A child of two years or three
> Go about and beg his bread,
> For father and mother both were dead.
> . . .
> Some had starved in that place to death,
> And some had stopped by eyes and breath,
> And some were crooked in their knees,
> And were now as lean as any trees.
> You saw a woman hold in her arm
> Her own dead child, with nothing warm,
> And babies sucking on the pap
> Within a dead woman's lap.
> There might find it last arrive
> That twelve were dead to one alive.
> And the dead knew nought of death
> So secretly they gave up their breath
> Without a noise or any cry,
> So if they slept, so did they die.[77]

5

CAMPAIGNS

After battles, captive soldiers who became non-combatants by virtue of their prisoner status were nonetheless commonly killed. Sieges witnessed the deaths of many civilians as they became inadvertently caught up in wars and the line between belligerent and non-belligerent became blurred (sometimes conveniently or deliberately so). But in most campaigns, there was no ambiguity whatsoever: the civilian population became a clearly defined target. This did not necessarily mean that other military objectives were any less important – strategy still ultimately resolved on castles and towns – but that taking war to the civilian populations beyond the protective walls of towns was an essential part of the war-making process. While some communities could escape the ravages of war untouched, others were, quite literally, devastated by them. The frequency of wars and their geographical extent could make them hard to avoid.

CAMPAIGNS IN MEDIEVAL WARFARE

Contrary to received wisdom, campaigning was not exclusively a seasonal occupation between spring (post-Easter) and harvest. The psycho-belligerent Bertran de Born would yearn for springtime not for the colourful flowers popping up everywhere, but for the colourful war banners being raised and unfurled. For some expeditions, weather and the agricultural cycle were indeed limiting factors, but for others they were not major considerations. Many campaigns started in November and January (as we shall see in the cases investigated below).

A familiar pattern is drawn out by Count Philip of Flanders' invasion of Picardy at the end of November, 1181, while Philip Augustus was campaigning in Champagne; following a Christmas truce, Franco-Flemish hostilities resumed in mid-January.

The launching of military operations at these times probably reflects a last push for gains and a strengthening of hands in the traditional Christmas round of peace talks and armistices, or an early start to the new campaign season to make gains before Easter. (Not that either Christmas or even Easter, the holiest time of the year, could guarantee a temporary cessation of military operations, as the devoutly bellicose Simon de Montfort displayed at Rochester in 1264.) Winter conditions could obviously be detrimental to expeditions, but summer campaigning was not ideal either: it ensured better food supplies and greater damage against the enemy, but also brought with it water shortages, dehydration and heat exhaustion. When Louis VI prepared his army for battle at Reims in August 1124, he formed wagons into circles where his men could retire from combat for water and rest.

As noted in the previous chapter, to follow a campaign is to follow the progress of an army from town to town, and from castle to castle. As always, there are exceptions to the rule, but these usually serve to highlight them. Smaller twelfth-century castles in northern England were frequently abandoned in advance of Scottish invasions through lack of preparation or relative weakness against opposition forces that were considered too strong for the castle's defences; the result was an operational focus on the more significant fortresses. The grand *chevauchées* (literally 'rides') of the English during the Hundred Years War were not sustained, despite their early successes; instead, the end of the conflict was heralded from the 1430s when stronghold after stronghold fell to the French as they picked them off one by one; such was the momentum gained that by the last French campaign of 1449–50, most fortresses simply submitted without resistance. Only a relatively few major sieges made medieval warfare periodically static; in reality, progress from one enemy stronghold to another could be very rapid.

The movement of one army necessitated counter-movements by its enemy, thus the warfare of the time could be extremely fluid, with armies always on the march. In 1216, King John employed diversionary tactics throughout eastern and southern England to draw enemy forces away from besieging his royal castles at Dover and Windsor. The rebels responded to this by attempting to cut off the King's retreat as he progressed along the Suffolk coast; they marched towards Cambridge to effect this, but John, on receiving intelligence, withdrew to Stamford. Here he heard that Lincoln was under siege and marched north to its relief; the rebels there moved on. Meanwhile, the rebel force that had failed to catch up with the King returned to London with the booty from their campaign. From here they proceeded to help their forces at Dover. And so it went on. The focus on strongholds actually made medieval warfare extremely dynamic. This combination of rapid and frequent movement of armies with year-round warfare meant that rural populations often found themselves in the path of the Mars juggernaut.

For the peasantry and inhabitants of undefended towns that lay in the way of armies as they moved from one theatre of war to another, there was good reason for trepidation. Even a small army on the move was an impressive sight, but a larger one was an enormous undertaking entailing a huge allocation of finance and resources, brought together through complex organization. For England in the Wars of the Roses, one historian has assessed that 'an army of 10,000 combatants plus several thousand non-combatants would be like one of the kingdom's major cities on the move'.[1] Even if a reasonably disciplined army were marching in peacetime, as through Europe on the way to the crusades, then the impact of such a large force on the rural community of villages and hamlets along its route would be enormous. This impact could be either relatively positive, through the market for food and goods, or negative, should military requisitioning be onerous and appropriating (medieval sources attest to loud complaints against princes' itinerant courts); but in a time of war and exigency, the swamping of an area with soldiers geared to combat brought with it justifiable fear and apprehension. These emotions escalated to terror when the soldiers served under the flags of opposing powers.

RAVAGING

What scared non-belligerents most was ravaging and its consequences: fear of death by the sword; fear of starvation from destroyed or seized crops; fear of captivity and ransom; fear of impoverishment from the destruction of their homes and their belongings being stolen. In other words, they shared the same dread as the inhabitants of a besieged town. A brief look at two campaigns reveals how ravaging was integral to an army on the march in contested territory.

During the dying days of Henry II's reign, Anglo-French conflict entered another phase. In July 1188, Henry crossed to Normandy with a large number of men. Philip Augustus dismissed the demands of high-level ambassadors sent by Henry and prepared for war. Philip's first action was to unleash a series of independent plundering expeditions into enemy territory. Bishop Philip of Beauvais, the French King's cousin, entered Normandy, where he burnt Aumale and 'other castles and towns, killed many men, and seized booty'.[2] Philip led his forces to Vendôme, which he captured, and marched towards Le Mans, torching villages along the way. Angevin forces under Duke Richard regained some land; by mid-August he had retaken Vendôme and razed it. Henry's contribution was to march along the border to Gisors, burning all in his path. Peace talks at Gisors failed and the war continued.

The first campaign of substance in the Hundred Years War was led by Edward III in 1339. It started with the failure to take Cambrai in northern France: logistical problems and the city's strength forced the English to lift the siege after nearly three weeks. Adopting an alternative strategy, they went on a cavalcade (*chevauchée*) across the region, incendiaries destroying something approaching two hundred villages and towns. Edward was attempting to goad the French into battle, but Philip VI of France refused to pick up the gauntlet. Instead, his forces prevented supplies reaching Edward's men while at the same time devastating his own lands in a deliberate scorched-earth policy, so as to deny the English resources from the land. As the leading authority on Edwardian warfare has noted, 'The campaign simply fizzled out. Philip had suffered a severe blow to his reputation, but Edward had expended a huge fortune and a full campaigning season without making any concrete gains'.[3]

Campaigns, especially when smaller in scale, took on the nature more of raids than of military expeditions. Yet, as the *chevauchées* of the Black Prince show, raiding and campaigning were often synonymous; it was a rare expedition indeed that did not embark upon widespread ravaging or take on the characteristics of raiding. Contemporary writings on war are replete with the advice that the successful waging of war relied upon ravaging. In the late twelfth century, Jordan Fantosme has the veteran warrior Count Philip recommending to King Louis VII of France that his ally, King William of Scotland, should invade England in the following way: 'Let him destroy your enemy and lay waste their land: let it all be consumed in fire and flames! Let him not leave them, outside their castles, in wood or meadow, as much as will furnish them a meal on the morrow. Then let him assemble his men and lay siege to their castles ... This is the way to fight them, to my way of thinking: first lay waste the land, then destroy one's enemies.'[4]

As Fantosme makes clear earlier in his chronicle, this was exactly how Count Philip waged his own wars, and to great effect. A military treatise written by Pierre Dubois in 1300, the *Doctrine of Successful Expeditions and Shortened Wars*, advocated complete abstention from sieges and battles, and instead the undertaking of a policy of sustained depredation in the countryside.

The consequences of ravaging to the rural population could be calamitous, as contemporary observers attest, especially the devastation wrought during the Hundred Years War. In the early fifteenth century, Thomas Basin wrote: 'From the Loire to the Seine the peasants have been slain or put to flight. We ourselves have seen vast empty plains absolutely deserted, uncultivated, abandoned, empty of inhabitants, covered with bushes and bramble.'[5]

These examples come from a period when the English were implementing a scorched-earth policy against a resurgent enemy. Yet the scenes they describe were repeated throughout the entire Middle Ages and are recorded in contemporary accounts in strikingly familiar terms, for ravaging was a constant of warfare. Over two centuries earlier, the *Chansons des Lorrains* vividly captured in words the incursion of a foreign army and how it affected non-combatants:

They start to march. The scouts and incendiaries lead; after them come the foragers who are to gather the spoils and carry them in the great baggage train. The tumult begins. The peasants, having just come out to the fields, turn back, uttering loud cries; the shepherds gather their flocks and drive them towards the neighbouring woods in the hope of saving them. The incendiaries set the villages on fire, and the foragers visit and sack them; the terrified inhabitants are burnt or led apart with their hands tied to be held for ransom. Everywhere alarm bells ring, fear spreads from side to side and becomes widespread. On all sides one sees helmets shining, pennons floating, and horsemen covering the plain. Here hands are laid on money; there cattle, donkeys and flocks are seized. The smoke spreads, the flames rise, and the peasants and shepherds flee in panic in all directions.[6]

The association of armies with such wanton destruction has helped to perpetuate Charles Oman's view that medieval 'strategy – the higher branch of the military art – was absolutely nonexistent. An invading army moved into hostile territory, not in order to strike at some great strategical point, *but merely to burn and harry the land'* (my emphasis).[7] Yet the details in the above passages adumbrate a military logic behind the ravaging that belies the oversimplified image of blundering, plundering armies staggering incontinently across the land. When the smoke clears, the reasons behind the fires manifest themselves.

William the Conqueror's Harrying of the North, 1069–70

William the Conqueror was one of the most successful – and ruthless – military commanders of the Middle Ages. With daring and great tactical skill, and also with masterly logistical organization, he won the Crown of England in that most famous of years, 1066. Winning the kingdom itself took somewhat longer, and involved a number of major campaigns across the length and breadth of a recalcitrant England as he fought to impose his authority on his conquest. This was 'government by punitive expedition'. [8] The most punishing of these was his operation in Northumbria and beyond over the winter of 1069–70. An Anglo-Saxon historian has noted: 'The Harrying of the North is perhaps the best known incident of William I's reign after the battle of Hastings itself. It received almost universal condemnation, at the time and later, but its actual effects are difficult to gauge.'[9]

William was kept busy by troubles in his duchy of Normandy, by the Welsh, by the Scots, by the English resistance and by the Danes, who felt that England was their rightful inheritance. Semi-independent and secessionist by nature, the North posed real difficulties for William and occupied much of his time. The great threat was the potential for northern discontents to ally with the Danes: a formidable challenge in its own right, but one heightened by the inevitable rebellions it would ignite around the country, leaving the Normans exposed and fighting on all fronts. This was the reality facing William in the late summer of 1069, when King Sven of Denmark launched a major expeditionary force to England, consisting of 240 ships under his sons and brother. Starting with Kent, the fleet made its way up to the Humber, raiding the east coast along its way. When there, it formed a base, probably in readiness for further Danish troops and a full-scale invasion, and precipitated a widespread uprising in Yorkshire. An Anglo-Danish force marched on York and took the city on 20 September, with few from the Norman garrison surviving the encounter. This was a major setback for William, 'the heaviest defeat which the Normans ever suffered in England',[10] and it represented the greatest emergency of his short reign so far. Revolts broke out across England, especially in the West and North-West, with Yorkshire being the political epicentre. There was a real possibility of a separate, hostile kingdom establishing itself in the North. 'The magnitude of the crisis indicates the importance of the ensuing campaign, and explains (though it does not excuse) its terrible sequel.'[11] William led a forced march north, causing the Anglo-Danish forces to retreat back to the Humber. He then headed west to deal with the uprising in Staffordshire while Norman divisions remaining in Lincoln decisively repulsed a move southwards by the leading Anglo-Saxon noble, Edgar the Atheling. Contained in the North, the Danes exploited William's absence to reoccupy York. William was by now in Nottingham, where he heard news of Danish preparations for York. Fighting his way across the Aire, he made for the city, by now in Danish hands, and 'plundered and utterly lay waste' the regions he passed through, effectively marking the start of the Harrying of the North.[12]

Instead of assaulting York, William repeated the successful strategy he had employed to bring London under subjugation in 1066: he ravaged the territory around the city, especially to the north and west. By so doing, he isolated York and limited the supplies that would reach its garrison and the Danish army in general. Pressures of time and manpower in the face of great unrest across the country denied William the option of a thorough investment of the city; besides, the presence of a large enemy force in the region would have made a siege a risky enterprise. The Danes withdrew to their base and William spent Christmas in the burned-out city, which had been torched in September. In an act designed to symbolize his regal authority, he had his royal paraphernalia brought up from Winchester so that the resplendent display would make an important political statement. Norman messengers sent by William to the Danish leadership offered an officially sanctioned bribe and liberty to forage along the coastline on condition that the army remained in the same area until the better weather of spring permitted a safe sea journey home. The offer was accepted (but not honoured when winter had finished). This temporary truce freed William to deal once again with a resurgence of resistance in Chester, the hardest part of which was a gruelling but impressive march across the Pennines in the heart of winter. The forces he left behind in Yorkshire executed his explicit and chilling orders to devastate the North.

The Danes agreed to the terms, as they were running desperately short of provisions on the Humber. Not only had the depredations of the Normans greatly aggravated their situation, but the region was still reeling from William's ravages at the beginning of the year, when he had laid waste the area in response to another rising in which Durham had been temporarily lost and some of his leading magnates killed. There is much to recommend the accepted sequence of events related in the above paragraph, but David Douglas's alternative timing is also worthy of consideration: that the Danes agreed to being bought off after William had subdued the Chester rebellion, as they saw their last English allies succumb to the Conqueror. This possibility should be born in mind when we consider the reason for William's savage destruction of the northern countryside.

The King sent out contingents of troops to devastate the region in a systematic and thorough fashion. Some sources mention it in a cursory fashion. The Anglo-Saxon Chronicle baldly states that 'King William marched into that shire and completely devastated it,' and that he 'plundered and utterly lay waste the shire'.[13] Henry of Huntingdon makes only an oblique reference to events: the King 'destroyed the English of that province'.[14] Hugh the Chantor records that 'York and the whole district round it' was 'destroyed by the Normans with sword, famine and flame' and offers some details of church destruction.[15]

If this were all that historians had to go on, the Harrying of the North would not, even with oral history, have become such a notorious event. But the harrying made more of an impression on other chroniclers, mainly writing in the early twelfth century, who were appalled by what had occurred. John ('Florence') of Worcester seems to have had access to a lost version of the Anglo-Saxon Chronicle, and his slightly longer report was important in influencing other chroniclers, who would embellish or add to his account with their own knowledge, sometimes supplemented by local testimony, verbal tradition and knowledge. John tells us that William assembled his army and 'hastened, with an angry heart, into Northumbria, where he did not cease for the whole winter to lay waste the land, to murder the inhabitants, and to inflict numerous injuries'. More tellingly, he describes the cumulative consequences of William's strategy of ravaging: '[S]o great a famine prevailed that men were forced to consume the flesh of horses, dogs, cats, and even that of human beings.'[16] William of Malmesbury writes that William 'ordered both the towns and fields of the whole district to be laid waste; the fruits and grain to be destroyed by fire or by water', adding that 'fire, slaughter and devastation' had left 'the ground, for more than sixty miles around, totally uncultivated and barren, remaining bare even to this present day'.[17]

Simeon of Durham, in keeping with the trend to become less restrained the further the writer was in time from events, augments John of Worcester's account with grim details. Corpses lay rotting in houses and in the streets, 'for no one was left to bury them, all being cut down either by the sword or by famine'; survivors fled in search of food or sold themselves into slavery; the land was therefore left without anyone to cultivate it for nine years; 'the dwellings were everywhere deserted, the inhabitants seeking safety in flight, or lying hidden in the woods or the fastness of the mountains'; no village between Durham and York remained inhabited.[18] It is little wonder that one of the Latin verbs used by writers to describe ravaging is *depopulare*. But the most vivid and passionate detailed narrative, and the one by which the harrying has become so infamous, stems from the quill of Orderic Vitalis. William

continued to comb forests and remote mountainous places, stopping at nothing to hunt out the enemy hidden there. His camps were spread out over an area of a hundred miles. He cut down many in his vengeance; destroyed the lairs of others; harried the land, and burned homes to ashes. Nowhere else had William shown such cruelty. Shamefully he succumbed to this vice, for he made no effort to restrain his fury and punished the innocent with the guilty. In his anger he commanded that all crops and herds, chattels and food of every kind should be brought together and burned to ashes with consuming fire, so that the whole region north of the Humber might be stripped of all means of sustenance. In consequence, so serious a scarcity was felt in England, and so terrible a famine fell upon the homeless and defenceless, that more than 100,000 Christian folk of both sexes, young and old alike, perished of hunger. My narrative has frequently had occasion to praise William, but for this act which condemned the innocent and guilty alike to die by slow starvation I cannot commend him.

Orderic goes on to lament the deaths of 'helpless children' and others, all the result of William's act of 'infamy' in initiating this 'brutal slaughter'.[19] Orderic may have been writing some sixty years after the events he describes, but as Ann Williams notes, 'He was born in Shropshire in 1075 and spent the first ten years of his life there, while memories of the Harrying of the North, and of Mercia, were still fresh. Orderic may well have heard tales from those who suffered from it'.[20] (The importance of oral tradition is increasingly being recognized by many medievalists.)

Some historians have tended to play down these reports as typical monkish hyperbole; however, just as this criticism has been overdone for clerics writing on war, so it is here, too. Undoubtedly, there is exaggeration, especially in Orderic's figure of over a hundred thousand dead, but there is more of substance than just the anti-Norman prejudice of a conquered people. William of Malmesbury warns against reproaching the king out of 'national hatred'; he, for his part, with both English and Norman blood flowing in his veins, vows not to conceal any of William's 'good deeds' or 'bad conduct'.[21] And Orderic himself went native in Normandy, having spent his entire life there after he was ten. The taciturnity of contemporary Norman sources also suggests that William's actions were so extreme they were best glossed over. It has rightly been noticed that the Anglo-Saxon Chronicle's brief remarks on the harrying are less dramatic than the more detailed and violent comments on the Danish ravaging of 1066. This may simply be a case of inconsistency in the chronicle, although it could be explained on other grounds: the Viking legacy in England was one of pagan pillaging; in some respects, Denmark was still missionary territory; and in 1066 William had not yet had the chance to plunder English monasteries (as he was to in 1070).

The English sources stress the effects of famine above all else; this was the worst killer. The Normans 'massacred many peasants outright, but the large number who must have escaped were ultimately doomed as completely'.[22] Ravaging in summer meant torching fields of crops; in winter it meant destroying stockpiles of food and grain stored from the last harvest for consumption in these very months of scarcity. The destruction of agricultural implements and corn for sowing compounded the loss by removing the very means to prepare for the next harvest, further adding to the sense of despair and futility by extending the famine for another year. Those that were able fled before the Normans targeted their villages, taking to the hills and forests with what they could. No wonder fear, fire and famine depopulated the area so catastrophically. Sixteen years on, the Domesday Book was reporting large expanses as still derelict. Refugees spread far and wide. Some travelled as far south as Evesham, where they were taken in by the abbey, thereby further contributing to the dissemination of news of the disaster through the monastic network.

Some historians who have taken the exaggerations of the chroniclers as an admonition to question the extreme severity of the harrying have also re-examined the Domesday Book evidence of 1086. This national survey of land ownership and values for tax offers a rare, official quantification of the state of holdings in the shires. The Domesday Book reveals many entries for 'waste' in the counties of the North and the Midlands, and this is taken as being indicative of damages caused by war. Thus, it is sometimes considered that the trail of destruction caused by a ravaging army on the move can be traced by the Domesday record. But recent scholarship has suggested that 'waste' was probably just an administrative term for financial imbalances that owed little to warfare, and, as a study of William's depredations around London in 1066 concludes, the 'assumption that war damage inflicts characteristic patterns which can almost always be detected in the record of

Domesday valuations is flawed'.[23] (However, Pipe Roll records from the reigns of Henry II and John tend to make the connection of waste to military activity more explicitly.) Despite the fact that Domesday attests to almost fifty per cent of Yorkshire being classified as waste or as being without resources sixteen years after the harrying, the extent of William's campaign of 1069–70 is still regarded sceptically by some.

However, more recent scholarship still, in the form of an important article by John Palmer on Domesday waste and the Harrying of the North, concludes that, as a result of military activity, 'the losses in Yorkshire were truly staggering'.[24] Different places recovered from the effects of the ravaging at different rates: in some cases, especially in the West, recovery occurred after a couple of years; in Yorkshire, it sometimes took decades. The French historian Robert Fossier actually believed that ravaging could be good for the land, with the ashes helping next year's productivity (farmers, after all, seasonally clear the post-harvest stubble off their fields by burning it). It is right to declare, as some have, that the medieval landscape was remarkably resilient; but that slightly misses the point. It was not the land that suffered so grievously, but its people. The depopulated area described by the chronicles could not tend itself. Survivors fled the region because they wished to avoid the initial onslaught, or because they feared more to come, and because there was little to stay for after the destruction. They did not return any time soon because they waited for the Normans to finish their operations and, with little if anything sown, there was nothing to sustain them if they did go back. Manors that did recover more quickly may have been those considered safe for an early return of tenants, or owned by lords who had access to resources that could facilitate recovery.

The harrying extended beyond Yorkshire to Shropshire, Staffordshire, Cheshire and Derbyshire. William's strategy specifically targeted the rural population; it was a military campaign not against castles or armies, but against non-combatants. There are two main reasons given to explain the severity of the campaign. The first and most widely countenanced is that William wanted to ensure that Northumbria would be in no position to threaten rebellion again for a very long time, and thereby crush any thought of separatism. By destroying the land and its produce, William was denying enemy forces provisions for an army in the field and crippling the infrastructure that provided the economic support for waging war. It is also worth adding that by depopulating the area he was scattering the manpower that might otherwise be recruited into an enemy army. There is some dispute as to how far the lands of the native aristocracy were targeted: that a particular estate one would have expected to be attacked can be seen to be doing well in the Domesday Book might suggest that the harrying was not as extensive as has been made out. But the richer estates are the very ones where the owners had the resources mentioned above to promote a faster recovery, especially when the magnates had come to an accommodation, temporary or otherwise, with William, and the complex web of politics, patronage and expediency was spun anew. Besides, as Palmer has noted, not only did the majority of the lands devastated in Yorkshire belong to rebel leaders, they were also hit hard.

The second reason for William's action is more compelling in my view. This explanation affords greater priority to the Danish threat. For William, a rebellion in England was far more serious when it was backed up with the considerable military capability of another state. The devastation of Yorkshire would equally deny an invading army the supplies necessary to sustain a campaign. The Count of Toulouse employed a scorched-earth policy in retreat from the advancing French during the Albigensian Crusade in 1226, denying them supplies for the crusaders and, critically, their animals. As mentioned above, Philip VI acted similarly in 1339 with the Black Prince. With its North Sea coastline, strength of resistance to Norman hegemony, and its distance from William's relatively secure base in the South, Yorkshire's seaboard offered Danish fleets an obvious bridgehead for operations in England.

It is no surprise that the Danish forces bottled in at the Humber came to terms with William when supplies disappeared along with allies. William's ravaging of the hinterland must have had in mind the need to dissuade the Danes on the Humber from making incursions back into the volatile region when spring came. Without the ability to forage and live off the land, any Danish operations would have been highly impracticable; when the Danes reneged on their deal with William, and King Sven sailed to the Danes on the Humber in the spring of 1070 (rather than the other way round as was the agreement), it is a measure of the success of William's ruthless campaign that they sailed down the coast and moved their new offensive southwards into East Anglia. As Stephen Morillo has explained, the fleet-based army of the Danes was unlike a baronial or continental one that could be contained in a base such as a town or a castle; the presence of ships gave it the freedom and mobility to withdraw and turn up somewhere else. Thus we may deduce that in comprehensively ravaging Yorkshire, William was ensuring that any future Danish fleet arriving there would be met with a barren wasteland incapable of supporting an invading army. William of Malmesbury actually makes this point in his *History*, writing that William ordered the coastal districts to be especially targeted. Yes, the Danes would appear elsewhere, but crucially it would not be to join up with allies in the hostile, inflammatory and separatist North. This was William's primary objective, and this is what the Harrying of the North achieved.

Historians have recognized the outstanding military achievements of William's early campaigns as king of England. The Harrying of the North did succeed in preventing any further rebellions: there were no more general uprisings during his reign. The Danish problem remained, but greatly diminished as the Norse were denied allies of substance and a northern power base to support them in England. The campaign of 1069–70 sealed William's conquest of England that had begun in 1066. The terrible devastation wrought by William was not just a military victory that spectacularly achieved its objectives, it was also 'an act of state, of a sort not confined to any period, and the political reasons at the time no doubt seemed as compelling as such reasons always do'.[25]

King David's Scottish Invasions, 1138

The marcher regions of the North were a problem for English kings throughout the Middle Ages and beyond. In 1138 the largest and most serious Scottish incursions across the border yet to occur were launched, prompting a chronicler of the time to write, 'The root and origin of all evil arose in that part of England called Northumbria to produce plunder and arson, strife and war'.[26] King David I of Scotland led no less than three invasions of England in the first half of that year (January, April and July), leaving the North in a constant state of war or war readiness. David has the reputation of being a conventionally pious king and statesman, 'the real architect of the medieval Scottish kingdom' over which his long reign exerted impressive 'civilising influences', and who 'ostentatiously adhered to the chivalric conventions of Anglo-Norman warfare'.[27] Yet these invasions marked a new level of savagery in the already bitter Anglo-Scottish conflict.

The present border with Scotland is rather different from that of the fluctuating one in the twelfth century. Scottish kings had genuine claims to much of the North of England, and in 1136 and 1138 David took advantage of the turmoil in England to assert his rights in Northumbria and Cumbria. This turmoil has defined the reign of Stephen of England. Following Henry I's death, in December 1135, Stephen seized the crown (and, just as vitally, the treasury) to usurp the anointed successor, Henry's daughter Matilda. Matilda was married to Count Goffrey of Anjou, one of the most powerful magnates in France, who put his huge resources behind Matilda's military attempts to sit on the throne as queen of England. To make matters worse for Stephen, David was Matilda's uncle. The death of a king was a traditional time of political unrest and the troubles built up to a storm that unleashed itself against Stephen in 1136 on all fronts: an Angevin incursion into Normandy, risings in Wales, trouble in the South-West, and invasions in the North. With each of the enemies taking strategic advantage from the movements of the others, Stephen became so hard pressed he had to 'let Wales and the Marches run riot in 1136',[28] leading to the worst Norman defeats in Wales for forty years. Instead, he led substantial armies against the rebels in the West Country and against the Scots in the North (he was to do the same again in 1138). Even his foes recognized Stephen's bravery and martial ability, most famously displayed before his capture at the battle of Lincoln in 1141; Stephen needed both in abundance, especially in the early years of his reign.

The Scottish invasion of 1136 (actually begun in the last week of December 1135) was a major affair, eliciting from Stephen a response that saw him march to Durham 'with an army that was greater than any in living memory in England'.[29] By this time (early February), David had already taken five major castles, but the sheer size of Stephen's host cowed the Scottish king into negotiation. The result was the first treaty of Durham, which gave to David the reward of Doncaster and Carlisle, while granting an early, and therefore important, success to Stephen. A few chronicles make a perfunctory mention of the military campaign. One notes that David ravaged and laid waste many districts, but, unlike accounts from Wales in the same year, there is no talk of atrocities. It was a very different story two years later.

The truce arranged at Durham expired in December 1137. The question of Northumbria needed addressing, but Stephen refused to entertain any thought of discussing the matter. War inevitably, and quickly, followed; David invaded England in mid-January. As we shall shortly see, the campaign marked an escalation in outright savagery. After a costly and fruitless siege at Wark, the Scottish king moved southwards, leaving a small force behind to contain the garrison and thereby safeguard his line of communications. While moving into the area north of Durham, David halted his brutal ravaging campaign and retreated on hearing of Stephen's approach in early February. Stephen raised the siege at Wark and embarked on some ravaging of his own in the Lowlands, only to return suddenly to England, probably due to a lack of supplies (although one chronicle hints, with some plausibility, that Stephen was not entirely certain of some of his leading men's loyalty).

David marched back into Northumbria on 8 April, intent on devastating the county of Durham and coastal Northumberland. This time, the situation was even more serious for Stephen. His enemies had coordinated their movements in Normandy, the West Country, and on the Welsh border. Stephen headed west, leaving Archbishop Thurstan of York and his northern barons to deal with the Scots, who were again meeting with considerable success. David's main force threatened Durham; amongst the religious establishments sought out and hit along the way was Stephen's own foundation at Furness Abbey. In June, another division defeated an English force eighty miles south of Carlisle. Apparently, ill-founded rumours of Stephen's imminent arrival put the Scots to flight once more. But they did not go far. The defection of the eminent northern baron Eustace fitz John to David, bringing with him manpower and strategic strongholds, incited the Scottish king to launch yet another invasion at the end of July, and one on a far larger scale than his previous expeditions.

It has been suggested that David planned to ravage beyond Yorkshire deep into England. His confidence and ambition had grown not only from his new northern ally, but from the knowledge that Stephen was busy in the South-East, successfully suppressing rebellions in Kent, where his wife was blockading Dover, and in the South and

West, where Stephen had invested a number of castles. As ever, the line of march was marked by the fires of the Scots' raiding parties until David reached the Tees in mid-August. Stephen spared some household knights to reinforce the royalist muster in York. On 22 August, the Scots were smashed at the battle of the Standard near Northallerton. King David barely managed to escape, leaving his infantry to be massacred. He retreated to Roxburgh and did not bother Northumbria again for some while.

This bald recital of facts about King David's three invasions of 1138 is of the type to be found in any number of history books relating any number of campaigns at any time. Such narratives are necessarily condensed to provide the essential details of campaigns and to recount the protagonists' movements, but they do little to capture the reality and horror that accompany them. For David's expeditions were marked by atrocity on a truly appalling scale. As David Crouch has written concerning the first six months of 1138, 'A harsher period of Stephen's reign had opened, and as his strategy hardened so, naturally, did that of his opponents.'[30]

The sources certainly seem to attest to this. John of Worcester is the most restrained. The invasion occurred only two years before he stopped writing his chronicle. Amid the Scots' burning of fields and depredation in the countryside, he records that the 'dreadful invasion' of Northumbria and surrounding area over six months meant 'many were captured, robbed, imprisoned and tortured; ecclesiastics were put to death for the sake of the property of their churches, and one can hardly account the number of the slain on either our side or theirs'.[31] (The comment on numbers is ambiguous; could it mean royalist troops also committed atrocities – as they surely did – or is it just a reference to combat deaths?)

Henry of Huntingdon, who had close ties with Lincoln (and hence was closer to the events of 1138) began writing his contemporary account of events from around 1133, in 'the present time', as he says. His rendition of the Scottish events sets the tone for reporting the invasion.

The King of Scotland ... commanded his men in barbarous deeds. For they ripped open pregnant women and tore out the unborn foetuses. They tossed children on the points of their lances. They dismembered priests on their altars. They put on to the bodies of the slain the heads cut off crucifixes, and changing them round, they put back on the crucifixes the heads of the dead. Everywhere that the Scots attacked would be filled with horror and barbarity, accompanied by the cries of women, the wailing of the aged, the groans of the dying, the despair of the living.[32]

Robert of Torigny had finished his chronicle by 1154. Although distant from events in Normandy, he was well travelled and well informed, not least from Henry of Huntingdon, who visited him in 1139, just a year after the invasion. Understandably, he closely follows Henry's details. Orderic Vitalis, who finished his chronicle in 1141, was also a Norman monk; his version also seems to follow Huntingdon, but is much shorter, concentrating on the pregnant women. The *Gesta Stephani*, written in the 1140s by either Bishop Robert of Bath or someone within his circle, agrees with Huntingdon that King David gave direct orders to his troops to wreak death and destruction everywhere they went: he 'sent out a decree through Scotland and summoned all to arms, and giving them free licence, he commanded them to commit against the English, without pity, the most savage and cruel deeds they could invent'. Frustratingly, just as the author is about to relate what happened during the invasion, substantial *lacunae* deprive us of important information: David is, 'organizing squadrons and battalions, against all the land, which was large and rich ... '[33]

The main source for the atrocities of 1138 is Richard of Hexham. Richard was a canon of the abbey at Hexham at the time of the invasion; he became prior in 1141, finishing his chronicle by 1154. Unsurprisingly, given his geographical location, his most pressing concerns were with the Scots rather than with the troubles of King Stephen further south. Richard heaps outraged opprobrium on the Scots of the first invasion in January: 'that cursed army, more atrocious than the whole race of pagans, neither fearing God nor regarding man, spread desolation over the whole province, and murdered every where persons of both sexes, of every age and rank, and overthrew, plundered, and burned towns, churches and houses.' He writes that the Scots took great sadistic pleasure in their grisly work, as 'they put to the sword and transfixed with spears' all they came across, not sparing the most vulnerable: the young, the old, the women and the sick. Non-combatants sought to escape the Scots by fleeing from their villages, but many were still cut down: the Scots 'massacred numberless persons in the wild' as they overran the province, ravaging everything 'by sword and fire'.[34] The hyperbole is palpable when he records – notably as hearsay – that when the Sots slaughtered a large group of children, they even dammed a brook to collect the blood for drinking.

The second invasion is reported in similar terms: 'The king of Scotland ... with his execrable army, once more returned to Northumberland, and with no less ferocity and cruelty than he had previously exhibited.' The pattern of brutal ravaging was repeated. Richard again details the areas of depredation, carefully specifying that the Scots struck targets they had missed first time around, and 'anywhere' that 'had escaped uninjured' previously. A division sent by David to Yorkshire under his nephew William was no less ruthless.

> Sparing no rank, no age, no sex, no condition, they first massacred, in the most barbarous manner possible, children and kindred in sight of their relatives, and servants in the sight of their masters, masters in sight of their servants, and husbands before the eyes of their wives; and then (horrible to relate) they carried off, like so much booty, the noble matrons and chaste virgins, together with other women. These naked, fettered, herded together, by whips and lashes they drove them before them, goading them with their spears and other weapons. This took place in other wars, but in this to a far greater extent. Afterwards, when they were distributed along with the other booty, a few of them from motives of pity restored some of them to liberty ... but the Picts and many others carried off those who fell to their share to their own country. And finally, these brutal men ... when tired of abusing these poor wretches like animals, made them their slaves or sold them for cattle to other barbarians.[35]

This is quite a catalogue of horror and, understandably, many historians have treated such reports with scepticism. For a start, familiar accounts are repeated with suspicious regularity later in English sources throughout the medieval period. To cite just one example from many, coming 160 years after the events described above, a letter from King Edward's court to Pope Boniface in 1301 complains about the savagery of the Scots in 1296 performing the same atrocities mentioned above, adding the cutting off of women's breasts and, in an echo of the Hexham Chronicle, even mentioning the large-scale slaughter of a group of schoolboys, burned alive having been blockaded in their school. Trying to determine what is real and what is prurient sensationalism for propaganda purposes is a difficult task; but extravagant embellishment or even outright fabrication of one incident does not automatically negate others. For example, the burning of the schoolboys is not only also included in the chronicle from Lancerost in the fourteenth century, but it is stated as occurring in the town of Hexham. Has Richard's story been embroidered over time into a new version, or are the letter and Lancerost Chronicle based on recent fact? Is the repetition of similar brutal acts a topos, or have the acts become a stock literary theme because they are actually perpetrated so frequently? Then there is the influence of Bible stories and stained-glass windows luridly depicting the slaughter of the innocents: which events are prompted by witnesses, and which are implanted in the minds of suggestible writers by the religious environment? Writing an accurate account of a battle or siege is difficult enough (even in the modern age), so how much more difficult it was to write about ravaging, when endless raiding parties split of from the main column to cause their damage.

The repetition may equally be due not to tradition, but to the reality of the situation. The fourteenth-century Lancerost Chronicle mentioned above, a local source like Hexham, records the Scottish wars in similar vein to the chroniclers of the twelfth century; its descriptions of ravaging and raids provide an 'accurate and realistic picture of the kind of war which characterised those parts'.[36] It is interesting to compare the descriptions of twelfth-century writers about the Harrying of the North in 1069–70 with the Scottish invasions of 1138. The earlier ravaging is also related in gruesome fashion, but the focus is on the after-effects, the consequences of the brutal military actions; for 1138, Richard of Hexham (and Henry of Huntingdon to a lesser extent) add explicit details of the act of atrocity itself, description of the action rather than of the effect. This may be to further demonize the enemy in an atmosphere of ethnic hatred, but it also may simultaneously represent the fears felt by the writers and their communities in the here-and-now of the war-torn North. Richard of

Hexham was writing from within the war zone. As he writes, 'In this raging and tempestuous period', the 'noble monastery of Hexham' was 'in the very midst of the collision, and placed as it were on the very route of these ruffians, so as to be surrounded by them on every side'.[37]

Much of what he did not see first-hand would have been reported by victims and eyewitnesses seeking refuge in the monastery or simply reporting to it. Similarly, it is the local writer Simeon of Durham who also offers the most violent images of Scottish incursions. Simeon's writing stops at 1129, but he writes of Scottish atrocities against the English fifty years previously in 1070 in the same way as Richard of Hexham (which is not surprising, as again there is a Hexham connection: the text has mid-twelfth-century interpolations from a monk at Richard's monastery). The Scottish king Malcolm

> ordered his troops no longer to spare the English nation . . . to carry them off captives under the yoke of perpetual slavery . . . Some aged men and women were beheaded with the sword; others were thrust through with spear . . . Infants . . . were thrown high into the air and in their fall they were received on the points of lances and pikes thickly placed in the ground. The Scots . . . delighted in this cruelty as an amusing spectacle.[38]

On occasion we must doubt Richard of Hexham's writing, but otherwise, as touched on above, he shows himself to be reasonably objective and factual for the time: while writing of the invasion, he is concerned to make an accurate record of the movements of the Scots and the places they did and did not attack; he allows that some Scots took pity on their captives and released them; that, despite his apocalyptic version, others were spared for ransom. He says that the sufferings are not unique, but typical of other wars, but that they have taken on a new intensity in the current conflict; and that the blood-drinking episode is unverified hearsay. It is more than likely – but not certain – that isolated incidents have become generalized; but this is not as important as the accumulation of individual atrocities and their total number, for it is this that captures the savage nature of the wars, and this that inflicted the greatest miseries on non-combatants.

It is worth bearing these points in mind when discussing propaganda, for it may well be the case that some of the atrocities were not fabricated to this end, but rather that actual atrocities were inflated for propaganda purposes. We do not have to accept Richard's account *in toto*, simply on the basis of self-contradiction. Clearly, it was not the case that the Scots killed everyone in their path, as Richard tells us of the fate of many women taken captive. He also writes of ransoms, but here it seems to relate to soldiers. Simeon is more distinct on this: 'Young men and maidens, and whomsoever seemed fit for toil and labour, were bound and driven before the face of their enemies, to be reduced in perpetual exile to slaves.'[39] Some of these women died of exhaustion on their march northwards. What is evident from the sources is that those most likely to be killed were any that resisted the slave drive – husbands, fathers and sometimes mothers – and the most vulnerable, as they had least value and would not easily keep up with an army on the warpath. Slavery was still prevalent on the Celtic fringe at this time, much to the horror of more civilized English writers (but, as we shall see in the next sections, that did not mean captives in England were no longer financial commodities to be bartered). Those that were not to be taken were slaughtered to get them out of the way, to terrorize others elsewhere who might resist, and also to undermine the authority of the English king by showing how incapable he was of protecting his own people. As with the sack of Jerusalem and any other number of atrocities, who died and who survived lay at the whim of the sword holder.

The most obvious example of propaganda writing is the episode of damming and drinking children's blood. Richard reports this with the qualification 'it is said'. This is an obvious example of placing the barbarous enemy way beyond even the worst behaviour expected from the most depraved people. Such a depiction of the Scots elevated conflict against them into a holy war. At the Battle of the Standard, the leading ecclesiastics consciously emphasized this aspect under the standards of the northern saints (from which the battle derives its name), calling for the English to be the means through which God would punish the Scots. The incessant slaying and decapitation of priests at the altar may well be propaganda based on truth. Churches were always the ultimate places of sanctuary, but were often sought out in vain. The Scots' treatment of them was not so different from that of others in this regard, as some examples from France indicate: in 1440, John Talbot burned to death over three hundred men, women and children taking refuge in a church in Lihons; the churches in Béziers were execution chambers; and when even a king of such renowned piety as Louis VII could torch a church full of non-combatants, as he did in Vitry in 1143, then their value as places of refuge clearly fluctuated according to the situation. It was only natural that priests should be at the altars of their churches with their flocks huddled in the aisles. It was also natural for them to be targeted as sources of wealth. And if Thomas Becket, archbishop of Canterbury, could be cut down in his cathedral by knights from the King's household, what hope was there for a humble parish priest faced by vicious, beggarly common soldiers intent on little but plunder? Babies impaled on swords and pikes and pregnant women being cut open were a constant of medieval warfare reporting and beyond, as woodcarvings and prints from the sixteenth century reveal, and as do written accounts from much later. We cannot identify with any certainty when and where they happened; but given other excesses committed in this and other wars of the Middle Ages, and also given the extra bitterness from a frontier war with ethnic hatreds, it is likely that something similar occurred in 1138 as the chroniclers say.

Vitriol and accusation of atrocities were not reserved for the Scots, but for all on the Celtic fringe. Thus, when the Welsh went raiding in 1136, the *Gesta Stephani* recounts that these 'men of an animal type . . . cleared the villages by plunder, fire and sword, burnt the houses, slaughtered the men. . . . Addicted to every crime, ready for anything unlawful, they spared no age, showed no respect for any order, were not restrained from wickedness either by time or by place'.[40] John of Worcester writes of the same event that it 'was the occasion of a vast and widespread destruction of churches, town wheat and cattle'. Of the two rounds of extensive killing, the second was the greater: 'There was so great a slaughter that (not taking into account those who were carried away into captivity) there remained 10,000 women whose husbands, with numberless children, had been either drowned, or burned, or put to the sword.'[41] Such reactions were prompted not only by disgust but also by a sense of cultural and political superiority bound up in the conscious English imperialism of the time, on which John Gillingham and R. R. Davies have written so insightfully. Expansion, conquest and domination – under the ever-useful imperial guise of a civilization mission – could be undertaken with a lighter conscience and with more support if the enemy could be labelled as bestial savages.

The fact that Scotland had elements (mainly the frightening Galwegians) that still practised the old-style warfare of slavery and slaughter only added credence to the reports of atrocity. King David and his cavalry could be relied upon to abide by the code of chivalry and take other knights for ransom, but some of his more unruly troops, utterly excluded from this code, were less likely to be so accommodating. It was a similar problem with the Welsh, who, as Gerald of Wales observed, cut off heads instead of taking prisoners, and massacred captives instead of taking ransom. The Irish were to receive the same treatment, when, non-coincidentally, the English moved into their home territory later in the century. The Irish themselves were accustomed in their power struggles to 'pursuing a policy of slaughter, plunder and burning' and decapitation on a horrific scale. In 1069 at Osriage in south-western Leinster they saw no reason to change their habits when King Dermot's Irish forces celebrated a victory with their new Norman allies:

> About 200 heads of his enemies were laid at Dermot's feet. When he had turned each one over and recognized it, out of an excess of joy he jumped three times in the air with arms clasped over his head, and joyfully gave thanks to the Supreme Creator as he loudly revelled in his triumph. He lifted up to his mouth the head of one he particularly loathed, and taking it by the ears and hair, gnawed at the nose and cheeks – a cruel and most inhuman act.[42]

If that was the mood in the literary world, how much more vicious things would have been on the battlefield. It fostered a sense of total war, in which the killing of the enemy without distinction between soldiers and non-combatants became virtuous. It was the same over four hundred years later. On the eve of Flodden in 1513, fought on the Scottish border, a Gaelic poet encourages such *guerre à outrance:*

> Let us make harsh and mighty warfare against the English. . . . The roots from which they grow, destroy them, their increase is too great, and leave no Englishman alive after you nor Englishwoman there to tell the tale. Burn their bad coarse women, burn their

uncouth offspring, and burn their sooty houses, and rid us of the reproach of them. Let their ashes float downstream after burning their remains, show no mercy to a living Englishman, O . . . deadly slayer of the wounded.[43]

This was a call for a war of extermination in which there was no room for compassion for the wounded or even women, as they would produce only more English enemies. As Matthew Strickland has commented on this passage, '[I]t is impossible to envisage such words coming from an Anglo-French courtly poet extolling the chivalric virtues of his patron'.[44] Not that English soldiers would be so sensitive. Unsurprisingly, those at Flodden reciprocated Scottish sentiment. According to a contemporary source, many 'Scottish prisoners could and might have been taken but they were so vengeable and cruel in their fighting that when the Englishmen had the better of them they would not save them, though it so were that diverse Scots offered great sums of money for their lives'.[45] Such was the spiral of violence that sometimes not even money could break it.

It has been suggested that the anti-Scottish feeling in English writing of the twelfth century was provoked by repugnance at the Scots' way of warfare, which was perceived as little more than slaving raids. This is a partial explanation. More obviously, the ethnic hatred on both sides was generated predominantly by war. This hatred was a form of aggressive, nascent national identity. As I have argued elsewhere, 'The effect of war on nationalist feelings is well documented; such feelings in England by the twelfth century had been nurtured by wars against the Celtic fringe.'[46] Some medievalists have commented on the patriotism displayed in the works of William of Malmesbury and Henry of Huntingdon. England had long held a sense of the 'other', a national identity shaped by reference to what people were not. Thus, the Old English word for Wales – *Wealhas* – means 'foreigners'. Contrary to the chronocentrism of some modern historians following the Gellner school of nationalism, national identity grew strongly in medieval England and, later, France, with war being the driving force in both cases (Anglo-French war, in fact). It was this added ingredient that made the Hundred Years War so deadly at times.

Scottish tactics and strategy were largely dictated by necessity. Their aristocracy, and hence the upper echelons of their army, were more similar than dissimilar to their English counterparts, and there were close courtly connections; any cultural gaps quickly narrowed over the twelfth century. Scottish campaigns did not consist merely of killing, pillaging and enslaving, but, especially in the border regions, of sieges, too: David's dogged and persistent preoccupation with Wark finally paid off when a starved garrison surrendered towards the end of 1138. However, ravaging was the primary tactic and, as the first treaty of Durham shows with Stephen granting Carlisle and Doncaster to David, another means by which to gain strongholds. The marked battle avoidance of David, hastily beating a retreat at the mere rumour of an advancing English army, was a practical response to the better armour, training and equipment of the English. His own infantry, lightly armoured and poorly disciplined, was no match for the English, as the Battle of the Standard bloodily demonstrated. But the further the Scots advanced into England, the less important sieges became (many castles were simply bypassed), as the intent was simply to plunder and thereby apply pressure in the hope of being bought off with territorial concessions. In this sense, a campaign became a raid, with the intention of moving as quickly, as destructively and as profitably as possible. The fate of the non-combatants – their homes, their goods, their lives – was not due to collateral damage but to the objectives of war.

How was it that King David, anxious to be esteemed as a chivalrous knight and considered 'civilized' by William Malmesbury, allowed his troops to act so homicidally and so brutally? As we have seen repeatedly, even the most renowned exponents of kingly chivalry did not hesitate to indulge in stark, brutal acts of carnage in their dedication to the military imperative. David was no different. Part of the problem was, as always, financial. Scotland, like Wales and Ireland, was not as economically developed as England; consequently, there were fewer coins circulating there. Rank-and-file Scottish troops rarely received wages and therefore depended on plunder and slavery instead. Anything that had a value and could be moved was taken as a form of pay. And as poverty was endemic on the Celtic fringe, there were always men ready to join a raiding party in search of relative riches. As with the Welsh, '[T]hese were men who lived by and for war, and for whom the equation of peace and prosperity was the very reverse of the truth'.[47] If David had not let these men loose on the rampage, then his armies would have been greatly reduced in strength as he did not have the means to pay them.

Booty was the concern of all soldiers, including the most noble of knights; but for the main infantry contingent of a Scottish army it was the be-all and end-all. Both Henry of Huntingdon and the author of the *Gesta Stephani* claim that King David gave specific orders to his troops to wage unrestrained war in the most savage way. This assertion is as hard to prove as it is to disprove; either way, David clearly understood what the Scottish style of warfare entailed and, indeed, depended on it to make gains. With understanding comes complicity. The King may have regretted the excesses of his troops, only to protest that there was little he could do to restrain them, suggesting that the best way to prevent them causing such misery was to end the war by coming to generous terms with him. It is a common ploy throughout military history. For David to wage war he relied on troops that were geared towards savagery, slavery and slaughter. As Keith Stringer has concluded: 'Their terror tactics were on a scale not experienced since the Conqueror's notorious Harrying of the North of 1069–70, and had the clear aim of so demoralizing Stephen and his northern supporters that they would be forced to accept Scottish conquests, or at least a peace that went some way towards meeting David's demands.'[48]

It was no different in the war of 1173–4, when Jordan of Fantosme has King William of Scotland calling for widespread ravaging, 'leaving not a house nor a church standing' and 'killing all the men'.[49] Some efforts were made at restraint in the Edwardian wars a century later, but they seem no less savage. And so it remained into the sixteenth century at Flodden.

This section has restricted itself to English reporting of Scottish atrocities. It therefore paints a very one-sided picture in which the Scots were the sole perpetrators of these horrors. That was certainly not the case in reality. A major theme of this book is that there were few, if any, medieval commanders who did not commit what we today would call a war crime; another theme is that violence begets violence. Thus the English assuredly committed their share of atrocities throughout the Anglo-Scottish wars in the Middle Ages, so it is worth reminding ourselves of the letter that John Balliol, King of Scotland, wrote to Edward I in 1296 renouncing his homage, using familiar language:

You yourself, and others of your realm (to your own knowledge, for surely you know not to be ignorant of what they do) have (as everyone knows) inflicted over and over again, by naked force, grievous and intolerable injuries, slights, and wrongs upon us and the inhabitants of our realm . . . by taking away, and receiving within your realm, both by land and sea, our chattels and those of our subjects; by slaying merchants and other inhabitants of our realm, and by forcibly seizing the men of our realm, taking them into your own. . . . For now you have come to the frontiers of our realm in a warlike array . . . and have crossed beyond into our realm, and brutally committed acts of slaughter and of burning.[50]

What did David's murderous invasions achieve? In some ways, quite a lot (although this is an area of dispute). By the second treaty of Durham in April 1139, David was effectively bought off for the time being. David's lordship of Carlisle and the rights of his son to the earldom of Huntingdon were confirmed, and his son was also granted the earldom of Northumberland. It is notable that, after his defeat at the Battle of the Standard, David retreated to Carlisle and not to Scotland. Here he held a major council with a papal legate and the leading men of his kingdom, lay and secular, and thus Carlisle was 'obviously treated as a chief place of Scottish government'.[51] Basically, Stephen acknowledged in the treaty the areas that David had made his own, freeing the English king to concentrate on his many troubles elsewhere.

Unfortunately for him, these troubles saw him in prison after his defeat at the Battle of Lincoln in 1141, leaving David to fill the political vacuum in the North by simply taking over government there without conflict. The northern chroniclers, who had so vehemently condemned the Scottish king and his troops for their atrocities, now fell over themselves in praising their new peace-loving, pious, virtuous and compassionate lord and master.

King John's Winter Campaign, 1215–16

The war of Magna Carta that began in England in 1215 was a long time in gestation, and King John was its feckless father. His oppressive and arbitrary government imposed a severe financial burden on his subjects, whom John exploited in an effort to gain the means by which he might recover his lost territories in France. These losses – above all, Normandy, which Philip Augustus annexed in 1204 after his stunning victory at Chateau Gaillard – cast a huge shadow over John's reign, one that could only be cast off by tangible results on the battlefield.

The help and support of his barons would have been a great advantage to John, but the King preferred to place what little trust he had in mercenaries. This required a lot of money, which John sought to extract from his barons, thereby dangerously alienating them: dispossessions 'by will', hostage-taking, fines, duplicate charters of sole ownership issued to different people and other unscrupulous measures left John isolated. He exacerbated his problems further by mishandling patronage, granting prized offices to foreigners and new men. Many of John's most intransigent and unrelenting agents were placed in the North, building up huge resentment there; it is no surprise that the 'northerners' are to be found heading the consequent rebellion.

John's singularly unpleasant character further reinforced his deserved reputation for being completely untrustworthy. This traditional view has, until recently, held sway for centuries. However, a revisionist school from the 1960s, propounding the idea that good kingship was less about chivalric charisma and military leadership, and more about keeping a nice tidy set of bookkeeping records, argued that John was in fact a pretty good king, after all. He was not. The fact that John was such a keen bureaucrat is a reflection of his failures elsewhere; he managed to find some useful employment in tax-raising schemes, but in little else. Thankfully, a counter-revisionist attack has attempted to set the academic record straight, although a popular more positive view of John still persists.

John deservedly had a very hostile press from contemporaries in England. Biased (but well-informed) monastic chroniclers heaped censure on him. Richard of Devizes describes him as a raging madman; the Barnwell chronicler labels him 'a pillager of his own people'; Matthew Paris believed that in dying John defiled Hell. Secular sources confirm these judgements. The biographer of the royalist William Marshal characterizes him as a suspicious and resentful ruler, heedless to reason, and blinded by pride. Even Anonymous of Béthune, whose master fought for John in the wars of this time, cannot find anything positive to say in his simple and damning summary: 'He had too many bad qualities'. A wholly unchivalrous king, he was, unlike Richard the Lionheart or Henry V, not a man to inspire confidence on the battlefield (or off it, either).

Yet some historians argue that his poor reputation as a military leader is undeserved; that he was, in fact, 'a shrewd strategist', that 'the inference he was a feeble soldier is false', that he was 'skilled in siegecraft' and that his military plans 'came incredibly close to success'.[52] In other words, he does not deserve his sobriquet, bestowed upon him by Gervase of Canterbury, of 'Softsword'. His campaign of 1215–16 may offer some support for this view, as even many of John's modern-day detractors concur that it was a total success.

By 1212, John had gained mastery over the British Isles. It was a short-lived triumph. A Welsh revolt demanded an immediate response. His first move was typically hard-hearted: killing the hostage sons of one of the Welsh leaders – two died after castration; the seven-year-old was hanged. His planned expedition to Wales was cancelled when he uncovered a baronial plot to assassinate him (or to abandon him to the Welsh). A carefully prepared French invasion of 1213 was successfully prevented by a combination of decisive military action (his half-brother William Longsword destroying the French fleet at Damme) and by supine diplomacy (John's submission of his realm as a fief of the Pope). John, in turn, placed high hopes on an Anglo-Imperial invasion of France in 1214, but the well-funded expedition was disastrously ended by defeat at the battle of Bouvines. Demands on the baronage to provide the finances for this disastrous campaign increased the number of baronial dissidents and finally provoked them into outright rebellion in May 1215. London opened its gates to the rebels, an early boost that did just a little to offset the extensive network of royal castles and foreign mercenaries being brought into the country to fight for John. A state of phoney war permitted time for the talks that led to Magna Carta in June, by which the barons hoped to restrain John's capricious and high-handed style of government and to ease their tax burden. John only signed the charter as a temporary, delaying measure, and repudiated it the following month, thus precipitating the war proper in September. John's new papal ally saw to it that the dissident barons were excommunicated; this did not, however, prevent the rebels from calling their forces the 'Army of God'. The rebels looked for allies of their own, enlisting the help of Alexander II of Scotland and enticing Prince Louis of France to aid them with the prospect of the throne. But Louis' main force would not arrive until well into the following year.

The barons had need of the French. Although strong in the North and East, they had little to match the resources at John's disposal, which were augmented further by his raiding of dissident estates near at hand and taking rebel castles in the South; John also had the strength of some 150 royal castles strategically placed throughout the country. The castles would be important for John's march up and down the country over winter, providing secure bases and field troops. The rebels held Rochester for a while, losing it to John by December after a dramatic siege. It was here that John was talked out of hanging the garrison by his captains, concerned that they might receive the same treatment if caught. Crucially, the rebels maintained their position in London where they received an advanced expeditionary force from Louis. In the North, King Alexander of Scotland went on the warpath and the northern barons made their submissions to him. On 20 December, John held a council of war at St Albans. A chronicler tells us that his primary concern was to find the means by which he could pay his mercenaries to defeat the barons. He split his army in two. One half, under William Longsword and John's senior mercenary captains, successfully subdued rebel hot spots in the South while containing the main force within London. Needless to say, they did this by sword and fire, as at Ely in Cambridgeshire, where Ralph of Coggeshall reports royalist soldiers burning the place: '[T]hey made great slaughter, as they did everywhere they went, sparing neither age, nor sex, nor condition, nor the clergy'.[53] John's role was to accomplish the same in a campaign northwards into rebel territory. It was a ravaging campaign the like of which England had not experienced in over half a century.

Rebel estates were torched and their castles taken. The garrison at Belvoir in Leicestershire surrendered when John threatened to starve to death their lord, William of Albiny, whom he had captured at Rochester. Such was the ferocity of the march that castle after castle was abandoned to him, and town after town hurried to open its gates to him. Anonymous of Béthune informs us that the constable of Pontefract placed himself at the King's mercy, while York paid John one thousand pounds to regain his goodwill. Roger of Wendover reports that the commanders of the baronial castles, 'when they heard of the king's advance, left their castles untenanted and fled to places of secrecy, leaving their provisions and various stores for their approaching enemies'.[54] Coggeshall confirms the efficacy of John's terror tactics: 'The king and his army ... depopulated the lands of the barons, incessantly dedicated to plunder and burning.... The Northern barons fled before his face while a few submitted themselves to the mercy of the merciless one.'[55] So swift was his progress that by 8 January he was outside Durham. From here he rushed to Newcastle when he learned that Alexander had set it alight. In retaliation, John burned and destroyed Berwick, a Scottish chronicle speaking of slaughter and torture.

Dunbar and Haddington received similar treatment before John headed south again in the last week of January. He may have been short of supplies, as the retreating Scots had destroyed their own areas to deny John provisions that would enable him to lengthen the campaign if he so wished; Matthew Paris said John returned south due to 'urgent necessity'. In effect, he had achieved most of his objectives and his government by punitive expedition had established his intentions. For the time being, there was little military resistance left in the North and so John could focus his attention on isolated pockets of resistance in the South. In March he began whittling away at these. But London still remained defiant.

How bad was the ravaging campaign? As ever, it is impossible to quantify such things. Of the sources closest to events, two otherwise superb ones for the war in England at the end of John's reign actually say little. The epic vernacular poem *History of William Marshal* is hardly ever mentioned in relation to the 1215 campaign, as all the author offers is a cursory mention of the mercenary 'men of Flanders, foreign knights and soldiers, who every day were set on pillage ... bent ... on laying waste' the land.[56] William Marshal was keeping the situation under control in Ireland at this time, which probably explains the reticence. The Old French *History of the Dukes of Normandy and Kings of England* is more interesting for its taciturnity. Like the *History of William Marshal*, it is normally a rich mine of information on the details of the war. The author's patron fought for John, and depicts many of the war's military encounters in great detail. But for specifics of the depredations, all he writes is that John went into Scotland 'ravaging the land' and that 'he burned and destroyed the town of

Berwick'.[57] The chronicle concerns itself more with actual combats, and its author may well have felt that, as with the Anglo-Norman chroniclers of the Scottish wars, his patron should not be sullied by mention of sordid and base details of war against non-combatants.

Two contemporary Latin sources provide the best information. Ralph of Coggeshall was abbot of the Cistercian house at Coggeshall in Essex during the time of these events. In 1215 the war came to his monastery: royalist troops 'entered violently', stealing treasure and taking away twenty-two horses belonging to the Bishop of London. He is cited above in relation to the barons fleeing before John's advance, burning, plundering and depopulating the barons' lands, and to the sacking of Ely, where he claims no one was spared. At Ely, he reports that the soldiers inflicted 'horrible tortures' on men to get at their money.[58] It is a short explanation that tells us so much about the nature of ravaging campaigns and why non-combatants were treated so cruelly.

By far our best source, but one treated with suspicion by many historians, is Roger of Wendover. However, as I have argued elsewhere, it is a mistake to dismiss Wendover too readily: 'the importance of Wendover's underestimated chronicle' is that the author 'excels at portraying the impact of war on society and how money truly constituted the sinews of war'.[59] Wendover has suffered in the shadow of the more illustrious Matthew Paris, who based the early part of his great chronicles on copying the chronicle of Wendover. In many ways, he was ideally placed to write on the war in England. Like Coggeshall, but much more so, he was in the middle of things. His great monastery of St Albans was visited by kings, papal emissaries, bishops, counts and leading court officials. John started his campaign here in December 1215 and the abbey was plundered by both sides in the war. As prior of Belvoir, a cell of St Albans near Lincoln, Wendover was located in the crucible of events. His patron was the William of Albiny captured by John at Rochester, and used by the King to coerce the castle by Wendover's priory to surrender at Christmas 1215. He witnessed armies marching through the Vale of Belvoir and, valuably, despite his patron's loyalties, he was just as prepared to condemn anti-royalist forces as royalist ones. Like most medieval writers, he was, of course, prone to exaggeration, but most of his details ring true.

Wendover devotes substantial space to cataloguing 'the various kinds of suffering endured' by the people of England; it is rare to see in a medieval chronicle such consideration given to actions against the population, as opposed to actions between armies. Wendover recounts that, at his war council in St Albans, John resolved 'to ravage the whole country with fire and sword'.[60] In his account of the first stages of the campaign, note how the financial purpose of ravaging is made clear: the destruction of the barons' economic base, and the extortion of money from non-combatants to supplement the troops' wages:

> Spreading his troops abroad, [John] burned the houses and buildings of the barons, robbing them of their goods and cattle, and thus destroying everything that came in his way, he gave a miserable spectacle to those who beheld it. . . . He ordered his incendiaries to set fire to the hedges and towns on his march, so that . . . by robbery he might support the wicked agents of his iniquity. All the inhabitants of every condition and rank who did not take refuge in a churchyard were made prisoners, and, after being tortured, were forced to pay a heavy ransom.[61]

William Longsword was doing the same in the South, where royalist soldiers were 'collecting booty and indulging in pillage; they levied impositions on the towns, made prisoners of the inhabitants, burnt the buildings of their barons, destroyed the parks and warrens, cut down the trees in the orchards and, having spread fire as far as the suburbs of London, they took away an immense booty with them'.[62] It is important to observe how, amid the seemingly wanton destruction of ravaging, that economic targets were picked out and hit.

It was the same after Christmas when John's forces progressed 'burning the buildings belonging to the barons, making booty of their cattle, plundering them of their goods and destroying everything they came to with the sword'. John gave his commanders orders to 'destroy all the property of the barons, namely their castles, buildings, towns, parks, warrens, lakes and mills . . . to finish the business with equal cruelty'.[63] This is targeted economic warfare. It was not unique to this campaign, but a feature of many others. Of a later ravaging expedition in Henry III's reign, Wendover specifies that the villages struck belonged to the enemy and that the soldiers were careful not to damage any estates where the lord was loyal to the King. This was ravaging as a disciplined weapon of medieval commanders.

There is some evidence that royalist forces were not so indiscriminate in their rampage during the winter of 1215–16. Court records reveal that one man had a hand cut off by the marshal of John's army for stealing a cow from a churchyard. Was he a token example to impress an ecclesiastical audience? Did the theft contravene a local agreement? Was he a soldier in John's pay? As discussed in chapter one, war provided cover for all manner of criminality, by non-combatants as well as by soldiers. Sometimes it was a genuine attempt to recoup losses incurred by the ravages of war; other times it was sheer opportunism, as judicial records of the time indicate. 'The war was an obvious excuse for violent lawlessness, and many were disseised of their property by their more powerful and unscrupulous neighbours. One Yorkshire squire frankly admitted that he had behaved so villainously that he dared not face a local jury.'[64]

James Holt has warned against amplification of the atrocity stories, citing that Ripon was spared any depredations when John's forces arrived there. There could be various reasons why Ripon itself was spared (politics or payment of protection or 'goodwill' money, for example); John, ever anxious for hard cash, frequently accepted cash and treasure in lieu of torching a place.

Disciplined ravaging required a strong captain imposing his will on his troops. But, as with Alexander's Scots, there was room for intentional ambiguity: John would keep his troops, especially his mercenaries, loyal and happy only by allowing them considerable licence to line their own pockets; at the same time, their excesses had the other useful and practical effect of crushing opposition and intimidating future resistance. It is notable how the ferocity of John's campaign resulted in many rebels flocking to him, craving forgiveness. All it took for a non-combatant to be made an acceptable target was that he or she should be a resident in a town or on an estate owned by a baronial opponent. Most non-combatants probably did not express a voluntary allegiance either way, and even royalist sympathizers in baronial territory would be very lucky indeed to escape the depredations. As with the residents of an enemy-held town, little time was wasted on ordinary non-combatants; discrimination was reserved for men of standing. Wendover records the ordeal of ordinary people caught up in John's ravaging campaign:

> The whole surface of the earth was covered with these limbs of the devil like locusts, who assembled ... to blot out every thing from the face of the earth, from man down to his cattle; for, running about with drawn swords and knives, they ransacked towns, houses cemeteries, and churches, robbing everyone, and sparing neither women nor children; the king's enemies wherever they were found were imprisoned in chains and compelled to pay a heavy ransom. Even the priests, whilst standing at the very altars ... were seized, tortured, robed and ill-treated. .... They inflicted similar tortures on knights and others of every condition. Some of them they hung up by the middle, some by the feet and legs, some by their hands, and some by the thumbs and arms, and then threw salt mixed with vinegar in the eyes of the wretched. ... Others were placed on gridirons over live coals, and then bathing their roasted bodies in cold water they thus killed them.

Some of these torture details may have religious origins (St Laurence, for example, was martyred on a gridiron) or bear resemblance to those depicted in the Anglo-Saxon Chronicle, but the suffering, as Ralph of Coggeshall confirms, was real enough. Wendover then makes clear the motivating factor behind the atrocities:

> The wretched creatures uttered pitiable cries and dreadful groans, but there was no one to show them pity, for their torturers were satisfied with nothing but their money. Many who had worldly possessions gave them to their torturers, and were not believed when they had given their all; others, who had nothing, gave many promises, that they might at least for a short time put off the tortures they had experienced once. This persecution was general through-out England, and fathers were sold to torture by their sons, brothers by their brothers, and citizens by their fellow citizens.[65]

This passage, perhaps more than any other, explains the atrocities committed by soldiers on non-combatants in medieval warfare (and other eras, too). It was all about money, about using the hollow legitimacy of war to steal from people who were deliberately, and conveniently, proscribed and thereby placed outside the laws of protection through no fault of their own. The tortures were not mindless sadism (though that undoubtedly played a part in some cases), but a means of extorting money. The worse the torture, the more the victim, and onlookers, would be terrified into giving what they had to stop further pain. Pain was the mangle that squeezed out every available drop of wealth.

Once again, we are confronted with some contradictory evidence. Widespread torture is, I believe, wholly believable as a common practice for the reason given above. But torture is not the same as killing. Undoubtedly, many victims died from their torture, and others were killed to shock potential victims into handing over their money. But what of the tales of slaughter? John Gillingam has argued that 'Ravaging and burning the countryside were essential ingredients of chivalrous warfare ... but killing unresisting non-combatants was not.'[66] Thus, as Orderic Vitalis recorded for Normandy in 1118, villagers who had been pillaged followed the raiding party 'planning to buy back their stock or recover it somehow'.[67] Despite some assertions that John's campaign of 1215 16 exceeded even the horrors of earlier Scottish invasions, this was evidently not the case. For one thing, John was not on a slaving mission; with no slavery in England, low-level prisoners were taken for the express purposes of ransoming back or torture: if relatives were killed, who would pay the ransom? Furthermore, the role of churches as sanctuaries appears to have been more respected in this conflict than in others. The cow thief who lost his hand had committed his crime in a churchyard. Wendover says of 1216 that 'goods were exposed for sale only in churchyards ... and no one dared go beyond the limits of churches'. [68]

It seems from Wendover that while people's lives were relatively safe in churches (although one mercenary captain does strike a non-combatant dead in a church doorway), goods and possessions were not, as the monasteries at Coggeshall and St Albans discovered. The references to pillaging of cemeteries is gruesome. Graves were dug up to get at any possessions buried with the person. Even corpses had a value: their going rate was usually half the ransom of a live hostage. But both Coggeshall and Wendover refer to widespread, deliberate killing, the latter declaring that at the end of the campaign, John had 'subdued all this country with dreadful slaughter'.[69] Inevitably, many of the deaths would have been in sacked towns such as Berwick; the scale of other deaths is probably exaggerated, but there would have been substantial civilian fatalities in a major campaign of ravaging, burning of buildings and torture that extended from St Albans into Scotland and back down again, and with the main backbone of the royal army comprising chiefly of hardened foreign mercenaries. Nor do we know of individual events, where a group of pillaging soldiers may have acted mercilessly either through drink, or after a recent combat, when adrenalin and bloodlust were still high, or lashed out in inarticulate revenge for a comrade killed in the action.

The much-repeated phrase 'sparing no one' in medieval chroniclers may not always be as clear as it sounds: in addition to its usual meaning of 'everyone, without exception, being killed', it occasionally signified that no one was spared the suffering or ignominy, which does not automatically mean death. This interpretation can explain many of the seeming inconsistencies of chroniclers' statements. Despite its scale, John's winter campaign was not as bloody as the invasions by the Scots or the risings of the Welsh. What marks it out as so shocking is the vivid, compassionate testimony of Wendover, in which the emphasis is placed not so much on killing as on the individual sufferings of ordinary people.

Judgement on the military success of John's campaign is mixed. The flight of his enemies; the destruction of their estates; the submission of so many rebels and their castles; and, not least, the plunder he gained with which he could satisfy his mercenaries: all were significant victories that impressed – and worried – contemporary writers. But the triumphs were, as so often with John, temporary and incomplete. Many of the northern rebels took their losses and disappeared, for the moment, over the border into Scotland. Most crucially, London survived as a rebel stronghold. John was in a strong position and, as Ralph Turner has observed, 'If significant French aid to the rebels had not arrived, King John simply could have camped outside London and waited for their surrender.'[70] But a second, powerful French contingent had arrived in London, securing their position further there as a base for Prince Louis's expected arrival with the main force. For all the dramatic impact of John rampaging up and down the country, the campaign was a lost opportunity. Yes, the money gained kept his mercenaries together for the future conflict, and reasserting his control over the country ensured a steady flow of more income; but if the rebels themselves had been temporarily weakened, their French allies were given time to prepare, strengthen and reinforce their planned campaign, too. John might have been better off keeping his mercenaries together with the promise of spoils from the biggest prize of all: London.

It is therefore hard to escape W. L. Warren's judgement of John's decision to go on campaign: 'This is a typical example of his reluctance to commit himself to decisive military action: the rebellion would have collapsed had London been recaptured. The rebel headquarters there were the nettle that he should have grasped and uprooted without flinching.' Then, in a brilliant but damning observation that highlights just one reason from many that made John such a poor war leader, he adds: '[O]ne cannot help feeling that a Richard or a Philip would have gone straight for the hardest task and sought a decisive victory. John had to pay dearly for taking the course of least resistance and seeking his ends by indirect means'.[71] The price was even higher for those who fell under the wheels of his campaign juggernaut. There was a longer-term price, too: the French duly arrived in force and the war escalated, lasting for another year and a half.

The Black Prince's Grand Chevauchée, 1355

The most famous ravaging expeditions of the Middle Ages, if not the most famous of all medieval campaigns, are those undertaken by King Edward III and his son Edward, the Black Prince, in the fourteenth century. Their *chevauchées* across France have become synonymous with the image of mounted soldiers riding hard and fast, pillaging and burning anything and everything in their path. But in reality, they are little different from any other ravaging campaigns: David's invasions in 1138 and John's campaign of 1215–16 are no less *chevauchées* than the ones in the Hundred Years War. In fact, the very term *chevauchée* is to be found in Old French sources from the late twelfth and early thirteenth centuries to describe the same style of warfare. The fourteenth-century *chevauchées* are sometimes singled out on account of their speed, but this gives the false impression that the whole operation was purely a mounted one; besides, the plunder gained – a central objective – was as much a limiting factor in the 1300s as it was in the 1100s. In 1215–16, John marched, in winter, from St Albans near London to Durham in two and a half weeks, seeing to government business along the way. The Black Prince's Grand *Chevauchée* of 1355 completed a round march of nearly seven hundred miles from Bordeaux to Narbonne in just under two months. Raid, *chevauchée* and, sometimes, campaign are interchangeable terms.

The *chevauchée* has been defined as 'a typical campaign' of the Hundred Years War, 'the aim of which was to inflict as much damage as possible on the enemy through the destruction of his resources'.[72] The Black Prince's campaign of 1355 achieved just that. His army of between six and eight thousand men, English and Gascon, left Bordeaux in early October to carry out a fast raid into the Languedoc. From the start, the main targets were lands in the hands of his enemy, Count Jean of Armagnac, a chief commander of the French king, John II. Though it was originally intended as a profitable diversionary tactic to co-ordinate with English forces operating in northern France, thereby dividing the enemy, a change of plans meant the campaign was now purely a raid. Gaining momentum from its successes along the way, the army eventually reached Narbonne on the eastern coast before returning to Bordeaux: a march from the Atlantic to the Mediterranean and back. It has been aptly described as 'a remarkable exercise in devastation and destruction ... perhaps the pre-eminent example of the *chevauchée* strategy' that 'assaulted over 500 villages, towns, castles and other settlements and strongholds'.[73]

To create the most damage possible, the army moved forward in three columns abreast, thus widening their path of depredation. On one Sunday alone (15 November), Edward's forces burned four towns including Fonjeaux and Limoux – while he rested in a religious house. Major strongholds were avoided, not least because French counter-strategy had meant they were strengthened in readiness. However, overconfidently, Edward could not resist marching up to Armagnac's base at Toulouse, a calculated insult to the Count. From here he moved on Carcassonne where, as we have seen earlier, he refused a pay-off from the city and burned its suburbs. Two French armies closed in on Edward as he made his way back to Bordeaux, but his reaction to them is disputed between those who believe he was trying to avoid battle, and those who think he was actively seeking one. A letter from the

Black Prince to the Bishop of Winchester gives the impression that Edward was goading the enemy, and that he headed home when it was clear that the French would not give battle. Armagnac seemingly made the conscious decision not to engage Edward, despite the damage to his lands. Edward arrived back in home territory on 2 December, with very few losses in men, and very great gains in wealth.

Our two main English eyewitness sources for the campaign are Edward himself and his chief secretary accompanying him. Both appear indifferent to non-combatants, coldly analysing the raid in factual military and financial terms. Edward's despatch restricts itself to trumpeting his successes ('not a day passed without a town, castle, or fortress being taken') and describing his army's pillaging in conventional terms: 'laying waste the countryside'; 'burnt and destroyed'; 'burning the town so that it was completely destroyed' (Carcassonne). His only acknowledgement of non-combatants is when they 'fled' to Carcassonne, 'took refuge in the castle' of Narbonne, and at Samatan, 'whose inhabitants left empty on our approach'.[74] His secretary, Sir John Wingfield, writing to the same recipient (the Bishop of Winchester), offers more details, but in the same conventional phraseology of burning, destroying and laying waste. His main concern is to express the great financial gains of the campaign: 'It seems certain that since the war against the French king began, there has never been such destruction in a region as in this raid. For the countryside and towns which we have destroyed in this raid produced more revenue for the king of France in aid of his wars than half his kingdom ... as I could prove from authentic documents found in various towns in the tax-collectors' houses.'[75]

A third source, Robert of Avesbury, adds a human dimension, but only in as much as he tells of the anxiety of the people of Montpellier, who 'feared lest they should suffer the same fate' as the people of Narbonne, and many of whom, from the town and surrounding countryside, 'went in terror to Avignon, with such property as they could carry, that they might be under the protection of the pope'.[76]

There is no mention of prisoners, ransoms or killings. There was plenty of the last of these: just south of Toulouse at Lacroix-Falgarde, light troops stormed the town and put many non-combatants to the sword; at Carcassonne, there was widespread rape. Nor is there much talk of booty, either. But booty there was, and prisoners, too. Jonathan

Sumption writes, 'The Prince was highly satisfied with the campaign. A great quantity of booty had been brought from Languedoc, enough to fill about 1,000 carts according to one report. The ransoms of French prisoners were collected gradually over the following months as contracts were enforced and promissory notes were cashed. Many of the Prince's followers became rich men.'[77]

However, he and other historians question the military value of the raid: 'No battles had been won, no territory conquered, and no castles garrisoned.'[78] Clifford Rogers disputes this assessment, claiming that Edward achieved a set of vaguer objectives: punishing rebels, aiding allies, and making gains to the enemy's disadvantage (certainly true economically). There was another, transient advantage to add to the very real financial one. The impact of the expedition astonished France, bringing fierce war to a region which had previously escaped it. The impact can be assessed from the quotations cited on pages 199 and 238–9, taken from accounts describing the effects of *chevauchée* in the Hundred Years War. By penetrating so deeply and successfully into a region regarded as safe, the Black Prince was showing the French people that he was more powerful than their king, who was too feeble to protect them. But the propaganda victory did not translate into hard political gains. Edward wanted 'to terrify the inhabitants into changing allegiance . . . but they still feared French revenge at a later date more than they feared the enemy at the gates'.[79] The dread of a future, retributive atrocity neutralized the dread of a present, aggressive one. The Black Prince showed he understood this equation at Limoges.

The 1355 campaign is also interesting as it raises the question of whether Edward had adopted a battle-seeking policy. This has generated an ongoing debate between medieval military historians which is too involved to engage in great detail with here. Clifford Rogers sparked the debate with a series of scholarly articles and a book that offer contemporary evidence of Edward III and the Black Prince actively pursuing battle with the French. Some of this evidence can be interpreted in different ways; for example, when Jean le Bel quotes the King as saying he will go to France 'and do battle with King Jean',[80] is this a genuine quote and, if so, is it merely figurative? The Christmas letters home from Edward and Wingfield also indicate this intent in 1355; but then, for the satisfaction of honour, they would, as they are unlikely to say that Edward fled from the French at the faintest whiff of them. Apart from the sheer riskiness of battle and the general strategy of commanders to avoid it, there is also the practical matter of plunder: why risk losing the incredible wealth gained in a battle that could see it, and much more besides, lost to the French? It is easy to determine what a King John of England would do – grab the easy money and run – but a wholly different and more robust personality such as the Black Prince is a different matter.

Did the Black Prince, as one chronicle suggests of his father the King, 'lay waste to all the country, so that he would be giving the Frenchmen sharper provocation to fight?'[81] Rogers makes a strong case for this, arguing that the serious political and military situation within France at the time (compounded by the recent reaping of the Black Death) left King John II vulnerable to a decisive blow. He sees the move on Toulouse in this light: more than a shameful insult, the display of destroying the area outside the city was intended to draw the garrison out into the field of battle. At one point in late November, Edward's troops were drawn up in battle order, but the French, though greater in number, drew off. Edward's advance guard caught up with some, capturing men-at-arms while massacring the poor carters. There are always exceptions to the general rule of battle-avoidance, and Edward may have been one of them, just as William the Conqueror was at Hastings, deliberately targeting King Harold's estates to provoke him into a battle that William needed. Hewitt wrote: 'Since it was impracticable to occupy France ... the enemy was to be weakened by the destruction of his resources. Devastation was a negative, economic means for the attainment of the ultimate, political end.'[82] This impracticability (although not completely insurmountable: colonization, allies and a subjugated and cowed population might have achieved a similar result) might have meant that Edward sought a decisive, crushing victory in battle to radically alter the political situation in one swoop. The refusal of the inhabitants at Carcassonne to submit revealed the limits of ravaging; and the approach of the French armies soon afterwards made battle-seeking more possible. Is it a coincidence that the English sources seem to suggest a greater willingness for battle after the failure at Carcassonne?

The great English *chevauchées* of the Hundred Years War became more infrequent after the Black Prince's death as they failed to achieve major political or military objectives. Thereafter, they still played a dominant role in warfare as raids had always done – the extent of devastation in fifteenth-century France was every bit as great – but sieges were to determine the outcome of the great conflict. The French had starting responding to the *chevauchées* by adding greater strength to the major fortresses, abandoning the countryside and shadowing the English army with forces of their own, thereby preventing raiding parties peeling off from the main columns. All the while they scrupulously avoided battle. It was an extremely successful strategy and one that must have crossed the keen military minds of Edward and his commander. It was nothing new: Duke William of Normandy was doing the same thing against his enemies three centuries earlier in the 1050s. If battle-avoidance proved so effective for the French, it was obviously detrimental to the English.

Ravaging had many adaptive advantages – provisioning for the army, weakening the enemy politically and economically, punishing dissidents, plunder – to which battle-seeking or battle-avoidance could easily be added. If a main purpose of Edward's *chevauchée* was to take on the French in a pitched battle, he obviously failed. But then, he had much to compensate him, as the chroniclers attest: such was the booty, Edward's men 'didn't know what to do with it all'.[83] Some of that plunder had come from garrisons and castles, but most of it came from non-combatants who, as usual, had paid the price of war. Jean de Venette reflects sadly on how the ravaging of the Hundred Years War has destroyed his home village and all the livestock, exposing the reality of military campaigning:

The English, destroyed, burned, and plundered many little towns and villages capturing or even killing the inhabitants. The loss by fire of the village where I was born is to be lamented, together with that of many others near by. The vines in this region were not pruned or kept from rotting. The fields were not sown or ploughed. There were no cattle or fowl in the fields. No wayfarers went along the roads, carrying their best cheese and dairy products to market. The eye of man was saddened by the looks of the nettles and thistles springing up on every side. Instead of houses and churches there was the lamentable spectacle of scattered, smoking ruins to which they had been reduced by devouring flames. What more can I say? Every misery increased on every hand, especially among the rural population, the peasants, for their lords bore hard upon them, extorting from them all their substance and poor means of livelihood.[84]

CONCLUSIONS

The cases of ravaging discussed above were chosen not just because England has hitherto come off rather lightly as a place of atrocity, but also because they highlight important aspects of this form of campaigning. The Harrying of the North is an example of a pre-emptive scorched-earth policy, carried out to prevent an enemy creating a power base in the region by denying him supplies and the economic infrastructure necessary to sustain a competing polity. The Scottish invasions of 1138 demonstrate another form of extreme ravaging, this time fuelled by border tensions, ethnic hostility and growing national identity. John's *chevauchée* of 1215–16 makes explicit the links between ravaging and acts of cruelty and how it could be a carefully targeted weapon. And the Black Prince's raid of 1355 shows how waging war in such a manner undermined the financial basis of an enemy and challenged its leadership's authority. Of course, most cases of ravaging exhibit many or even all of these features, and others, too.

Before an army destroyed it gathered – or seized and stole. Military logistics were always to the forefront of a commander's mind. An army could take with it only limited provisions; these had to be supplemented by living off the land an army passed through. If ravaging had no military or political objectives, it would have still occurred for this reason. What an army gained an area lost, for, as has been succinctly noted, 'one man's foraging is another man's ravaging'.[85] What an army could not use it destroyed so that the enemy could not benefit from it, either through supply of goods or through the taxation levied on them.

Historians can sometimes lavish too much attention on the text of *De Re Militari* (or, more accurately, *Epitoma Rei Militaris*) Vegetius' late Roman handbook on war – he was, after all, just a donkey doctor – but the blindingly obvious recommendations in his beginner's guide to warfare are much quoted for the eternal, common-sense truths they propound, a pertinent one being: 'On any expedition, the single most effective weapon is that food should be sufficient for you while famine should break the enemy'.[86] Ravaging achieved just that. Commanders considering the impact of their troops travelling across friendly or neutral territory would ensure their troops bought what they needed, keeping his men under better control than the inflated prices. Henry V famously kept his troops in check during his invasion of Normandy: he treated the duchy as his sovereign territory and wished to impress his just lordship on its inhabitants. Duke William of Normandy only just managed to keep his invasion force gathered at Dives in line in 1066 by regular pay and markets. On Louis VIII's long march through friendly lands as he headed south to Avignon in 1226, he brought with him cattle and fodder from his own provinces. Conversely, three centuries later, when Charles V failed to pay his troops in 1527, they sacked Rome utterly.

Maintaining discipline and restricting ravaging were always easier in friendly territory, but could also be achieved (or at least the urge to loot could be channelled) in the field of operations. We have seen how ravaging could be accurately targeted against specific areas and enemy estates and to the extent that particular buildings in a town or village could be singled out. Even the Black Prince's *chevauchées*, infamously symbolic of the destruction of medieval warfare, were focused affairs. During the raid into Languedoc of 1355, the captain of Arouille immediately surrendered his castle and three local towns under his control; all were spared. The following year, on his way to victory at Poitiers, Prince Edward's forces inflicted huge damage on the western borders of the Limousin region, only to stop their depredations abruptly and briefly at Bellac: the widow there had connections with the English royal family.

Ravaging was also employed as a diversionary tactic. When in 1216 John heard that his castles at Windsor and Dover were besieged, he immediately embarked on a ravaging expedition of his enemies' estates at harvest time, successfully drawing them away from the sieges. Similarly, it was a device for goading a reluctant enemy into battle. This did not work on Count Baldwin of Flanders, who reassured his men as they watched his territory being burned by his enemies: 'They can't take the land with them.'[87] Baldwin, like Alexander II, David I, Louis VIII and any number of other leaders, was prepared to torch his

own lands to hinder an advancing enemy. A scorched-earth policy –
counter-ravaging as a defence mechanism – turned the tables on the
enemy presence. Count Raymond of Toulouse used it effectively
against the French at Avignon in 1226:

> The provisions of the [French] soldiers failed them and numbers of
> the troops died; for the count of Toulouse, like a skilful soldier, had,
> before the arrival of the French, removed out of their way all kinds
> of provisions, together with the old men, women, children, and the
> horses and cattle, so that they were deprived of all kind of sus-
> tenance. And it was not only the men who suffered, but also the
> horses and cattle of the army perished from hunger; for the count
> had ordered all the fields throughout the district to be ploughed up,
> so that there was no supply of fodder for the cattle except what had
> been brought from the French provinces; therefore large bodies of
> troops were obliged to leave the camp to seek provisions for the men
> and food for the horses, and on these trips ... they often suffered
> great losses from attacks by the count of Toulouse who, with his
> troops, lay in ambush for them.[88]

This passage is instructive as it shows Count Raymond protecting his
people by destroying their land and forcibly removing them from their
homes to prevent their being taken hostage for ransom. Their miseries
may have been compounded by hungry enemy soldiers becoming
further antagonized by the lack of food and booty, increasing
their hostility and inducing more violent behaviour against non-
combatants.

Brutality was likely to be intensified when colonial motives and
ethnic tensions came to the fore. It was one thing for a non-combatant
to have his land ravaged either as a warning or as a political measure,
but another to be physically ejected from his home area. This was the
fate of the inhabitants of Petit-Andely when the French took the town
at the siege of Château Gaillard; they were replaced by French colonists.
It was the frequent fate of the defeated in many towns; population
displacement was a significant feature of medieval warfare. An alternative way of achieving the same effect was to take not just homes,
but also liberty and life.

As in siege warfare, fear was considered a necessary part of many campaigns, a way of breaking resolve and encouraging either capitulation or coming to terms. The destructive nature of ravaging heightened fears. It worked well for John in 1215, when he met little resistance heading north; his cruel reputation had worked similarly against the Scots in 1209; and David's barbaric Galwegian troops played their part in forcing Stephen to negotiate in 1136 and 1138. There are endless examples of fear working; but it could operate both ways, as the Black Prince discovered at Carcassonne. There is also plenty of evidence to show that it could be counterproductive, as we have seen. Roger of Wendover reports that in the Welsh Marches, English troops occasionally followed the Welsh tradition of decapitating enemies. Welsh raiders of Hubert of Burgh's lands were beheaded when caught in 1231, Burgh delivering the heads to King Henry III. Prince Llewelyn, in typical Celtic border practice, then slaughtered non-combatants, women and children included, in churches. In 1245, Matthew Paris relates the return of a contingent of English troops to camp with the heads of one hundred Welshmen killed in – or just after – a skirmish, and how the Welsh decapitated everyone in a number of towns that they took in 1258. The English even offered bounties for Welsh heads. The belief that this might decrease Welsh raiding parties was not borne out. Frederick Suppe, who has studied this grisly practice, concludes that the only real benefit for the English was that such savagery vented their anger and frustration and gained a little 'psychological retaliation'; the evidence 'suggests that brutality only incited the Welsh to reciprocate. Terror, then, was no military deterrent.'[89] What worked in one place did not necessarily work in another. This was the cycle of atrocity that remained unbroken in the Middle Ages.

Successful ravaging was an economically efficient way of waging war, while imposing onerous expenses on the enemy. The raider could hope to reimburse the costs of his campaign through plunder, protection money and ransom; to the defender fell the heavy cost of lost productivity and lost taxes with the simultaneous need for vast outlays of capital on defences (town walls did not come cheap). The ultimate objective of major campaigns was political. Ravaging was part of the process in the pursuit of political gains. It intended to show the subjects of an enemy ruler how unprotected they were, and how much better they would be under a lord who could wield real power. Hence the

Black Prince raided the Languedoc when King John of France was politically weakened. Christopher Allmand has neatly summarized the purpose of ravaging thus: 'A war of successful raids might shake confidence further by showing that, as kings, they lacked the power to fulfil one of their prime roles, the defence of their people. ... In this way, their credibility would be undermined and weakened.'[90] Ravaging subverted the whole basis of the contract between a lord and his people. As the thirteenth-century *Schwabenspiegel* states: 'We should serve our lords for they protect us; if they do not protect us, justice does not oblige us to serve them'.[91]

When they were not protected, they generally took to the hills and forests with what they could carry or drive before them; as one fourteenth-century Frenchman put it, he joined the 'country people who were fleeing to the fields, ditches, caves and woods like desperate men'.[92] Sometimes, they simply joined in, looking for their share of spoils: victims as perpetrators. This happened on a relatively small scale in John's winter campaign of 1215–16, but it went much further in the Hundred Years War. When caught, these people would justify their actions through necessity. Nicholas Wright offers examples of this in his studies on the effect of the war on the French countryside. In the late fourteenth century, Jean le Jeusne explained that he was forced into joining a company of twelve men who lived by brigandage because it was the only way to survive. When the fighting calmed down, he returned to his peaceful occupation as a labourer. When two armed men entered the village of St Romain in 1373 with the purpose of forcing money from its inhabitants, the whole village was evacuated and took refuge in woods. Ten of their bravest men returned after a week and discovered three pillagers in one of their houses. After a violent struggle, they took the three men to the river and drowned them.

But vigilante action was not encouraged: it undermined what remained of the authority of the justice system. In 1375 a poor weaver of Vernon was kept in a small wicker basket for ten days and forced to pay a huge sum of sixty gold francs for having taken part in the killing of a pillager. However, involvement was welcomed when it contributed to the war effort. On their hurried retreat to London in 1217, the French soldiers defeated at Lincoln passed through towns where the inhabitants ambushed them with bludgeons, killing many.

No doubt the French were plundered just as they had plundered the townspeople. But opportunism in war was nothing new, as we saw in chapter two, with the case in 1050 of two serfs who joined those plundering their lord's lands. They were captured and blinded.

It has been suggested by some historians that the killing of non-combatants rose with the demise of slavery, as people lost their value. Non-combatant men were often killed on ravaging expeditions simply to deny the enemy any chance of recruiting them as soldiers; and anyone might be killed, for reasons already discussed. But on most occasions, non-combatants were just as likely to be taken hostage, as John's 1215 campaign reveals. The ransoms from non-combatants were not inconsiderable. Philippe Contamine provides evidence of this in a paper on ransom and booty in English Normandy towards the end of the Hundred Years War, in which he notes: 'Certainly, it is striking to see that the ransoms of supposed non-combatants are not very inferior to those of soldiers.'[93] They were frequently comparable. Contamine cites the case of the unfortunate Jean Guérard, a poor man of thirty-four years, married and with a child. He was taken by French soldiers in 1419, and again in 1420; he was made to pay twenty *moutons d'or* on both occasions. In 1425 he was taken for a third time, this time by English soldiers, and ransomed for twenty *écus*.

Even in death, it could be hard to avoid the clutches of soldiers. As mentioned, corpses could be ransomed at half the price of a living person, if they were to be ransomed at all. The Scottish invasion of Ireland coincided with the Great Famine of 1317. Foraging was understandably very poor. As a consequence, one chronicler tells us that the soldiers were 'so destroyed with hunger that they raised the bodies of the dead from the cemeteries'.[94] No wonder the banners of an approaching army on campaign so terrified non-combatants.

6

MEDIEVAL SAVAGERY?

Modern research has devoted much time to examining man's ability to act cruelly. Investigations such as the infamous Stanford experiment reveal how quickly people can adapt to violent and sadistic modes of behaviour. The modern military, struggling in the twentieth century with the natural reluctance of man to kill, has funded research which has led to combat training that develops a conditional reflex to killing the enemy, or 'targets'. Chemical reactions triggered in sequence in the brain also play their part, prompting responses that enable a man to end the life of another. This library of research can shed useful light on the soldier's role in atrocities in both our age and the Middle Ages, but it can have only a limited application to the earlier time. Yes, medieval soldiers were conditioned in a fashion – that is what training and propaganda have always done since civilization began – but it goes deeper than that, and is more basic. The eminent psychologist Philip Zimbardo, of Stanford Prison Experiment fame, has examined the psychology of evil in his recent book *The Lucifer Effect: How Good People Turn Evil*, in which he wisely concludes that research 'might be as thick as a phone book', but to really comprehend what happens, 'we have to understand the person in the situation'.[1]

The situation is all-important. If a medieval soldier was ordered to kill a non-combatant, it was unlikely that he would refuse, lest he become a victim too. (The sources do not attest to there having been many conscientious objectors.) The basis of this book has been to explain atrocities in the light of the military imperative, the calculated decision that acts of savagery and mass executions would further military objectives. But on plenty of occasions, individual acts of atrocity were committed without express commands. In many cases there has been a tacit – or at least unrecorded – understanding that soldiers would behave in this way; certainly, the expectation of such behaviour was never remote. King David of Scotland may not have encouraged the chivalrous knights of his royal household to behave in the same way as his brutal infantry, but that does not mean he did not appreciate the military effect of rampaging footsoldiers. In this book we have come across events where the matter of life and death was at the whim of the soldier. Killing could be quite arbitrary: a soldier might strike down a non-combatant one day, but not the next. It could all depend on whether a campaign had been gruelling or not; whether a comrade had been killed by disease or combat; whether booty and opportunity had been good so far; or any number of other factors too myriad to explore.

The very nature of a war was a significant determinant. Those fought in border regions, as on the Celtic fringe in England, the Reconquista in Spain, or the crusades in the Holy Land or Baltic, were particularly marked by a harshness that became endemic and ingrained. Even a conflict like that between England and France – paragons of chivalry – could become more brutalized over time, as the Hundred Years War shows. Ideas of chivalry evolved accordingly: although many writers still decried the treatment of non-combatants, many others, especially self-justifying literary warriors, simply chose to accept that targeting non-combatants was an acceptable part of chivalrous warfare. However, whatever the theatre of war, there were always exceptions to the savagery – examples of civilized behaviour and tolerance – indicating that the conflict need not be the way it is, and challenging the justification for certain acts. The fact that atrocities could spark a wave of reciprocation and a downward spiral of violence occasionally stayed the hand of a commander; but in any given situation he might determine that a display of power and brutality was what was needed to help him win his objectives. Sadly, more often than not he would have been right in this assessment.

For the ordinary soldier, belonging to a larger group of his contingent within an army was usually of great importance. Often far from home and, of course, in hostile territory, his immediate combat unit, however loosely defined or organized, constituted his comrades and support. Research on soldiers in combat shows that in the wars of recent history, men have fought not so much for their country or a cause, but for their fellow soldiers. This 'primary-group cohesion', a bonding strengthened by experiences in war, is an important part in understanding soldiers' behaviour. In the American Civil War one southern corporal wrote that a soldier on leave was always anxious to get back: 'There is a feeling of love – a strong attachment for those with whom one has shared common dangers, that is never felt ... under any other circumstances.' An officer who fought at the Battle of Shiloh in 1862, reflected that those 'who had stood shoulder to shoulder during the terrible days of that bloody battle were hooped with steel, with bands stronger than steel'.[2] Every modern conflict reaffirms these attitudes.

Unfortunately, this noble and honourable aspect of soldiering has its dark side. Primary group cohesion can also lead troops into committing atrocities. The terrible Russian advance into Berlin in 1945 resulted in rape on a massive scale; it is an easy task to fold a thousand years of history to place the following passage in the medieval period: 'Marauders and rapists acted as a rule under the influence of alcohol, and they acted in bands, and thus under peer pressure – venting a collective rage pent-up from years of oppression ... One can well imagine the taunts at those unwilling to engage in a virile attack on German women. ... Officers stood by passively during gang-rapes, or made sure every man had his turn.'[3]

Christopher Browning's seminal study of a German death squad, *Ordinary Men: Reserve Police Battalion 101 and the Final Solution in Poland*, disturbingly shows how unexceptional men would actively choose to participate in the execution of civilians, men, women and children: 'Within virtually every social collective, the peer group exerts tremendous peer pressure and sets moral norms. If the men of Reserve Police Battalion 101 could become killers under such circumstances, what group of men cannot?'[4] As with the Russians in Berlin, so men wanted to join in with their mates and not risk being taunted as weaklings. The sordid monetary interest was also always present. The Russians, like the Germans before them, plundered as they advanced. Executed Jews often meant clothes, jewellery and other property for the killers; careerist officers saw opportunities for promotion.

Hard as it is to understand for those of us lucky enough not to have fought in war, many soldiers have found the experience of combat an enjoyable one. Another soldier who took part in the Battle of Shiloh declared: 'I never felt before, the excitement which makes a man want to rush into the fight, but I did that day.'[5] Ernest Jung, a modern, Prussian version of Bertran de Born, wrote of his time at war in books like *Storm of Steel*, celebrating the First World War as a fundamental element to be experienced and enjoyed. In her important book *An Intimate History of Killing*, Joanna Bourke devotes a whole chapter to 'The Pleasures of War', describing this phenomenon in modern warfare and how it has contributed to atrocity. Bloodlust becomes an urge to sate. Niall Ferguson has also helped dispel the myth that the industrial carnage of the First World War was mitigated by the civilized – chivalrous, we could say – behaviour of troops and officers. A sergeant on the Somme wrote that combat left a man 'half-mad with excitement . . . when you start a man killing, you can't turn him off again like an engine'; another soldier spoke of 'the swift thrill of approaching death . . . a wonderful sensation not to be missed'. The execution of German prisoners was often officially sanctioned. One bloodthirsty English colonel instructed his men: 'You may meet a German who says, "Mercy! I have ten children!" Kill him! He may have ten more.' Another officer told his sergeant to 'blood his men' by executing some German prisoners. After the massacre began, the sergeant looked around and asked: 'Where's 'Arry? . . . 'Arry 'asn't 'ad a go yet.' After Harry, 'a timid boy', was 'given his man to kill', he became 'like a man-eating tiger in his desire for German blood'.[6]

These impulses were – and are – experienced by many soldiers in all wars. Some war correspondents witness all manner of horrors and yet become addicted to war and acknowledge the enjoyment, or thrill, that they and soldiers derive from it, 'the shared and terrible love of it all', as one puts it.[7] It would be strange to single out the Middle Ages as being any different. In a predominantly illiterate society, there are no thoughts recorded by the common soldier. But absence of evidence is not evidence of absence. We do, however, have plenty of testimony to what we would recognize as primary-group cohesion among the knightly classes; bonding was part of the process of chivalry. Jean of Bueil wrote in the fifteenth century that 'war is a joyous thing':

You love your comrade so much in war . . . A great feeling of loyalty and of pity fills your heart on seeing your friend so valiantly exposing his body to execute and accomplish the command of the Creator. And then you are prepared to go and die or live with him, and for love not to abandon him. And out of that there arises such a delectation, that he who has not experienced it is not fit to say what delight it is . . . A man who does that feels so strengthened, so elated, that he does not know where he is.[8]

The sentiments expressed are strikingly similar to the modern quotes above, and many other modern recollections of comradeship in war. Such bonding is evident in ancient Greek epics and was a major literary theme of medieval chivalric works, as exemplified in the relationship between Roland and Oliver in *The Song of Roland*. By the twelfth century, 'military friendship transcends all others'.[9] It seems to me that this enjoyment of war, its compulsion, is sometimes masked by the appeal to higher motives of country, cause or religion. Such an appeal is, of course, similarly used to justify atrocities or more mundane mercenary motives. Freud believed that war strips us of the accretions of civilization and lays bare the primal man in each of us. War is co-eternal with man's nature.

Why, then, should the Middle Ages be regarded any differently? Why should the medieval soldier behave any differently from the modern one? Historians have to treat medieval sources with great care, allowing for the influences of bigotry, patronage, ignorance of events, religion and literary devices. Many medieval military historians will allow, as it is so often put, 'a kernel of truth' in atrocity stories but stress the undoubtedly exaggerated nature of the reports, and that individual acts are inflated into generalities. So if one chronicle hears of an especially gruesome act – say, taking a real example from one medieval writer, the cutting off of women's breasts (one of Edward I's complaints to the Pope about Scottish atrocities) – then others copy it and it escalates into a typical action of other soldiers on any given occasion. But in reality, there were relatively few writers, especially in the earlier part of the Middle Ages. If a writer hears of one gruesome event, how many other non-writers have heard it, too, and at different times and in different places? What are the odds that the atrocity chanced to occur just once, near to a monastery where a monk was just happening to write a chronicle at the same time, and whose writings have just happened to survive to the present day? Some of these accounts took on biblical descriptions (St Agatha had her breasts cut off) and others became repeated literary themes (topoi) which historians are always on the look-out for, but these may be an expression of limitation for writers who did not witness the important event, or who wished to embellish it.

The medieval example just given of cutting off women's breasts rings warning bells of such extreme, almost gratuitous writing. Yet here is a marine from Vietnam who used to sport a necklace of ears: 'We used to cut their ears off. We had a trophy. If a guy would have a necklace of ears, he was a good killer, a good trooper. It was encouraged to cut ears, to cut the nose off, to cut the guy's penis off. A female, you cut her breasts off. It was encouraged to do these things. The officers expected you to do it or something was wrong with you.'[10] Similar stories are repeated from Europe at the very end of the twentieth century, in the Serbian wars. Again, these are modern examples that can explain medieval atrocities, so why are the medieval ones so readily dismissed, qualified or watered down?

There are a number of main reasons. First, there is the necessary tendency to question medieval writers, especially when they are monastic. If one moment a monk is writing incredulous, plainly ridiculous miracle stories, such as Wendover's cautionary tale, mentioned earlier (above, p. 10), of a little black suckling pig draining a washerwoman dry for taking in laundry on a Sunday, and in the next paragraph he recounts an atrocity, then there is a natural tendency towards scepticism. Secondly, many writers are dismissed as hysterical monks given to hyperbole, especially when their monastic lands suffer some minor, relatively inconsequential damage by soldiers, or have their horses and grain taken. Thirdly, writers primarily wrote to please their patrons, and so their bias has to be accommodated when interpreting and filtering their texts. Fourthly, there is too much credence given to religious and chivalric texts and to the laws of war that were so often only intermittently applied. Most historians recognize that these ideals and laws were arbitrarily applied, and then not often to noncombatants, but the continuing influence and knowledge of these texts sometimes still disproportionately informs viewpoints. Fifthly, there is a natural and understandable tendency for a reader not to want to believe the horrors being related, sometimes partly from a misplaced or unconsciously displaced notion that these things simply do not happen now, and therefore they did not then; and if they did, they are exceptions. Finally for our purposes of summary here, there is no evidence in the form of film, photographs or the reporting of prize-winning and trusted journalists to indisputably fix an atrocity in a definite time and place, and with real people as the victims. Technology permits us to have libraries of atrocity evidence for modern wars; medieval society had to rely on writers to record them – and that usually meant monks.

The atrocity stories from medieval chronicles are too readily discounted or diluted because they do not conform to modern standards of evidence-gathering. Yet so often the sensationalism of medieval reports is the reality of modern ones. The parallels are striking. The killing of prisoners is also a feature of recent warfare. We have seen this for the First World War; in the Second World War, a 'no prisoner' policy was often employed by Americans fighting in the Far East, and German prisoners were killed during the D-Day landings; many prisoners were similarly despatched in Vietnam. Civilians are targeted, whether in bombing raids or in direct attacks on villages and towns. The British dropped chemical bombs in Iraq in the 1920s; Saddam Hussein later used chemical weapons on the Kurds. The Germans had a policy of burning villages and towns when entering and leaving Russia; villages were torched in Vietnam and, at My Lai, inhabitants massacred. In the Middle Ages peasants took to the hills and forests to avoid princes on punitive expeditions; Greek men did the same in the Second World War to avoid expected German reprisals. Useless mouths were expelled from Paris in 1870, and were cited by defendants at the Nuremberg trials. Prisoners in the Second World War who died on marches in the Far East and on the German retreat form Eastern Europe are not so dissimilar to those non-combatants caught in the Scottish raids and whipped forward into slavery, or expiring along the way; and the slaying of those who might impede the slave drive is affirmed by a nineteenth-century Nigerian slave who has said that the old and very young had to flee or be cut down.

What of the most shocking medieval cases, the ones most likely to be met with disbelief? Monks writing of priests being beheaded at the altar might suggest special pleading, but the clergy were marked for horrific torture and death in the Spanish Civil War. Henry of Huntingdon's gruesome account of troops entertaining themselves by swapping around severed heads was replayed with revolting imagination by Japanese troops during the Rape of Nanking. Photographs from Italy in the Second World War show civilian militia joyfully parading the head of a partisan on a pole. In Vietnam, sunglasses, cigarettes and excrement were carefully placed on the head of a North Vietnamese corpse. In Spanish Morocco, troops in Franco's forces rode around with heads swinging from their bridles.

What of cannibalism at Château Gaillard, Rouen and other sieges and campaigns? Again, this has been widely reported and verified whenever famine or starvation threatens: remember the survivors of the *Essex*, found still clutching the gnawed bones of their dead crewmates? In the Second World War starving Japanese soldiers were permitted to eat the flesh of prisoners. But even stories like these are routinely dismissed. The siege of Leningrad produced many stories of cannibalism. 'Such nightmarish circumstances', notes the authority John Erickson, 'long discounted and disbelieved, require some substantiation.' He offers this by citing a top-secret Soviet report form February 1942 which details '886 investigated cases between early December 1941 and February 15, 1942, alone'.[11] No wonder children were warned not to venture down alleyways.

War does not change much when men are operating in the field. In parts of the developing world, especially in Africa, the nature of warfare is pretty much the same as in early medieval Europe. It is also worth repeating my impressions at the opening of this book: watching the post-Yugoslavian war unfold on the news in the 1990s, I was struck by how much even European warfare resembled that of the Middle Ages: donkeys transporting supplies up hills to the Serbian forces during the long siege of Sarajevo; burning villages and ethnic cleansing; and atrocities like the massacre of seven to eight thousand Muslim men and boys at Srebrenica, the purpose of which was to reduce the manpower available to the opposing army. Everywhere, terror and atrocity are present as a manifestation of the military imperative.

It has always been this way. Besieged by Julius Caesar at Alesia in 52 BC, Vercingetorix expelled his useless mouths, wives, children and parents, and saw them die slowly in front of the walls as Caesar refused to allow them to pass or be taken into slavery. Thucydides' *History of the Peloponnesian Wars* tells of whole islands having their men massacred. Going back three thousand years, the inscription on the

Moabite stone tells of King Moab's wars against the Israelites. He boasts of slaughtering all in the cities he wins: 'I took it and killed them all – 7,000 men, boys, women, girls and female slaves.'[12]

Atrocities still abound in our world in recent years: Rwanda, former Yugoslavia, Iraq, Sudan, the Congo, to name the best known. The Middle Ages were no different. As a recent study of medieval genocide thinking concludes: 'Modern ethnic slaughter does not necessarily depend for its occurrence upon the governmental and technological resources usually associated with modernity; when popular moods and mentalities favour extreme action, the most basic means often suffice.'[13] As this book has attempted to show, medieval warfare favoured extreme actions. But their medieval barbarities were far from unique. Medieval commanders would have approved of General 'Bloody Eyes' Skobelev's belief expressed when, after slaughtering thousands (perhaps as many as fifteen thousand) Turks, he declared: 'The duration of peace is in direct proportion to the slaughter you inflict on the enemy.'

Gerald of Wales was well aware of the cruelties of war. Sadly, his call for a more humane type of warfare was not heeded: 'When the turmoil of battle is over and [the warrior] has laid aside his arms, ferocity too should be laid aside, a human code of behaviour should be once more adopted, and feelings of mercy and clemency should be revived in the spirit that is truly noble.'[14] War is always with us, and so this call remains just as pertinent in the twenty-first century as it was in the Middle Ages. Sadly, it is unlikely to be heard above the gunfire and exploding bombs forever claiming their victims in execution of the military imperative.

NOTES

(Place of publication is London unless otherwise stated)

CHAPTER 1: VIOLENCE

1 Brian Holden Reid, 'Rationality and Irrationality in Union Strategy, April 1861–March 1862', *War in History*, 1 (1) (1994), 23.
2 G. N. Garmonsway (ed. and trans.), *The Anglo-Saxon Chronicle* (1972), 135.
3 Henry of Huntingdon, *The History of the English People, 1000–1154*, ed. and trans. Diana Greenway (Oxford, 2002), 7.
4 Johan Huizinga, *The Waning of the Middle Ages* (New York, 1949; original edn 1919), 11, 12, 24.
5 Barbara Tuchman, *A Distant Mirror: The Calamitous Fourteenth Century* (New York, 1978), 134–5.
6 Suger, *The Deeds of Louis the Fat*, ed. and trans. Richard Cusimano and John Moorhead (Washington, 1992), 116.
7 John Hudson, *The Formation of the English Common Law: Law and Society in England from the Norman Conquest to Magna Carta*, (1996), 74. The following three paragraphs draw heavily on this important survey.
8 Henry Summerson, 'Attitudes to Capital Punishment in England, 1200–1350', in Michael Prestwich, Richard Britnell and Robin Frame (eds), *Thirteenth Century England 8* (Woodbridge, 2001), 25.
9 Cynthia Neville, 'Homicide in the Ecclesiastical Court of Fourteenth-Century Durham', in Nigel Saul (ed.), *Fourteenth-Century England 1* (Woodbridge, 2000), 14.
10 Trevor Dean, *Crime in Medieval Europe* (2001), 16. A number of the following examples are to be found in this book.
11 Henry Moore, *The History of the Persecutions of the Church of Rome and Complete Protestant Martyrology;* (1809), 256–7. As the title may suggest, this is not an unbiased work; it heavily utilizes John Foxe's *Acts and Monuments* of 1563, more popularly known as *Foxe's Book of Martyrs*.
12 Richard Evans, *Rituals of Retribution: Capital Punishment in Germany, 1600–1987* (1997 edn; originally Oxford, 1996), 28. This massive scholarly work, though taking the Early Modern period as its starting point, can hardly be

bettered for its discussion of the role of capital punishment in society, its observations holding true for the medieval world.

13 George Scott, *A History of Torture*, (1940), 246. My thanks to Ian Grant for locating this and other books on torture. I have been unable to determine whether goats have a particular liking for brine, although farmer John Booth informs me that goats do enjoy salt-licks.

14 Robert Bartlett, *England Under the Norman and Angevin Kings, 1075–1225*, (Oxford), 2000, 185.

15 Dean, *Crime in Medieval Europe*, 125.

16 Evans, *Rituals of Retribution*, 31.

17 Ibid., 28.

18 Claude Gauvard, 'Justification and Theory of the Death Penalty at the *Parlement* of Paris in the Late Middle Ages', in Christopher Allmand (ed.), *War, Government and Power in Late Medieval France* (Liverpool, 2000), 198.

19 Philipa Maddern, *Violence and Social Order: East Anglia, 1422–1442* (Oxford, 1992), 232.

20 Dean, *Crime in Medieval Europe*, 81. See also the findings in Nancy Wicher, 'Selective Female Infanticide as Partial Explanation for the Dearth of Women in Viking Age Scandinavia', in Guy Halsall (ed.), *Violence and Society in the Early Medieval West* (Woodbridge, 1998).

21 Barbara Hanawalt, 'Violence in the Domestic Milieu of Late Medieval England', in Richard Kaeuper (ed.), *Violence in Medieval Society* (Woodbridge, 2000), 201.

22 Dean, *Crime in Medieval Europe*, 82.

23 Summerson, 'Attitudes to Capital Punishment', 133.

24 Hudson, *Formation of the English Common Law*, 160.

25 Michael Goodich, *Violence and Miracle in the Fourteenth Century* (Chicago, 1995), 155.

26 Cynthia Neville, 'War, Women and Crime in the Northern Border Lands in the Later Middle Ages', in Donald Kagay and L. J. Andrew Villalon (eds), *The Final Argument: The Imprint of Violence on Society in Medieval and Early Modern Europe* (Woodbridge, 1998), 169.

CHAPTER 2: WAR

1 C. Warren Hollister, 'Royal Acts of Mutilation: The Case Against Henry I', in *Monarchy, Magnates and Institutions in the Anglo-Norman World* (1986), 296–7.

2 Suger, 79–80. Other translations substitute 'mutilation' with 'castration'.

3 H. Ellis (ed.), *The Chronicle of John Hardyng* (1812). I have modernized the Old English.

4 J. E. A. Joliffe, *Angevin Kingship* (1963), 98.

5 Paul Hyams, 'What Did Henry III of England Think in Bed and in French about Kingship and Anger?', in Barbara Hanawalt (ed.), *Anger's Past: The Social Uses of an Emotion in the Middle Ages* (Ithaca, 1998), 123. I have translated the Latin.

6 Richard Barton, 'Zealous Anger and the Renegotiation of Aristocratic Relations in 11th- and 12th-Century France', in ibid.; 159.

7 Marc Bloch, *Feudal Society* (Chicago, 1961), *passim*.

8 Richard Kaeuper, *War, Justice and Public Order: England and France in the Later Middle Ages* (Oxford, 1988), 226.

9 Benjamin Arnold, *Princes and Territories in Medieval Germany* (Cambridge, 1991), 235.

10 Malcolm Vale, 'Trial by Battle in the Later Middle Ages', in Richard Kaeuper (ed.), *Violence in Medieval Society* (Woodbridge, 2000), 164.

11 Froissart, *Chronicles*, ed. and trans. Geoffrey Brereton (Harmondsworth, 1978), 151.

12 Suger, 141.

13 Ibid.

14 Kelly de Vries, 'Harold Godwinson in Wales: Military Legitimacy in Late Anglo-Saxon England', in Richard Abels (ed.), *The Normans and Their Adversaries* (Woodbridge, 2001), 85.

15 Matthew Strickland, 'Against the Lord's Anointed: Aspects of Warfare and Baronial Rebellion in England and Normandy, 1075–1265', in George Garnett and John Hudson (eds), *Law and Government in Medieval England and Normandy* (Cambridge, 1994), 60.

16 A. L. Brown, *The Governance of Late Medieval England* (1989), 18.

17 Maddern, *Violence and Social Order*, 12. I have modernized the Old English.

18 John Gillingham, *Richard Coeur de Lion* (1994), 95, 101 and *passim* for these and many other similar examples.

19 W. Paden, T. Sankovitch and P. Stalen (eds and trans.), *The Poems of Bertran de Born* (Los Angeles, 1986), 392, 380.

20 Helen Nicholson (ed. and trans.), *Chronicle of the Third Crusade* (Aldershot, 1997), 163.

21 Ibid.

22 Francesco Gabrieli (ed. and trans.), *Arab Historians of the Crusades* (1969), 213.

23 Nicholson, *Chronicle of the Third Crusade*, 204.

24 Peter Edbury (ed. and trans.), *The Conquest of Jerusalem and the Third Crusade* (Aldershot, 1996), 105.

25 John Appleby (ed. and trans.), *The Chronicle of Richard of Devizes* (1963), 78.

26 Nicholson, *Chronicle of the Third Crusade*, 223.

27 Cited in Sean McGlynn, 'Philip Augustus: Too Soft a King?', *Medieval Life*, 7 (1997), 24.

28 Ibid. 25.

29 Simeon of Durham, A *History of the Kings of England*, ed. and trans. J. Stevenson (Lampeter, 1987), 43.

30 Matthew Strickland, *War and Chivalry: The Conduct and Perception of War in England and Normandy, 1066–1217* (Cambridge, 1996), 90.

31 Walter Ullman, *Medieval Political Thought* (1975), 157.

32 H. E. J. Cowdrey, *Popes, Monks and Crusaders* (1984), VII, 44.

33 Kaeuper, *War, Justice and Public Order*, 146.

34 Blaise Pascal, cited in Michael Burleigh, *The Third Reich* (2000), frontispiece.

35 John Beeler, *Warfare in Feudal Europe* (Ithaca, 1971), xii.

36 Timothy Reuter, '*Episcopi cum sua militia:* The Prelate as Warrior in the Early Staufer Era', in Timothy Reuter (ed.), *Warriors and Churchmen in the Middle Ages* (1992), 85.

37 W. A. Pantin, *The English Church in the Fourteenth Century* (Toronto, 1980), 212.

38 *Anglo-Saxon Chronicle*, 186.

39 Gillian Spraggs, *Outlaws and Highwaymen: The Cult of the Robber in England from the Middle Ages to the Nineteenth Century* (2001) (cited in *London Review of Books*, 9 May, 2002, 32).

40 J. M. Wallace-Hadrill, 'War and Peace in the Earlier Middle Ages', *Transactions of the Royal Historical Society*, 25 (1975), 162.

41 Maurice Keen, *The Laws of War in the Later Middle Ages* (1965), 8.

42 Ibid., 64–5.

43 Frederick Russell, *The Just War in the Middle Ages* (Cambridge, 1976), 306, 308.

44 Guy Halsall, 'Playing By Whose Rules? A Further Look at Viking Atrocity in the Ninth Century', *Medieval History*, 2 (2) (1992), 2.

45 Ibid., 7.

46 Matthew Strickland, 'Slaughter, Slavery or Ransom: The Impact of the Conquest on Conduct in Warfare', in Carola Hicks (ed.), *England in the Eleventh Century* (Stamford, 1992), 43.

47 John Gillingham, *The English in the Twelfth Century: Imperialism, National Identity and Politics* (Woodbridge, 2000), 209–10.

48 Keen, *Laws of War*, 180.

49 Hyams, 'What Did Henry III Think . . .', 107.

50 Orderic Vitalis, *The Ecclesiastical History*, ed. and trans. Marjorie Chibnall (Oxford, 1969–81), vi, 240.

51 Roger of Wendover, *Flowers of History*, ed. and trans. J. A. Giles (Lampeter, 1996), ii, 397. I have slightly modernized the translation.

52 Ibid., 397–8.

53 Robert Stacey, 'The Age of Chivalry', in Michael Howard, George Andreopoulis and Mark Shulman (eds), *The Laws of War: Constraints on Warfare in the Western World* (New Haven, 1994), 33.

54 Ibid. 34, 35.

55 Richard Kaeuper, *Chivalry and Violence in Medieval Europe* (Oxford, 1999), 3.

56 Cited in Philippe Contamine, *War in the Middle Ages* (Oxford, 1984), 290.

57 Maurice Keen, 'Chivalry, Nobility and the Man-at-Arms', in Christopher Allmand (ed.), *War, Literature and Politics in the Late Middle Ages* (Liverpool, 1976), 45.

58 The Latin, literally 'by iron and flame', is *ferro flammisque*. Roger of Wendover uses this phrase on a number of occasions, e.g. Roger of Wendover, *Flores Historiarum*, ed. and trans. H. G. Hewlett, Rolls Series, 1886–1889, ii, 98, 161, 163 for the original Latin.

CHAPTER 3: BATTLES

1 Orderic Vitalis, ii, 218.
2 John Gillingham, 'An Age of Expansion, *c.*1020–1204', in Maurice Keen (ed.), *Medieval Warfare: A History* (Oxford, 1999), 76.
3 *Anglo-Saxon Chronicle*, 199.
4 Roger of Wendover, ii, 364.
5 A. J. Holden, D. Crouch and S. Gregory (eds), *History of William Marshal* (2002), i, 395 (hereafter *History of William Marshal*).
6 S. Weinberg, *Glory and Terror* (New York, 2004), 61.
7 Henry Riley (ed. and trans.), *Annals of Roger of Hoveden* (Lampeter, 1997), ii, 140–1. I have used the superior translation in John Gillingham, *Richard 1* (1999), 127.
8 R. A. Brown (ed. and trans.) *The Norman Conquest* (Woodbridge, 1985), 35.
9 Froissart, cited in Contamine, *War in the Middle Ages*, 256–7.
10 Gabrieli, *Arab Historians of the Crusade*, 135.
11 Einhard and Nokter, *Two Lives of Charlemagne*, trans. Lewis Thorpe (Harmondsworth, 1969), 61.
12 Ibid., 62–3.
13 A. B. Scott and F. X. Martin (eds and trans.), *Expugnatio Hibernica* (Dublin, 1978), 59 (hereafter Gerald of Wales, *Expugnatio*).
14 G. H. Opren (ed. and trans.), *Song of Dermot and the Earl* (Lampeter, 1994), 111.
15 Gerald of Wales, *Expugnatio*, 59–65 for the debate.
16 C. P. Melville and M. C. Lyons, 'Saladin's Hattin Letter', in B. Z. Kedar (ed.), *The Horns of the Hattin* (London and Jerusalem, 1992), 211.
17 D. S. Richards (ed. and trans.), *The Rare and Excellent History of Saladin*, (Aldershot, 1992), 75.
18 Gabrieli, *Arab Historians of the Crusade*, 138.
19 Melville and Lyons, 'Saladin's Hattin Letter', 212.
20 Nicholson, *Chronicle of the Third Crusade*, 34.
21 Ibid.
22 Richards, *The Rare and Excellent History of Saladin*, 74.
23 Nicholson, *Chronicle of the Third Crusade*, 34.
24 Richards, *The Rare and Excellent History of Saladin*, 164–5.
25 Gabrieli, *Arab Historians of the Crusade*, 349.
26 Gillingham, *Richard I*, 167.
27 Marianne Ailes and Malcolm Barber (eds and trans.), *The History of the Holy War* (Woodbridge, 2003), ii, 108; Nicholson, *Chronicle of the Third Crusade*, 229.
28 Gabrieli, *Arab Historians of the Crusade*, 224.
29 Ailes and Barber, *The History of the Third Crusade*, 108; Nicholson, *Chronicle of the Third Crusade*, 231.
30 Peter W. Edbury (ed. and trans.), *The Conquest of Jerusalem and the Third Crusade: Sources in Translation* (Aldershot, 1996), 108.
31 Cited in Gillingham, *Richard I*, 170.

32 Edbury, *The Conquest of Jerusalem*, 180.

33 Nicholson, *Chronicle of the Third Crusade*, 231; Richards, *Saladin*, 165.

34 Anne Curry (ed. and trans.), *The Battle of Agincourt: Sources and Interpretations* (Woodbridge, 2000), 82 (hereafter, Curry). This is a superbly comprehensive (and convenient) collection of all relevant medieval sources.

35 Ibid., 47.

36 Ibid., 52.

37 Ibid., 37.

38 Ibid., 37.

39 Ibid., 47.

40 Ibid., 62.

41 Ibid., 92–3.

42 Ibid. 107; Anne Curry, *Agincourt: A New History* (Stroud, 2005), 248.

43 Curry, 53.

44 Ibid. 39–40.

45 Ibid., 108.

46 Ibid., 131.

47 H. T. Riley (ed.), *Annals of John of Trokelow* (London, 1886), 87.

48 Curry, *Agincourt: A New History*, 250.

49 Keith Dockray (ed.), *Henry VI, Margaret of Anjou and the Wars of the Roses: A Source Book* (Stroud, 2000), 112.

50 Ibid., 133.

51 Alistair Dunn, 'A Kingdom in Crisis: Henry IV and the Battle of Shrewsbury', *History Today*, 53 (8) (2003), 32.

52 Roger of Wendover, ii, 508.

53 Froissart, 93.

54 Richard W. Kaueper and Elspeth Kennedy (eds and trans.), *The Book of Chivalry of Geoffroi de Charny* (Pennsylvania, 1996), 99.

55 Cited in J. F. Verbruggen, *The Art of Warfare in Western Europe During the Middle Ages* (Woodbridge, 1997), 44.

56 Ibid., 45.

57 Ibid., 48.

58 Suger, 32–3.

59 Joinville and Villehardouin, *Chronicles of the Crusades*, ed. and trans. M. R. B. Shaw (Harmondsworth, 1963), 252–3.

60 Cited in Huizinga, *The Waning of the Middle Ages*, 82, n.1.

CHAPTER 4: SIEGES

1 R. A. Brown, *English Castles* (1976), 198.

2 John France, *Western Warfare in the Age of the Crusades, 1000–1300* (1999), 126.

3 H. F. Delaborde, *Oeuvres de Rigord et de Guillaume le Breton* (Paris, 1882), ii, 198.

4 Michael Prestwich, *Armies and Warfare in the Middle Ages: The English Experience* (1996), 300.

5 Keen, *Laws of War*, 124.

6 Orderic Vitalis, iv, 218.

7 R. Howlett (ed.), *Chronicles of the Reigns of Stephen, Henry II and Richard I*, 4 vols, Rolls Series, i, 331.

8 Steven Runciman, *The First Crusade* (Cambridge, 1980), 188.

9 H. E. Mayer, *The Crusades* (Oxford, 1988), 56.

10 Edward Peters, *The First Crusade: The Chronicle of Fulcher of Chartres and Other Source Materials* (Pennsylvania, 1988), 110.

11 Susan Edgington, *The First Crusade* (1996), 9.

12 Peters, *First Crusade*, 205.

13 Rosalind Hill (ed. and trans.), *Gesta Francorum* (1962), 91–2.

14 Peters, *First Crusade*, 92.

15 Ibid., 260–1.

16 Carol Sweeetenham (ed. and trans.), *Robert the Monk's History of the First Crusade* (Aldershot, 2005), 200–2.

17 Ibid., 200.

18 Peters, *First Crusade*, 256.

19 Ibid., 92.

20 Ibid., 90.

21 David Hay, 'Gender Bias and Religious Intolerance in Accounts of "Massacres" of the First Crusade', in Michael Gervers and James M. Powell (eds), *Tolerance and Intolerance: Social Conflict in the Age of the Crusades* (Syracuse, 2001), 6.

22 Hill, *Gesta Francorum*, 91.

23 Peters, *First Crusade*, 248–9.

24 Delaborde, *Oeuvres*, ii, 197.

25 Ibid., i, 217.

26 Ibid., ii, 199.

27 Ibid., 200.

28 Ibid., 199.

29 Ibid., 199–200.

30 Wendover, ii, 311–13.

31 W. A. Sibly and M. D. Sibly (eds and trans.), *The History of the Albigensian Crusade: Peter of Les Vaux-de-Cernay's Historia Albigensis* (Woodbridge, 1998), 50.

32 Janet Shirley (ed. and trans.), *The Song of the Cathar Wars* (Aldershot, 1996), 19.

33 Ibid., 20.

34 Joseph Strayer, *The Albigensian Crusades* (New York, 1971), 62.

35 Cited in Malcolm Barber, *The Cathars* (Harlow, 2000), 211 and n. 20.

36 W. A. Sibly and M. D. Sibly (eds and trans.), *The Chronicle of William of Puylaurens* (Woodbridge, 2003), 33.

37 Sibly and Sibly, *History of the Albigensian Crusade*, 50–1.

38 Shirley, *Song of the Cathar Wars*, 21–2.

39 Ibid.

40 Ibid.

41 Ibid.

42 Sibly and Sibly, *History of the Albigensian Crusade*, 237.

43 Roger of Wendover, ii, 281.

44 Froissart, 176.

45 Clifford J. Rogers (ed.), *The Wars of Edward III: Sources and Interpretations* (Woodbridge, 1999), 192.

46 Froissart, 178.

47 Ibid., 179.

48 Richard Barber, *Edward: Prince of Wales and Aquitaine* (Woodbridge, 1978), 226; 125 for the following Walsingham quote.

49 Richard Barber (ed.), *Life and Campaigns of the Black Prince,* (1979), 137.

50 Rogers, *Wars of Edward III*, 193.

51 Barber, *Edward*, 226.

52 Michael Jones, 'War and Fourteenth-Century France', in Anne Curry and Michael Hughes (eds), *Arms, Armies and Fortifications in the Hundred Years War* (Woodbridge, 1994), 117.

53 Barber, *Life and Campaigns*, 137.

54 Froissart, 176.

55 Rogers, *Wars of Edward III*, 193.

56 Jim Bradbury, *The Medieval Siege* (Woodbridge, 1992), 161.

57 Froissart, 177–8.

58 Christopher Allmand (ed.), *Society at War: The Experience of England and France during the Hundred Years War* (Woodbridge, 1998), 132.

59 Matthew Strickland, 'A Law of Arms or a Law of Treason? Conduct in War in Edward I's Campaigns in Scotland, 1296–1307', in Richard W. Kaeuper (ed.), *Violence in Medieval Society* (Woodbridge, 2000), 76.

60 Prestwich, *Armies and Warfare*, 239.

61 John Barnie, *War in Medieval English Society: Social Values in the Hundred Years War, 1377–99* (New York, 1974), 75.

62 David Green, *Edward the Black Prince* (Harlow, 2007), 92.

63 Michael Prestwich, *The Three Edwards: War and State in England, 1272–1377* (2003), 164.

64 Barber, *Edward*, 226.

65 *History of William Marshal*, ii, 301.

66 Hill, *Gesta Francorum*, 19–20. Here I have used in preference William Zajac's translation from William Zajac, 'Captured Property on the First Crusade', in Jonathan Phillips (ed.), *The First Crusade: Origins and Impact* (Manchester, 1997), 155.

67 Keen, *Laws of War*, 112.

68 Roger of Wendover, ii, 396–7 (slightly amended).

69 Peter Thompson (ed. and trans.), *Contemporary Chronicles of the Hundred Years War* (1966), 271.

70 Froissart, 106.

71 Roger of Wendover, ii, 339.

72 John Gillingham, 'William the Bastard at War', in Christopher Harper-Bill, Christopher Holdsworth and Janet Nelson (eds), *Studies in Medieval History Presented to R. Allen Brown* (Woodbridge, 1989), 150.

73 Otto of Freising, *The Deeds of Frederick Barbarossa*, trans. by Charles Mierow (Toronto, 1994), 284.

74 Ibid., 285.

75 Peter Speed (ed.), *Those Who Fought: An Anthology of Medieval Sources* (New York, 1996), 171.

76 Otto of Freising, *Deeds of Frederick Barbarossa*, 285.

77 A. R. Myers (ed.), *English Historical Documents*, iv (1969), 220–2.

CHAPTER 5: CAMPAIGNS

1 J. Gillingham, *The Wars of the Roses: Peace and Conflict in Fifteenth-Century England* (1981), 45.

2 Delaborde, *Oeuvres*, i, 45.

3 Clifford J. Rogers, 'The Age of The Hundred Years War', in Keen, *Medieval Warfare*, 146–7.

4 R. C. Johnston (ed. and trans.), *Jordan Fantosme's Chronicle* (Oxford, 1981), 33–5.

5 Speed, *Those Who Fought*, 213.

6 Cited in Achille Luchaire, *Social France at the Time of Philip Augustus* (1912), 261.

7 C. W. C. Oman, *The Art of War in the Middle Ages* (Ithaca, 1953; originally 1885), 61.

8 William E. Kapelle, *The Norman Conquest of the North, 1060–1135* (1979), ch. 5.

9 Ann Williams, *The English and the Norman Conquest* (Woodbridge, 1995), 40.

10 F. M. Stenton, *Anglo-Saxon England* (Oxford, 1971), 603.

11 D. C. Douglas, *William the Conqueror* (1964), 211.

12 *Anglo-Saxon Chronicle*, 204.

13 Ibid., 203, 204.

14 Henry of Huntingdon, 28.

15 R. Allen Brown (ed.), *The Norman Conquest: Documents of Medieval History* (1984), 120.

16 'Florence' of Worcester, *A History of the Kings of England*, trans. by J. Stephenson (Lampeter, no date: c.1990), 137 (hereafter John of Worcester).

17 William of Malmesbury, *A History of the Norman Kings*, trans. J. Stephenson (Lampeter, 1989), 25.

18 Simeon of Durham, 137–8.

19 Orderic Vitalis, ii, 230–3.

20 Williams, *The English and the Norman Conquest*, 43.

21 William of Malmesbury, *History of the Norman Kings*, 5.

22 Kapelle, *Norman Conquest of the North*, 118.

23 John Palmer, 'The Conqueror's Footprints in Domesday Book', in Andrew

Ayton and J. L. Price (eds), *The Medieval Military Revolution: State, Society and Military Change in Medieval and Early Modern Europe* (1995), 37.

24 John Palmer, 'War and Domesday Waste', in Matthew Strickland (ed.), *Armies, Chivalry and Warfare in Medieval Britain and France* (Stamford, 1998), 259.

25 R. Allen Brown, *The Normans and the Norman Conquest* (Woodbridge, 1985), 170.

26 K. R. Potter (ed.), *Gesta Stephani* (Oxford, 1955), 33.

27 Donald Matthew, *King Stephen* (2002), 70; D. D. R. Owen, *William the Lion: Kingship and Culture, 1143–1214* (East Linton, 1997), 12; Matthew Strickland, 'Killing or Clemency? Ransom, Chivalry and Changing Attitudes to Defeated Opponents in Britain and Northern France, 7–12th Centuries', in Hans-Henning Kortum (ed.), *Krieg im Mittelalter* (2001) (from www.deremilitari.org/strickland, 17).

28 G. W. S. Barrow, 'The Scots and the North of England', in Edmund King (ed.), *The Anarchy of King Stephen's Reign* (Oxford, 1994), 265.

29 Henry of Huntingdon, 68.

30 David Crouch, *The Reign of King Stephen, 1135–54* (2000), 74.

31 John of Worcester, 191.

32 Henry of Huntingdon, 69–70.

33 *Gesta Stephani*, 36–7.

34 Richard of Hexham, 'History of the Acts of King Stephen', in J. Stephenson (trans.), *Contemporary Chronicles of the Middle Ages* (Lampeter, 1988), 61.

35 Ibid., 61–2.

36 Christopher Allmand, 'The Reporting of War in the Middle Ages', in Diana Dunn (ed.), *War and Society in Medieval and Early Modern Britain* (Liverpool, 2000), 20.

37 Richard of Hexham, 61–2.

38 Simeon of Durham, 139.

39 Ibid.

40 *Gesta Stephani*, 9–10.

41 John of Worcester, 188.

42 Gerald of Wales, *Expugnatio*, 37.

43 K. H. Jackson (ed.), *A Celtic Miscellany* (Harmondsworth, 1971), 239–41.

44 Strickland, 'A Law of Arms', 49.

45 Cited in Niall Barr, *Flodden* (Stroud, 2001).

46 Sean McGlynn, 'Britain and Europe: A Medieval Comparison', in *Politics*, 16 (3), (1996), 172.

47 R. R. Davies, *The First English Empire: Power and Identities in the British Isles, 1093–1343* (Oxford 2000), 131.

48 Keith J. Stringer, *The Reign of Stephen* (1993), 31.

49 Johnston, *Jordan Fantosme's Chronicle*, 127.

50 E. L. G. Stones (ed. and trans.), *Anglo-Scottish Relations, 1174–1328* (Oxford, 1965), 140–5.

51 Barrow, 'The Scots and the North of England', 246.

52 Alan Lloyd, *King John* (1973), 392; Ralph V. Turner, *King John* (Harlow, 1994), 258.

53 J. Stephenson (ed.), *Radulphi de Coggeshall Chronicon Anglicanum*, Rolls Series (1875) (hereafter Ralph of Coggeshall).

54 Roger of Wendover, ii, 349.

55 Ralph of Coggeshall, 178–9.

56 *History of William Marshal*, ii, 225.

57 F. Michel (ed.), *Histoire des Ducs de Normandie et des Rois d'Angleterre* (Paris, 1840), 164.

58 Ralph of Coggeshall, 177–8.

59 Sean McGlynn, 'Roger of Wendover and the Wars of Henry III, 1216–1234', in Björn K. U. Weiler and Ifor W. Rowlands (eds), *England and Europe in the Reign of Henry III, 1216–1272* (Aldershot, 2002), 197–8.

60 Roger of Wendover, ii, 351, 349.

61 Ibid., 349.

62 Ibid.

63 Ibid., 351, 353.

64 A. L. Poole, *From Domesday Book to Magna Carta* (Oxford, 1955), 481.

65 Roger of Wendover, ii, 353.

66 John Gillingham, 'Conquering the Barbarians', *The English in the Twelfth Century*, 45.

67 Orderic Vitalis, vi, 250.

68 Roger of Wendover, ii, 352.

69 Ibid.

70 Turner, *King John*, 255.

71 W. L. Warren, *King John* (1978), 248–9.

72 Barnie, *War in Medieval English Society*, 10.

73 David Green, *The Battle of Poitiers, 1356* (2002), 32.

74 Rogers, *Wars of Edward III*, 153.

75 Barber, *Campaigns of the Black Prince*, 52.

76 W. J. Ashley, *Edward III and his Wars, 1327–1360* (1887), 166.

77 Jonathan Sumption, *The Hundred Years War: Trial by Fire* (1999), 185.

78 Ibid.

79 Barber, *Edward*, 185.

80 Cited in Clifford J. Rogers, *War Cruel and Sharp: English Strategy under Edward III, 1327–1360* (Woodbridge, 2000), 296.

81 Ibid., 301.

82 H. J. Hewitt, *The Organization of War under Edward III, 1338–62* (Manchester, 1966), 117.

83 Cited in Rogers, *War Cruel and Sharp*, 323.

84 Rogers, *Wars of Edward III*, 169. (I have abridged this longer version.)

85 Gillingham, 'William the Bastard at War', 149.

86 N. P. Milner (ed. and trans.), *Vegetius: Epitome of Military Science* (Liverpool, 1993), 65.

87 W. Arndt (ed.), *Gisleberti Chronicon Hanoniense* (Hanover, 1869). An English

translation is now available: Gilbert of Mons, *Chronicle of Hainaut*, ed. and trans. Laura Napran (Woodbridge, 2005).

88 Roger of Wendover, ii, 479.

89 Frederick C. Suppe, *Military Institutions on the Welsh Marches: Shropshire, 1066–1300* (Woodbridge, 1994), 22.

90 Christopher Allmand, *The Hundred Years War: England and France at War, c.1300–c.1450* (Cambridge, 1988), 55.

91 Cited in Susan Reynolds, *Fiefs and Vassals* (Oxford, 1994), 37.

92 Nicholas Wright, *Knights and Peasants: The Hundred Years War in the French Countryside* (Woodbridge, 1998), 90.

93 Philippe Contamine, 'Rançons et Butins dans la Normandie Anglaise, 1424–1444', in Actes du 101e Congrès National des Sociétés Savantes (Lille, 1976), *La Guerre et la Paix: Frontières et Violences au Moyen Age* (Paris, 1978), 258.

94 Green, *Edward the Black Prince*, 35.

CHAPTER 6: MEDIEVAL SAVAGERY?

1 Philip Zimbardo, *The Lucifer Effect: How Good People Turn Evil* (2007) 487.

2 Susan Mary Grant, 'For God and Country: Why Men Joined Up for the US Civil War', in *History Today*, 50 (7) (2000), 23–4.

3 John Connelly, 'Rampaging', *London Review of Books*, 22 June 2006, 30.

4 Christopher Browning, *Ordinary Men: Reserve Police Battalion 101 and the Final Solution in Poland* (Harmondsworth, 1998), 189.

5 Grant, 'For God and Country', 24.

6 Niall Ferguson, *The Pity of War* (Harmondsworth, 1998), 377 and *passim*. See Bourke (below, n.10) for a variation of the German fathers theme.

7 Anthony Lloyd, *Another Bloody Love Letter* (2007).

8 Cited in Huizinga, *Waning of the Middle Ages*, 76.

9 Matthew Bennett, 'Military Masculinity in England and Northern France, c.1050–c.1215', in D. M. Hadley (ed.), *Masculinity in Medieval Europe* (1999), 88.

10 Joanna Bourke, *An Intimate History of Killing: Face to Face Killing in the Twentieth Century* (1999), 42.

11 John Erickson, Review, *Times Literary Supplement*, 28 August 1998.

12 F. F. Bruce, *Israel and the Nations: The History of Israel from the Exodus to the Fall of the Second Empire* (Sheffield, 1983), 38. My thanks to Dr Anthony Cross for bringing this book to my attention.

13 Len Scales, 'Bread, Cheese and Genocide: Imagining the Destruction of Peoples in Medieval Western Europe', in *History*, 92 (3) (2007), 300.

14 Gerald of Wales, *Expugnatio*, 61.

15 George Orwell, 'Looking Back on the Spanish War', *Essays* (1984), 219. (See also his comments on atrocities in 'Notes on Nationalism', ibid., 307, 316.)

SELECT BIBLIOGRAPHY

The following titles are the ones most directly relevant to this book. This is by no means a comprehensive bibliography. With some exceptions, I have not included general political and military histories. As there is a huge amount published on medieval warfare – far too much to list here – I have included some historiographical surveys and review articles which discuss some of the literature in this field. For primary sources, I have attempted to list the most accessible English translations available. Place of publication is London unless otherwise stated.

Ailes, M. and Barber, M. (eds and trans), *The History of the Holy War* (Woodbridge, 2003)

Allmand, C., 'The Reporting of War in the Middle Ages', in Diana Dunn (ed.), *War and Society in Medieval and Early Modern Britain* (Liverpool, 2000)

Allmand, C. (ed.), *Society at War: The Experience of England and France during the Hundred Years War* (Woodbridge, 1998)

Allmand, C., *The Hundred Years War: England and France at War, c.1300–c.1450* (Cambridge, 1988)

Allmand, C., *Henry V* (1992)

Allmand, C., 'War and Non-Combatants in the Middle Ages', in Keen, *Medieval Warfare*

Appleby, J. (ed. and trans.), *The Chronicle of Richard of Devizes* (1963)

Arndt, W. (ed.), *Gisleberti Chronicon Hanoniense* (Hanover, 1869)

Arnold, B., *Princes and Territories in Medieval Germany* (Cambridge, 1991)

Ashley, W. J. *Edward III and his Wars, 1327–1360* (1887)

Ayton, A., *Knights and Warhorses: Military Service and the English Aristocracy under Edward III* (Woodbridge, 1994)

Bachrach, B., Rogers, C. J., De Vries, K. (eds), *Journal of Medieval Military History* (Woodbridge, 2002)

Baraz, D., *Medieval Cruelty* (Ithaca, 2003)

Barber, M., *The Cathars* (Harlow, 2000)

Barber, R., *The Knight and Chivalry* (Woodbridge, 1995)

Barber, R., *Edward: Prince of Wales and Aquitaine* (Woodbridge, 1978)

Barber, R. (ed.), *Life and Campaigns of the Black Prince* (1979)

Barnie, J., *War in Medieval English Society: Social Values in the Hundred Years War, 1377–99* (New York, 1974)

Barr, N., *Flodden* (Stroud, 2001)

Barrow, G. W. S., 'The Scots and the North of England', in Edmund King (ed.), *The Anarchy of King Stephen's Reign* (Oxford, 1994)

Bartlett, R., *The Hanged Man: A Story of Miracle, Memory, and Colonialism in the Middle Ages*, (Princeton, 2004)

Bartlett, R., *England Under the Norman and Angevin Kings, 1075–1225* (Oxford, 2000)

Bartlett, R., *The Making of Europe: Conquest, Colonization and Cultural Challenge, 950–1350* (Harmondsworth, 1993)

Barton, R., 'Zealous Anger and the Renegotiation of Aristocratic Relations in 11th– and 12th–Century France', in Rosenwein, *Anger's Past*

Beeler, J., *Warfare in Feudal Europe* (Ithaca, 1971)

Bennett, M., *Agincourt 1415: Triumph Against the Odds* (1991)

Bennett, M., 'Military Masculinity in England and Northern France, c.1050–c.1215', in D. M. Hadley (ed.), *Masculinity in Medieval Europe* (1999)

Boardman, A. W., *The Battle of Towton* (Stroud, 1996)

Bloch, M., *Feudal Society* (Chicago, 1961)

Bourke, J., *An Intimate History of Killing: Face to Face Killing in the Twentieth Century* (1999)

Bradbury, J., *The Medieval Siege* (Woodbridge, 1992)

Brown, A. L., *The Governance of Late Medieval England* (1989)

Brown, R. A., *The Normans and the Norman Conquest* (Woodbridge, 1985)

Brown, R. A., *English Castles* (1976)

Brown R. A. (ed.), *The Norman Conquest: Documents of Medieval History* (1984)

Browning, C., *Ordinary Men: Reserve Police Battalion 101 and the Final Solution in Poland* (Harmondsworth, 1998)

Bruce, F. F., *Israel and the Nations: The History of Israel from the Exodus to the Fall of the Second Empire* (Sheffield, 1983)

Christiansen, E., *The Northern Crusades* (Harmondsworth, 1997)

Church, S. D., *King John: New Interpretations* (Woodbridge 1999)

Connelly, J., 'Rampaging', *London Review of Books*, 22 June 2006

Contamine, P., *War in the Middle Ages* (Oxford, 1984)

Contamine, P., 'Rançons et Butins dans la Normandie Anglaise, 1424–1444', in Actes du 101e Congrès National des Sociétés Savantes (Lille, 1976), *La Guerre et la Paix: Frontières et Violences au Moyen Age* (Paris, 1978)

Contamine, P. and Guyotjeannin, D. (eds.), *La Guerre, la Violence, et Les Gens au Moyen Âge* (2 vols) (Paris, 1996)

Contamine, P., Giry-Deloison, C. and Keen, M. (eds), *Guerre et Société en France, en Angleterre et en Bourgogne, XIVe–XVe Siècle* (Lille, 1991)

Coulson, C., *Castles in Medieval Society: Fortresses in England, France, and Ireland in the Central Middle Ages* (Oxford, 2003)

Cowdrey, H. E. J., *Popes, Monks and Crusaders* (1984)

Crouch, D., *The Reign of King Stephen, 1135–54* (Harlow, 2000)

Curry, A. (ed. and trans.), *The Battle of Agincourt: Sources and Interpretations*, (Woodbridge, 2000)

Curry, A., *Agincourt: A New History* (Stroud, 2005)

Davies, R. R., *The First English Empire: Power and Identities in the British Isles, 1093–1343* (Oxford, 2000)

Davis, R. H. C., *King Stephen* (Harlow, 1997)

Dean, T., *Crime in Medieval Europe* (2001)

Delaborde, H. F., *Oeuvres de Rigord et de Guillaume le Breton* (Paris, 1882)

DeVries, K., *Infantry Warfare in the Early Fourteenth Century* (Woodbridge, 1996)

DeVries, K., 'Harold Godwinson in Wales: Military Legitimacy in Late Anglo-Saxon England', in Richard Abels (ed.), *The Normans and Their Adversaries* (Woodbridge, 2001)

Dockray, K., *Henry V* (Stroud, 2004)

Dockray, K. (ed.), *Henry VI, Margaret of Anjou and the Wars of the Roses: A Source Book* (Stroud, 2000)

Douglas, D. C., *William the Conqueror* (1964)

Dunbabin, J., *Captivity and Imprisonment in Medieval Europe, 1000–1300* (Basingstoke, 2002)

Dunn, A., *The Great Rising of 1381* (Stroud, 2002)

Dunn, A., 'A Kingdom in Crisis: Henry IV and the Battle of Shrewsbury', *History Today*, 53 (8) (2003)

Edbury, P. W. (ed. and trans.), *The Conquest of Jerusalem and the Third Crusade: Sources in Translation* (Aldershot, 1996)

Edgington, S., *The First Crusade* (1996)

Ellis, H. (ed.), *The Chronicle of John Hardyng* (1812)

Erickson, J., Review, *Times Literary Supplement*, 28 August 1998

Evans, R., *Rituals of Retribution: Capital Punishment in Germany, 1600–1987* (1997)

Ferguson, N. *The Pity of War* (Harmondsworth, 1998)

Fiorato, V., Boylston, A. and Knüsel, C., *Blood Red Roses: The Archaeology of a Mass Grave from the Battle of Towton AD 1461* (Oxford, 2000)

Fletcher, R., *Bloodfeud: Murder and Revenge in Anglo-Saxon England* (Harmondsworth, 2002)

'Florence' of Worcester, *A History of the Kings of England*, trans. by J. Stephenson (Lampeter, no date: *c*.1990)

Foot, S., 'Violence Against Christians? The Vikings and the Church in Ninth-Century England', *Medieval History*, 1 (3) (1991)

France, J., *Western Warfare in the Age of the Crusades, 1000–1300* (1999)

France, J., *Victory in the East: A Military History of the First Crusade* (Cambridge, 1994)

France, J., 'Recent Writing on Medieval Warfare: From the Fall of Rome to *c*.1300', *Journal of Military History*, 65 (2), (2001)

Froissart, *Chronicles*, ed. and trans. Geoffrey Brereton, (Harmondsworth, 1978)

Gabrieli, F. (ed. and trans.), *Arab Historians of the Crusades* (1969)

Garmonsway, G. N. (ed. and trans.), *The Anglo-Saxon Chronicle* (1972)

Gauvard, C., 'Justification and Theory of the Death Penalty at the *Parlement* of Paris in the Late Middle Ages', in Christopher Allmand (ed.), *War, Government and Power in Late Medieval France* (Liverpool, 2000)

Gilbert of Mons, *Chronicle of Hainaut*, ed. and trans. Laura Napran (Woodbridge, 2005)

Gillingham, J., *The English in the Twelfth Century: Imperialism, National Identity and Politics* (Woodbridge, 2000)

Gillingham, J., *Richard Coeur de Lion* (1994)

Gillingham, J. *The Wars of the Roses: Peace and Conflict in Fifteenth-Century England* (1981)

Gillingham, J., 'William the Bastard at War', in Christopher Harper-Bill, Christopher Holdsworth and Janet Nelson (eds), *Studies in Medieval History Presented to R. Allen Brown* (Woodbridge, 1989)

Gillingham, J., 'An Age of Expansion, *c*.1020–1204, in Keen, *Medieval Warfare*

Given, J. B., *Society and Homicide in Thirteenth-Century England* (Stanford, 1977)

Gonthier, N., *Le Châtiment du Crime au Moyen Âge* (Rennes, 1998)

Goodich, M., *Violence and Miracle in the Fourteenth Century* (Chicago, 1995)

Grant, S. M. 'For God and Country: Why Men Joined Up for the US Civil War', in *History Today*, 50 (7) (2000)

Green, D., *Edward the Black Prince* (Harlow, 2007)

Green, D., *The Battle of Poitiers, 1356* (2002)

Grimsley, M. and Rogers, C. J. (eds), *Civilians in the Path of War* (2002)

Halsall, G., 'Playing By Whose Rules? A Further Look at Viking Atrocity in the Ninth Century', *Medieval History*, 2 (2) (1992)

Hammond, P. W., *The Battles of Barnet and Tewkesbury* (Stroud, 1990)

Hanawalt, B., 'Violence in the Domestic Milieu of Late Medieval England', in Richard Kaeuper (ed.), *Violence in Medieval Society* (Woodbridge, 2000)

Hanawalt, B. and Wallace, D. (eds), *Medieval Crime and Social Control* (Minneapolis, 1999)

Hanley, C., *War and Combat, 1150–1270: The Evidence of Old French Literature* (Woodbridge, 2003)

Harriss, G. L. *Henry V: The Practice of Kingship* (Oxford, 1985)

Hay, D., 'Gender Bias and Religious Intolerance in Accounts of "Massacres" of the First Crusade', in Michael Gervers and James M. Powell (eds), *Tolerance and Intolerance: Social Conflict in the Age of the Crusades* (Syracuse, 2001)

Henry of Huntingdon, *The History of the English People, 1000–1154*, ed. and trans. Diana Greenway (Oxford, 2002)

Hewitt, H. J., *The Organization of War under Edward III, 1338–62* (Manchester, 1966)

Hill, R. (ed. and trans.), *Gesta Francorum* (1962)

Holden, A. J., Crouch, D. and Gregory, S. (eds), *History of William Marshal* (2002–6)

Hollister, C., 'Royal Acts of Mutilation: The Case Against Henry I', in *Monarchy, Magnates and Institutions in the Anglo-Norman World* (1986)

Holt, J. C., *The Northerners* (Oxford, 1992)

Howlett, R. (ed.), *Chronicles of the Reigns of Stephen, Henry II and Richard I*, 4 vols, Rolls Series, (1884)

Hudson, J., *The Formation of the English Common Law: Law and Society in England from the Norman Conquest to Magna Carta* (1996)

Huizinga, J., *The Waning of the Middle Ages* (New York, 1949; original edn, 1919)

Hyams, P., 'What Did Henry III of England Think in Bed and in French about Kingship and Anger?', in Rosenwein (ed.), *Anger's Past*

Jackson, K. H. (ed.), *A Celtic Miscellany* (Harmondsworth, 1971)

Johnston, R. C. (ed. and trans.), *Jordan Fantosme's Chronicle* (Oxford, 1981)

Joinville and Villehardouin, *Chronicles of the Crusades*, ed. and trans. M. R. B. Shaw (Harmondsworth, 1963)

Joliffe, J. E. A. *Angevin Kingship* (1963)

Jones, M., 'War and Fourteenth-Century France', in Anne Curry and Michael Hughes (eds), *Arms, Armies and Fortifications in the Hundred Years War* (Woodbridge, 1994)

Kaeuper, R. W., *Chivalry and Violence in Medieval Europe* (Oxford, 1999)

Kaeuper, R. W., *War, Justice and Public Order: England and France in the Later Middle Ages* (Oxford, 1988)

Kaeuper, R. W. and Kennedy, E. (eds and trans), *The Book of Chivalry of Geoffroi de Charny* (Pennsylvania, 1996)

Kagay, D. J. and Villalon, L. J. A. (eds), *The Circle of War in the Middle Ages* (Woodbridge, 1999)

Kapelle, W. E., *The Norman Conquest of the North, 1000-1135* (1979)

Keen, M. *Nobles, Knights and Men-at-Arms* (1996)

Keen, M., *Chivalry* (1984)

Keen, M., *The Laws of War in the Later Middle Ages* (1965)

Keen, M. (ed.), *Medieval Warfare: A History* (Oxford, 1999)

Keen, M., 'Chivalry, Nobility and the Man-at-Arms', in Christopher Allmand (ed.), *War, Literature and Politics in the Late Middle Ages* (Liverpool, 1976)

Lloyd, A., *Another Bloody Love Letter* (2007)

Lloyd, A., *King John*, (1973)

Luchaire, A., *Social France at the Time of Philip Augustus* (1912)

Maddern, P., *Violence and Social Order: East Anglia, 1422–1442* (Oxford, 1992)

Mannix, D., *The History of Torture* (Stroud, 2003; originally 1964)

Matthew, D., *King Stephen* (2002)

Mayer, H. E., *The Crusades* (Oxford, 1988)

McGlynn, S., *The Invasion of England 1216* (Stroud, forthcoming 2008)

McGlynn, S., 'Roger of Wendover and the Wars of Henry III, 1216–1234', in Björn K. U. Weiler and Ifor W. Rowlands (eds), *England and Europe in the Reign of Henry III, 1216–1272* (Aldershot, 2002)

McGlynn, S., 'Politics and Violence in the Late Middle Ages', *Canadian Journal of History*, 26 (3) (2001)

McGlynn, S., 'The Useless Mouths', *History Today*, 48 (6) (1998)

McGlynn, S., 'Medieval Warfare', *European Review of History–Revue Européene d'Histoire*, 4 (2) (1997)

McGlynn, S., 'Britain and Europe: A Medieval Comparison', in *Politics*, 16 (3) (1996)

McGlynn, S., 'The Myths of Medieval Warfare', *History Today*, 44 (1), (1994)

McGlynn, S., 'Philip Augustus: Too Soft a King?', *Medieval Life*, 7 (1997)

Melville, C. P. and Lyons, M. C., 'Saladin's Hattin Letter', in B. Z. Kedar (ed.), *The Horns of the Hattin* (London and Jerusalem, 1992)

Meron, T., *Henry's Wars and Shakespeare's Laws: Perspectives on the Law of War in the Middle Ages* (Oxford, 1993)

Messenger, C. (ed.), *Reader's Guide to Military History* (London, 2001)

Meyerson, D., Thiery, D. and Falk, O., *'A Great Effusion of Blood?': Interpreting Medieval Violence* (Toronto, 2004)

Michel, F. (ed.), *Histoire des Ducs de Normandie et des Rois d'Angleterre* (Paris, 1840)

Milner, N. P. (ed. and trans.), *Vegetius: Epitome of Military Science* (Liverpool, 1993)

Moore, H., *The History of the Persecutions of the Church of Rome and Complete Protestant Martyrology* (1809)

Morillo, S., *Warfare Under the Anglo-Norman Kings* (Woodbridge, 1994)

Myers, A. R. (ed.), *English Historical Documents*, iv (1969), 220–2

Neville, C., *Violence, Custom and Law: The Anglo-Scottish Border Lands in the Later Middle Ages* (Edinburgh, 1998)

Neville, C., 'Homicide in the Ecclesiastical Court of Fourteenth-Century Durham', in Nigel Saul (ed.), *Fourteenth-Century England I* (Woodbridge, 2000)

Neville, C., 'War, Women and Crime in the Northern Border Lands in the Later Middle Ages', in Donald Kagay and L. J. Andrew Villalon (eds), *The Final Argument: The Imprint of Violence on Society in Medieval and Early Modern Europe* (Woodbridge, 1998)

Nicholson, H., *Medieval Warfare* (Basingstoke, 2004)

Nicholson, H. (ed. and trans.), *Chronicle of the Third Crusade* (Aldershot, 1997)

Nirenberg, D., *Communities of Violence: Persecution of Minorities in the Middle Ages* (Princeton, 1996)

O'Callaghan, J. F., *Reconquest and Crusade in Medieval Spain* (Pennsylvania, 2004)

Oman, C., *The Art of War in the Middle Ages* (Ithaca, 1953; originally 1885)

Opren, G. H. (ed. and trans.), *Song of Dermot and the Earl* (Lampeter, 1994)

Orderic Vitalis, *The Ecclesiastical History*, ed. and trans. Marjorie Chibnall (Oxford, 1969–81)

Otto of Freising, *The Deeds of Frederick Barbarossa*, trans. by Charles Mierow (Toronto, 1994)

Owen, D. D. R., *William the Lion: Kingship and Culture, 1143–1214* (East Linton, 1997)

Paden, W., Sankovitch, T. and Stalen, P. (eds and trans), *The Poems of Bertran de Born* (Los Angeles, 1986)

Palmer, J., 'War and Domesday Waste', in Matthew Strickland (ed.), *Armies, Chivalry and Warfare in Medieval Britain and France* (Stamford, 1998)

Palmer, J., 'The Conqueror's Footprints in Domesday Book', in Andrew Ayton and J. L. Price (eds), *The Medieval Military Revolution: State, Society and Military Change in Medieval and Early Modern Europe* (1995)

Pantin, W. A., *The English Church in the Fourteenth Century* (Toronto, 1980)

Peters, E. (ed.), *The First Crusade: The Chronicle of Fulcher of Chartres and Other Source Materials* (Pennsylvania, 1988)

Phillips, G., *The Anglo-Scot Wars, 1513–1550* (Woodbridge, 1999)

Poole, A. L. *From Domesday Book to Magna Carta* (Oxford, 1955)

Potter, K. R. (ed.), *Gesta Stephani* (Oxford, 1955)

Power, D., *The Norman Frontier in the Twelfth and Early Thirteenth Centuries* (Cambridge, 2004)

Powers, J. F., *A Society Organized for War: The Iberian Municipal Militias in the Central Middle Ages, 1000–1284* (Berkeley, 1988)

Prestwich, M., *The Three Edwards: War and State in England, 1272–1377* (2003)

Prestwich, M., *Armies and Warfare in the Middle Ages: The English Experience* (1996)

Reid, B. H., 'Rationality and Irrationality in Union Strategy, April 1861–March 1862', *War in History*, 1 (1) (1994)

Reuter, T., '*Episcopi cum sua militia:* The Prelate as Warrior in the Early Staufer Era', in Timothy Reuter (ed.), *Warriors and Churchmen in the Middle Ages* (1992)

Reynolds, S., *Fiefs and Vassals* (Oxford, 1994)

Richard of Hexham, 'History of the Acts of King Stephen', in J. Stephenson (trans.) *Contemporary Chronicles of the Middle Ages* (Lampeter, 1988)

Richards, D. S. (ed. and trans.), *The Rare and Excellent History of Saladin* (Aldershot, 1992)

Riley, H. T. (ed. and trans.), *Annals of Roger of Hoveden* (Lampeter, 1997)

Riley, H. T. (ed.), *Annals of John of Trokelow* (London, 1886)

Roger of Wendover, *Flowers of History*, ed. and trans. J. A. Giles (Lampeter, 1996)

Rogers, C. J., *War Cruel and Sharp: English Strategy Under Edward III, 1327–1360* (Woodbridge, 2000)

Rogers, C. J. (ed.), *The Wars of Edward III: Sources and Interpretations* (Woodbridge, 1999)

Rogers, C. J., 'The Age of the Hundred Years War', in Keen, *Medieval Warfare*

Rosenwein, B. (ed.), *Anger's Past: The Social Uses of an Emotion in the Middle Ages* (Ithaca, 1998)

Runciman, S., *The First Crusade* (Cambridge, 1980)

Russell, F., *The Just War in the Middle Ages* (Cambridge, 1976)

Saunders, C., Le Saux, F. and Thomas, N., *Writing War: Medieval Literary Responses to War* (Woodbridge, 2004)

Scales, L., 'Bread, Cheese and Genocide: Imagining the Destruction of Peoples in Medieval Western Europe', in *History*, 92 (3), (2007), 300

Scott, A. B. and Martin, F. X. (eds and trans), *Expugnatio Hibernica* (Dublin, 1978)

Scott, G., *A History of Torture* (1940)

Seward, D., *Henry V as Warlord* (1987)

Shirley, J. (ed. and trans.), *The Song of the Cathar Wars* (Aldershot, 1996)

Sibly, W. A. and Sibly, M. D. (eds and trans), *The Chronicle of William of Puylaurens* (Woodbridge, 2003)

Sibly, W. A., and Sibly, M. D. (eds and trans), *The History of the Albigensian Crusade: Peter of Les Vaux-de-Cernay's Historia Albigensis* (Woodbridge, 1998)

Simeon of Durham, *A History of the Kings of England*, ed. and trans. J. Stevenson (Lampeter, 1987)

Speed, Peter (ed.), *Those Who Fought: An Anthology of Medieval Sources* (New York, 1996)

Spraggs, G., *Outlaws and Highwaymen: The Cult of the Robber in England from the Middle Ages to the Nineteenth Century* (2001)

Stacey, R., 'The Age of Chivalry', in Michael Howard, George Andreopoulis and Mark Shulman (eds), *The Laws of War: Constraints on Warfare in the Western World* (New Haven, 1994)

Stenton, F. M., *Anglo-Saxon England* (Oxford, 1971)

Stephenson, J. (ed.), *Radulphi de Coggeshall Chronicon Anglicanum*, Rolls Series (1875)

Stones, E. L. G. (ed. and trans.) *Anglo-Scottish Relations, 1174–1328* (Oxford, 1965)

Strayer, J. *The Albigensian Crusades* (New York, 1971)

Strickland, M., *War and Chivalry: The Conduct and Perception of War in England and Normandy, 1066–1217* (Cambridge, 1996)

Strickland, M. (ed.), *Anglo-Norman Warfare* (Woodbridge, 1992)

Strickland, M., 'Killing or Clemency? Ransom, Chivalry and Changing Attitudes to Defeated Opponents in Britain and Northern France, 7–12th Centuries,' in Hans-Henning Kortum (ed.), *Krieg im Mittelalter* (2001) (from www.deremilitari.org/strickland)

Strickland, M., 'A Law of Arms or a Law of Treason? Conduct in War in Edward I's Campaigns in Scotland, 1296–1307', in Richard W. Kaeuper (ed.), *Violence in Medieval Society* (Woodbridge, 2000)

Strickland, M., 'Against the Lord's Anointed: Aspects of Warfare and Baronial Rebellion in England and Normandy, 1075–1265', in George Garnett and John Hudson (eds), *Law and Government in Medieval England and Normandy* (Cambridge, 1994)

Strickland, M., 'Slaughter, Slavery or Ransom: The Impact of the Conquest on Conduct in Warfare', in Carola Hicks (ed.), *England in the Eleventh Century* (Stamford, 1992)

Stringer, K. J., *The Reign of Stephen* (1993)

Suger, *The Deeds of Louis the Fat*, ed. and trans. Richard Cusimano and John Moorhead (Washington, 1992)

Summerson, H., 'Attitudes to Capital Punishment in England, 1200–1350', in Michael Prestwich, Richard Britnell and Robin Frame (eds), *Thirteenth Century England 8* (Woodbridge, 2001)

Sumption, J., *The Hundred Years War: Trial by Fire* (1999)

Suppe, F. C., *Military Institutions on the Welsh Marches: Shropshire, 1066–1300* (Woodbridge, 1994)

Sweetenham, C. (ed. and trans.), *Robert the Monk's History of the First Crusade* (Aldershot, 2005)

Thompson, P. (ed. and trans.), *Contemporary Chronicles of the Hundred Years War* (1966)

Tuchman, B., *A Distant Mirror: The Calamitous Fourteenth Century* (New York, 1978)

Turner, R. V., *King John* (Harlow, 1994)

Turner, R. V. and Heiser, R. H., *The Reign of Richard Lionheart: Ruler of the Angevin Empire, 1189–1199* (Harlow, 2000)

Ullman, W., *Medieval Political Thought* (1975)

Ullman, W., *Principles of Government and Politics in the Middle Ages* (1961)

Vale, M., *War and Chivalry: Warfare and Aristocratic Culture in England, France and Burgundy at the End of the Middle Ages* (Athens, Georgia, 1981)

Vale, M., 'Trial by Battle in the Later Middle Ages', in Richard Kaeuper (ed.), *Violence in Medieval Society* (Woodbridge, 2000)

Verbruggen, J. F., *The Art of Warfare in Western Europe During the Middle Ages* (Woodbridge, 1997)

Wallace-Hadrill, J. M., 'War and Peace in the Earlier Middle Ages', *Transactions of the Royal Historical Society*, 25 (1975)

Warren, W. L., *King John* (1978)

Weinberg, S., *Glory and Terror* (New York, 2004)

White, S., 'Feuding and Peacemaking in the Touraine around the Year 1000', *Traditio*, 42 (1986)

Wicher, N., 'Selective Female Infanticide as Partial Explanation for the Dearth of Women in Viking Age Scandinavia', in Guy Halsall (ed.), *Violence and Society in the Early Medieval West* (Woodbridge, 1998)

William of Malmesbury, *A History of the Norman Kings*, trans. J. Stephenson (Lampeter, 1989)

Williams, A., *The English and the Norman Conquest* (Woodbridge, 1995)

Wright, N., *Knights and Peasants: The Hundred Years War in the French Countryside* (Woodbridge, 1998)

Zajac, W., 'Captured Property on the First Crusade', in Jonathan Phillips (ed.), *The First Crusade: Origins and Impact* (Manchester, 1997)

Zimbardo, P., *The Lucifer Effect: How Good People Turn Evil* (2007)

INDEX

275